Natural tucker

Born in Adelaide, John Downes got his BA at Flinders University
in Political Science, Asian Studies and Education. He taught school
for three years in private and state high schools, most happily with
delinquent and disenchanted youth.

He was introduced to cooking by a lady who cooked him a stew!
It turned out to be a French Provincial stew and he wondered what
he had been eating for the past 22 years. The transition from acquiring taste-buds to a lacto-vegetarian diet was intuitive. The books of
George Ohsawa, the oriental philosopher-physician, gave him insight
into the place of food in man's physical and spiritual development
and the importance of balance of food and energy.

John Downes opened a macrobiotic restaurant called Goodness
Gracious in Adelaide in 1976 and a take-away food bar at Flinders
University. Later he moved to NSW and with some friends re-
established Goodness Gracious at Byron Bay where it became a combination of Natural Food store, restaurant and bookshop. This
became a 'Country and Eastern kitchen'. He moved from Byron Bay
in early 1978, taught macrobiotic and vegetarian cooking for a term
at the South Australian School of Food and Catering, Regency Park.

He has studied traditional Oriental medicine with the East-West Foundation in Sydney and in Boston, USA. In Melbourne, he revived a bakery in
Greville Street, Prahran, called Feedwell Foundry, which was very popular
for the many breads and pastries baked in its wood-fired brick oven. The
sale of the building saw the destruction of this beautiful oven. The search
for another wood-fired oven took four years, and has resulted in The Natural
Tucker Bakery at 809 Nicholson Street, North Carlton, Melbourne, which
produces delicious traditional leaven or 'sourdough' breads – the only bread
of its type in Australia. 'Natural Tucker' bread is becoming very popular.
John Downes is also teaching at the newly opened Australian Shiatsu
College in Melbourne and is about to open his own cooking school. John
is married, with three children.

By the same author:
The Natural Tucker Bread Book

Natural tucker

Traditional, eastern and wholefood cooking

John Downes

Hyland House Melbourne

First published in 1978 by
Hyland House Publishing Pty Limited
10 Hyland Street
South Yarra
Melbourne
Vic. 3141
Revised edition 1982
Reprinted 1982
Reprinted 1984
Second revised edition 1986

Downes, John Vincent.
Natural tucker.

Index
Bibliography
ISBN 0 908090 07 2 Paperback
0 908090 11 0 Cased

1. Cookery. 2. Cookery (Natural foods). I. Title.

641.5

Cover design by Leone Stott.
Illustrated by Carol Ruff
Design by Peter Yates
First edition typeset by Savage & Co. Pty. Ltd.
36 Costin St., Valley, Brisbane
Revisions typeset by Acton Graphic Arts Pty. Ltd.
8A Church St., Hawthorn, Vic. 3122
Printed by The Dominion Press, Blackburn, Victoria

Contents

Contents

Preface to the 1986 edition

'The art of a sculptor consists, it is said, in chiselling out of the wood an already existent image.'

It has been ten years since I first put pen to paper with this book in mind, and during that period we have witnessed many changes. Natural Foods are becoming more widely accepted in the general community and by medical professionals, who can no longer afford to deny the seminal role they play in the maintenance of health and prevention of disease. No matter what negative crusading is launched, more and more people have *experienced* an important change in their basic physical health by eliminating processed foods and embracing a more natural diet.

The tenets of natural diet may not be provable in a mechanical scientific fashion, but many don't seem to care about that any more, since the experience of wellbeing is what is important − not whether it shows on some contrived scientific apparatus or checklist. This *experience* underlines the inadequacy of our 'scientific' culture − for it doesn't matter if scientists can't say why it works! Even if the *experience* is regarded as a placebo or psychosomatic − this simply shows that there is more to life than what can be objectively and scientifically tested in a control situation.

Hence my statements relating to transmutation and the ability of humans to synthesise vitamin C have caused problems for some. The scientific maxim is that we can't do it − and this may well be true under certain circumstances. The key to understanding this is an acceptance of the idea of biochemical individuality. Even scientific data has shown a wide range of variability in the biochemical function and nutritional requirements of various people. The classic case of British Navy men being given vitamin C to cure their scurvy is never expanded to show that, on exactly the same diet, not all of the sailors had scurvy or showed signs of getting it − in fact the physician who recommended the lemon/lime juice cure also recommended that tension and psychological stress be avoided as a part of the treatment. Clearly, we use varying quantities of nutrients, according to how we function metabolically and view the world in a spiritual sense. The whole question of diet is a very big one which requires subtlety and an openness of understanding. There may be some hard and fast rules but there are also some tremendous and vital variables.

Just a final note about vitamin C for those who need it — there *is* documented scientific evidence to support the idea that vitamin C can be manufactured in the human body. Please read chapter 18 of Rudolph Ballentine's excellent book *Diet and Nutrition* (The Himalayan Institute, Penn., USA, 1978). This does not mean *you* can and I do not recommend that you pursue any fanatical dietary extremes. My illustration is simply for the purpose of freeing us from rigid dietetic beliefs and opening our perspective to the vastness of life.

This edition has been considerably revised and I hope you enjoy it.

Acknowledgments

I would like to express my deep gratitude to those who helped in so many ways. To my friend, John Day, who was critical and inspiring, his untimely death being a great blow to many who knew him. My ever-vigilant and all-correcting wife, Maar, friend David and sister Gerry. Richard at Book People, Carol Art for Art's sake, my mother and father, Anne and Al who made it possible. Thank you!

I am indebted also to Healtheries of New Zealand Limited who helped supply the New Zealand shopping guide.

For John C. Day, 'Daisy',
to whose dream this
book is dedicated.

Introduction

It is an extraordinary indication of our degeneration as useful beings that we have such poor judgement about the relationship between what we eat and our vitality. But even more basic is our inability to prepare foods which bring us life.

How many people would be desperate if they could not use cans, packets and convenience foods? For whom is such food convenient? It lacks the warmth of preparation and energy that is put into it by a loving mother/father or devoted cook ... this warmth is vital. The type of cooking and food preparation presented in this book is the most basic of all. It does not require great skill or intellect, simply practice and intuition. Basic cooking and food preparation should be straightforward.

'Basic' means being able to nurture oneself physically and spiritually, without having to resort to another person's (or factory's) judgement. Cooking develops your judgement and the judgement of those around you. Approach it with interest and a desire to feed yourself properly. Don't expect wonders overnight and don't be put off by failure, this is merely a vehicle for learning. Warmth and togetherness can't be bought in a can.

I have tried to present food which is based on traditional knowledge yet fulfils the requirements of today. It is reasonable that we should assimilate and use the thousands of years of experience our species has. Of course, traditional peoples did not have to make a decision as to whether white bread or wholemeal was better for them ... or whether they should swallow 20 vitamin C tablets because of the onset of a cold. There was an understanding among peoples of what foods are the best for maintaining strength and vitality; it is this understanding which has been lost.

Many will disagree and claim that we should 'go with the flow' so far as food habits are concerned ... that sugar consumption and meat/dairy based diets are nutritionally the best and most suitable for this age.

Modern scientific nutritionists have laid out clearly the minimum required daily doses of niacin, thiamin, riboflavin and food iron, etc. Yet by the standards of today's nutritionists, most of our ancestors would be dead, and life on earth could not have evolved. The diets of peoples such as the Sumerians and Egyptians may have been dangerously low in vitamin C and protein and calcium and iron and thiamin and riboflavin, according to some modern nutrionalists, yet they established ordered civilisations, accumulated wisdom and built structures which we would have trouble emulating today. Most Asians alive today shouldn't be . . . their diets are supposedly not adequate. There is a gap between theory and practice as far as nutrition is concerned. For example, I have been living on a diet which, according to most authorities, would leave me weak, undernourished and unproductive . . . my children should have rickets and scurvy.

There are thousands in a similar position who know through experience that most of the statements of modern nutritionists are based on theoretical assumptions which suit the economy more than the body. This is why I advocate using traditional knowledge of food . . . it works. The theory is 'transmutation'. Scoffed at for years, this 'theory' has finally been proven in experiments at the University of Ghent and the Laboratory of the Société des Agriculteurs de France, even though it has been 'proven' in unrecognised experimentation many times. The idea of transmutation is that when an individual eats a balanced diet of wholegrains, vegetables, seeds, nuts, fruit and lean animal food, in that order, his body is capable of changing or transmuting elements to supply all of his needs.

This especially relates to vitamins, of which our ancestors did not need supplements. Vitamin C can be manufactured in the body from balanced 'whole' foods which contain very little of this substance, and by exposure to sunlight. How many oranges does an eskimo eat? The balancing mechanism of the body is such that if there is a deficiency, it can be readjusted. The mechanism of transmutation is severely damaged by the consumption of foods high in vitamins and by processed foods. For example, if you ingest mountains of vitamin C, 90 per cent will be flushed out and 10 per cent can be utilised. However, next time your body requires vitamin C, transmutation doesn't work any more, and the only way to get the vitamin is from another source.

By returning to a more balanced, less extreme diet, your body will be able to return to full efficiency. Otherwise, you will become physically addicted to vitamin supplements. Even more basic than the idea of transmutation, although closely allied to it, is the idea of chewing food adequately. Many nutritionists today, when labelling a food with 50 mg of iron, for example, consider that this is completely available for absorption into the body. They do not adequately consider the processes of digestion . . . so really this food might as well be introduced intravenously. Chewing is a vital mechanism which predigests carbohydrate (especially) and energises the digestive system, stimulating juices and organs in preparation for the food ingested. It is a principal dietetic failure today that we do not chew our food properly and gain its full benefit. Lack of chewing causes blocking of intestines and bowels, constipation, poor nutrition, anaemia and low vitality. Many of today's foods are great for not chewing. The ice creams and sugar cakes, sloppy instant foods, can almost be swallowed whole. Drastic things happen if meat is not chewed adequately. This causes intestinal putrefaction with toxic physical and mental conditions. Soft food which can be swallowed with little chewing, is for infants and invalids. Healthy, vigorous people should use their teeth and gums and chew well. Otherwise, if people consume soft-quality food and don't chew much, they will develop a similar nature to an invalid or a child and soft, flabby tissue-texture.

When sick you should chew all food at least 100 times. At other times, chew food to a liquid before swallowing. This does not fit into the fashion of 'stuff and swallow', and neither will you if you chew well.

Many people today, in particular the young, are seeking alternative diets. They become vegetarians or vegans or lacto-vegetarians or macrobiotic or new age raw food folk or simply replace their sugar candies and cakes with raw sugar candies and cakes. At the same time, some of these people search for alternative medicine because our present day medical practice has so many shortcomings. Some in this sphere have found that they are able to heal themselves and their friends by following one or another traditional idea of natural medicine. They have also found that such healing does not always work on their friends who do not eat well.

If you eat clean, whole foods in a balanced fashion, you become amenable to natural medicine. Westerners cannot understand the Chinese preoccupation with ginseng. Western medical teams have analysed it to the atom and claim it has very little value as a healing herb. Yet the Chinese regard it as a cure-all. If eating a grain/vegetable diet, ginseng is a strong herb which can favourably alter the balance within your body. It does not work on heavy meat eaters or people with strong constitutions, or on people who consume tonnes of it. Similarly, acupuncture is nowhere near as successful in the west as in the east. This is due to the fact that westerners have bodies in which the vital meridians are distorted and clogged by mucous deposits as a result of poor eating. It is also due to the fact that when an oriental person becomes sick, the individual accepts blame, not seeing this as the fault of some micro-organism. Thus, oriental people in general have a better 'healing mentality' than westerners, who prefer to have drugs heal them . . . by remaining outside the healing process as though they were car engines having a radiator flush. Some who advocate systems of diet or healing are themselves the ones who need healing. There are many who hide under the guise of naturopath or chiropractor who are no better than many western doctors. Their knowledge is book learning and experience simply confuses them. Much harm has been done to the natural foods movement by charlatans and those who speak without experience. 'Natural foods' has in some respects become a cult and this is the opposite to what it should be. Some who follow extreme diets are exclusive and fanatic about food and tend to crusade their particular brand of health. They are worse off than most 'rubbish' eaters. Food alone cannot cure . . . mentality must develop along with physical health, correct eating can only *lead* to an unencumbered or free mentality. So many of us today think we have a free mentality when it is simply alternative and self-satisfied. Therefore we do inestimable damage to the development of real freedom and human evolution. The 'elimination of toxins', which seems to be a fashionable requirement of health today is not only physical, but spiritual.

I am not prescribing what you should eat. The recipes in this book are intended to be examples which show how my friends and I evolved a diet suited to ourselves. As such, the recipes are merely a guideline. Some I do not use regularly, and others not at all. I have included them because they are valuable in transition. Take time and change your food slowly. This will provide a chance to adapt and enjoy without becoming neurotic about eating.

Australia

'Australia has indeed achieved a much better national standard of nutrition, but possibly the biggest obstacle now to overcome is improvement in the standard of food preparation in the home and in processing factories. Faced with a bewildering array of foodstuffs, Australians appear to make poor use of this variety in promoting their own health and well being. They often make poor choices in foods they take regularly. Perhaps we now have too much tucker in Australia.'

Elizabeth Ashcroft in *Tucker in Australia*.

Since the settlement of this country, many aspects of Australian life have been derivative. Australians still eat as though they lived in Europe. This is perhaps our biggest obstacle to the attainment of health. This country has a much warmer climate than the Europe our ancestors left behind them, yet there has been a distinct lack of intuition on the part of Australians in their adaptation to our environment. Australia has almost the highest meat consumption in the world, second only to New Zealand. Traditionally, peoples who live in hot climates eat a very small proportion of meat and animal products. The Aboriginal is no exception to this, and their animal food was indigenous and not of the imported variety. The fact that we must make extensive alteration of the landscape and constant medication of our dairy and beef herds indicates that such animals are not suitable to the Australian environment. But because our forebears ate such foods, we carry on regardless. With reference to our immediate ancestors, their diet and the settlement of this nation, three authors in *Tucker in Australia* claim:

'Not only do the[se] five hungry years of Australia's early infancy mirror the life of 18th century England, but they also give some hint of one aspect of the pattern of Australians living for one hundred and fifty years to come. Perhaps the early agricultural struggles and failures and the drought of 1790–1791 are in part responsible for what many feel to be the Australian attitude towards the soil — to regard it, not as a bounteous mother who, having been cherished, will in return nourish her offspring, but as a churlish thing from whom a living must be wrung with sweat and tears'.

'In an attempt to balance out the effect of our large proportion of animal food consumption, Australians eat large quantities of sugar, extreme acid food such as tomatoes, and potatoes, and become awash in huge volumes of alcoholic beverages. Consumption of alcohol is increasing dramatically to the point where we consume, on average, more than 300 ml of alcoholic beverage per head per day. As a result of these food trends, Australia has one of the highest death rates due to degenerative disease, such as cancer and heart disease, in the world. The net result of such disease and consequent elaborate health care systems is that by the year 2000 our health care bill will equal our gross national product!' (Bryan Furnass in *The Impact of Environment and Lifestyle on Human Health*). All of the advances made by medical science in reducing the infant mortality rate due to infectious disease, and hence reducing mortality overall, are now being neutralised by increasingly lower life expectancy, especially for males. This shortening of life span is clearly due to our diet and our obsession with alcohol. It appears that Australian males are the main victims of degenerative disease, and at a ridiculously early age. Look at our beer guts and distorted masculine physiques, the Australian male's addiction to meat, and his obviously unharmonious or aggressive temperament. Australian society is characterised by a lack of appreciation of all things aesthetic, and if we are what we eat, it is no wonder. Michio Kushi argues that in terms of evolution, we should eat products which are our biological opposites and furthest from us on the evolutionary scale. This is a statement of natural law which has governed man's intuition about diet for eons. By consistently consuming mammals such as cow and sheep, we are almost cannibalistic, in that we are merely more sophisticated mammals. Some meat eating has always had its place in most traditional diets, but our outrageously carnivorous obsession is leading to physical and spiritual degeneration which can never be cured by all of the advances medical science has to offer.

My interest is that we Australians learn to eat according to our climate and learn from the examples of traditional ethnic peoples around us; not only Asian peoples but our own Aboriginal inhabitants.

Obviously we cannot emulate the diet of the Aborigines, but we can learn from them. Aboriginal mythology and natural science is not cute and obscure, but an indication of the mentality of people who lived within their environment. Much of this knowledge is now defiled and most Aborigines have been lured into our sweet life. But these people still have much to teach us because they lived comfortably within an ecology which we now distort and pillage. It is up to us to let go of our superior mentality and see this country clearly, as the Aborigines once did and in some cases still do.

'It will be interesting to look in on the Australian family in the year 2000. Will we see a highly sophisticated group in an air-conditioned, multi-storey, kitchenless apartment, eating a pre-cooked frozen meal of pre-fabricated meat and vegetables, reconstituted in a micro-wave oven, and sipping synthetic fruit juice, formulated liquids or perhaps even swallowing modular pills? Or will we find they have returned to nature and do-it-yourself living, as naked and hirsute they eat their stone-milled, wholemeal, home baked bread, 'organic' vegetables and home brewed beer?'

Caroline Turner in *Tucker in Australia*.

This is viewing our future in comical extremes. What concerns me is whether there will be a future for man on this planet if we continue to practise our egocentric, wasteful and amoral mode of life.

1

Food quality

Why imported foods?

Many of the recipes and remedies in this book are Asian traditional foods. The use of such imported foods can be criticised by those who want to be self-sufficient. But such foods are useful because they provide nutrients and qualities which make the transition from industrial food easier, and the maintenance of a wholesome way of eating more convenient to a larger number of people. Foods such as miso, shoyu, umeboshi plums, noodles and grain-honey will be produced in Australia in the near future. This is obviously desirable.

Traditional European foods are becoming more widely produced and available, for their role as the nourishment of our ancestors is important in overcoming the effect of present-day industrial food. Such foods tend to redevelop the 'grass roots' which many westerners feel they have lost, and continually seek. Most important is that the traditional or natural foods of Australia become more widely known and available. For example, the 'umeboshi plum' may sound strange to many, but a very similar food was produced by the Aboriginal inhabitants of this country.

Salt

Use unrefined sea salt. This should have a slightly grey tinge.

Traditionally, three things are good in small measures but bad in large — salt, yeast, hesitation. Some prefer to live without salt. After you eliminate stored animal salts from your system, a proportion of salt is a catalyst for activity.

If you eat wholefoods and use unrefined sea salt you will never get hard arteries from salt as this goes hand in hand with poor or unbalanced eating. Salt is one of man's most traditional seasonings — don't be neurotic about it.

A desirable way of consuming salt is as a seasoning ground with roasted sesame, or occasionally, sunflower seeds. This mixture should be slightly salty, not overbearing. The ratio of salt to seed should be 1:8–12. The oil from the seeds coats the salt and the body uses it more efficiently. This also prevents the salt from making you thirsty. Roast kombu, nori or wakame seaweed in a slow oven. When it is very dry, crush finely in a grinder. Add this to sesame salt in the same ratio as salt. Valuable minerals can be obtained in this way, as well as a unique flavour.

Natural soy sauce (shoyu) commonly called tamari, is an excellent seasoning, containing valuable ferments, enzymes, aminos, etc. It is made from soya beans, wheat, sea salt and water, aged for about two years. There are many imitations around — the real thing is unmistakeable after a while. Use in cooking or as a dip for tempura. Don't put it directly on your grains as it makes them less digestible because the oil from the soya beans coats the rice. All brands except those sold from natural food stores should be treated with suspicion. Place a drop of soy sauce in a glass of clean water. Shoyu sinks immediately to the bottom. Chemical pretenders start to dissolve soon after entering the water.

Miso is another way of consuming salt in a balanced form.

If you use sesame or sunflower seed-salt, shoyu and miso, and add a pinch when cooking grains in winter, you should not normally need more salt. Most of us have it stored in us from meat-eating days as undesirable 'animal quality salt'. If you are a vegetarian and getting cranky and short-tempered, examine your salt intake. Go without for a while to see if salt is the cause — adjust your intake accordingly.

You can eliminate stored salt after a period of good eating. Hot ginger baths and a drink of bancha tea containing two teaspoons of finely-grated radish are a help in getting rid of stored salt. Bancha tea with a salted plum, 5 drops of ginger juice and ½ teaspoon soy sauce — brewed for a few minutes — can also help to replace old salt with good quality salt and minerals.

Salt bought in supermarkets usually contains sugar and/or silico-aluminates or some additives to make it free-flowing. The bulk of this produce (99 per cent) is pure sodium chloride. When you buy or make natural salt, only three-quarters of its bulk is sodium chloride. The rest is valuable minerals. Even the sea salt from commercial sources has been refined.

If your salt goes damp during winter, it is probably all right. Best of all, if you live near the sea take an earthenware pot to the beach, light a driftwood fire and make your own salt by boiling off the water. Don't do it in Port Phillip Bay or in any other such cesspool. Salt can be omitted in any of the recipes in this book for those on a salt-free diet.

Oils

Coloured, thick, nutty-smelling oils are usually the ones for you. Some cold pressed oils are as chemical as their supermarket counterparts. Go by colour, smell and texture rather than label.

Corn oil, white and dark sesame and sunflower oil are good for everyday use. Use olive oil for that delicious Mediterranean flavour; corn oil for amazing cakes, crumbles and salad dressings. Use dark sesame oil sparingly, adding a tiny amount at the end of cooking — a truly remarkable flavour. Chinese stores carry it — be sure to get one from the People's Republic as these seem less purified.

I use peanut, white sesame and sometimes soy oil for wok-frying, a Chinese peanut oil or grapeseed oil for deep frying, Santa Sabina olive oil for European dishes and ghee, peanut oil or coconut oil for South-east Asian and Indian food.

Soy oil will burn at lower temperatures than other oils. Unfortunately, some tasty vegetable oils are not available in Australia. If you want to avoid using oil, sauté using a little water.

Flour

Flour is poorly labelled in Australia, there being no distinction between flour which has been milled from soft wheat and that from hard wheat. Soft wheat produces soft flour which is most suitable for cakes, pastries and chapatti. Hard wheat is generally better for bread, since it contains more gluten and sustains a higher rise. Hard wheat flour is sometimes called strong flour. It produces hard pastries too! Hard wheat is darker, sometimes almost translucent, whereas soft wheat is white or yellow. Hard wheat flour is sandy in texture. Soft wheat flour is soft — talc-like.

I mill my own wheat at home for bread and pastry, having a stock of the appropriate wheats. If you require lighter flour, simply sift your flour to remove the coarsest bran. This is also the best flour for chapatti. Good flour supplies can be had from Lowan Wholefoods, Continental mill in Victoria and Demeter. When buying wheat, purchase organic or biodynamic quality.

See *The Natural Tucker Bread Book* for an in-depth discussion of wheat and flour.

Water

If you live in Adelaide, move out, buy a water filter or set up a rain tank. Adelaide's water will eventually poison the city. From the reaches of the Murray in New South Wales to its outlet in South Australia, this river collects DDT, pesticides and chemicals from a thousand sources. The water is then chlorinated and fluoridated and piped to you. Nothing is done to remove soluble poisons. Adelaide will be the artery degeneration centre of Australia soon — it has too big a population for its water resources. This applies to most cities — clean water is vital. You work with it, wash with it, drink it and it is almost all of you, so if it is clean you can be too.

Grains

Try to buy your grains from reputable people. You support their efforts to provide clean food and benefit by having them around. (See Chapter 18.)

Lowan Wholefoods and Demeter are the major grain suppliers I have found. Lowan's grains are especially high quality. Four Leaf in South Australia also have excellent grain products. Biodynamic brown rice is available in Victoria through Biodynamic and Demeter outlets, McAdam Square, Croydon, Ceres and Soul Foods, see Shopping, page 185.

Grains should all be of a similar size and colour. If grain is broken, shrivelled and badly marked in high proportion, it is low grade.

Northern (West Queensland) wheat is darker and slimmer than its southern counterpart which is light-gold and plump. Rice should smell sweet and nutty. Unsprayed long-grain rice from North Queensland is very tasty but not as sustaining as the small-grain variety from New South Wales.

Lowan Wholefoods have excellent hulled millet, rolled and whole oats, buckwheat, rolled barley and wheat. Look carefully at nuts, seeds, grains for too many flaws, marks, or shrivels. Spiral have good unhulled sesame seeds. Nearly all sesame seeds available in health food stores are hulled and bleached. These are not 'wholesome'. Unhulled sesame seeds are grey-fawn and taste very different to the processed ones. Chinese groceries have unhulled black sesame seeds which are very good. Most tahina (sesame butter) available has emulsifying agents and added oil. Avoid this as it is very poor quality. Spiral sesame purée is made from unhulled sesame seeds and tastes so different to commercial tahina it is quite astounding. This is what I refer to when 'natural tahina' is mentioned in the text.

Miso

There are seven types of quality miso available commercially. These are the six available in good food outlets in Australia.

Kome: Sometimes called white or red miso, it is aged for 3 – 12 months. Kome is a light brown to red-brown colour and made from soya beans and partially hulled white rice.

Mugi: This is made from soya beans and barley. It has noticeable pieces of soya beans, and is brown; aged for 1½–2 years. It is saltier and stronger in taste than kome miso, and is good for winter soups. More suited to winter and colder climates, such as Melbourne and Adelaide, it is generally the most suitable miso for all-round use.

Hatcho: This is very dark brown to black, and is usually a purée because of longer fermentation (3 years). This is made from soya beans alone and is very strong and salty. You should only use this one in a cold climate winter. I believe it makes you short-tempered if used excessively or in warm weather. Suitable for hearty soups.

Mame: Young hatchomiso.

Genmai: Brown rice miso which is of the highest quality. I recommend it for all-round use.

Natto: Barley, soya, vegetable and seaweed combination with very short fermentation. Delightfully sweet.

Soba: Delicious buckwheat miso.

White (Shiro): Low salt miso made from soybeans and white rice. Sweet in flavour – good for summer use, in dips, spreads.

Vegetables

Perhaps the most varied type of vegetable in Australia is the pumpkin. There are sweet, watery, hard, powdery, pale and dark varieties. Some are so sweet it's remarkable. Try to use those which have firmer flesh rather than the watery

ones, as the latter have much less food value. Look for pumpkins that have dark-coloured flesh and aren't huge. It is better to buy a whole, small pumpkin than ready-cut pieces.

Queensland Blue and Windsor varieties have dark green skin and excellent flesh. Butternuts can be anaemic, but then so will their skin colour — so look for darker ones.

The 'Jap' pumpkin which I think is a type of Hokkaido pumpkin, is available in New South Wales and Queensland and is sweet enough to search out! Gramma Trombone is good for sweet pies, as is rice marrow. Many huge, rambling pumpkins are fruit rather than vegetable, and are flavourless and watery. Tiny Acorn pumpkins, called Golden Nugget, are worth growing for their unique texture and flavour. Try to avoid peeling pumpkins, as their skin is perfectly edible. Insert your thumbnail into the skin, if the skin can be pierced then it is edible.

Chinese vegetables such as cabbage, spinach, mustard cabbage, coriander, long white turnip or radish (daikon), winter melon, bitter melon, snake beans, snow peas, taro, are all worth hunting for. You will find these in quite a few suburban vegetable shops in Sydney and Melbourne, especially in ethnic areas. Little Bourke Street in Melbourne, Dixon Street, Haymarket in Sydney, and Fortitude Valley in Brisbane are Chinese produce areas, and here you will find these vegetables. There are very few Chinese stores in Adelaide, but sometimes these vegetables appear in the central market.

Chinese cabbage is becoming more popular and is available in quite a few vegetable shops today. Chinese vegetables are often organic, but often *not*, so wash carefully.

Search out the mustard cabbage with thick, juicy stems, which are an unusual light green colour. It is delicious stir-fried in oil/ginger for two minutes — sprinkled with water and shoyu, covered for one minute and served brilliant emerald green.

Greek and Italian shops have beautiful green leafy vegetables such as kale and chicory. Don't be afraid to ask how to cook them, you might learn more than you bargained for.

If you live where giant bamboo is growing, look for bamboo shoots. These are like cones coming out of the ground. Strip back the leaves and rind, and slice the tender inner core. Drop into boiling salted water and cook until the shoots turn quite ivory and loose their acrid odour (30 minutes). Then use in stir-frying. As these are a strong food, don't eat too many.

The range of vegetables available is quite extraordinary when you look. It is a pity that some people only cook cauliflower, pumpkin, potato, carrot, swede by boiling them. To be eating mainly grains and vegetables gives you an infinite variety of foods and combinations. Meat restricts scope because the meal is centred on the meat and everything has to be a 'side' dish designed to provide relief from the bulk of meat. This restricts the ability of the body to utilise all of its sensory apparatus and become more a part of the whole world. Some claim that once humans had abilities far beyond our own. Our sense of *deja-vu*, having seen something before, or having been in a situation before, is a lingering remnant of such capacity. The accuracy of some clairvoyants and abilities of certain 'faith healers' are also abilities which were once more widespread. It is because of degeneration in our diet, specially in the last 500 years, that such capacities as we have are blocked by mucous, fat or other deposits of matter in our systems.

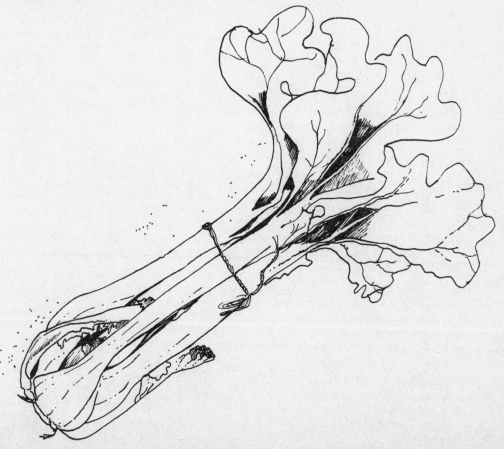

The Aboriginal inhabitants of Australia and the Indians of the Americas had knowledge which few modern people can comprehend because it seems to be of such obscure, simple or superstitious quality. In reality, it is a knowledge concerning the balance of all life with the Earth and within the universe ... something we now pursue like musical chairs through philosophy and atomic physics. Aborigines had this awareness because they were what they ate — all things that flourish naturally. It may not be possible for many people today to achieve such capacities, but it is certainly possible to restore such seemingly trifling abilities as memory, sight, co-ordination, smell, hearing. Our degeneration is eating this far into our senses. How many people do we know today who score perfectly on all of these simple functions? If we were made 'in God's image,' by today's standards, He would have died of a stroke at fifty-five!

2

Utensils

Preparing your own food means acquiring skill at man's most basic craft. Become a craftsman — vegetables must be chopped or cut properly for correct cooking and so they look a delight on the plate.

To do this properly, acquire a good vegetable knife.

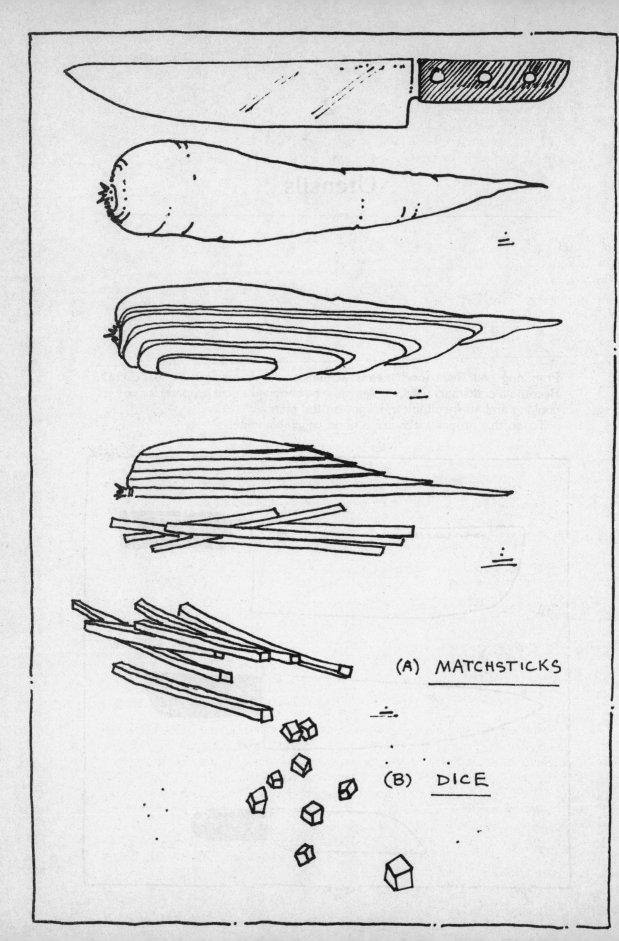

(A) MATCHSTICKS

(B) DICE

Those shown are the best knives I have used to date. They are Asian, and Asian food-stores are the best to scour for cooking utensils. Most European cooking equipment is designed for meat based cooking and is usually impractical for use with vegetables. Small and light Chinese cleavers are also useful.

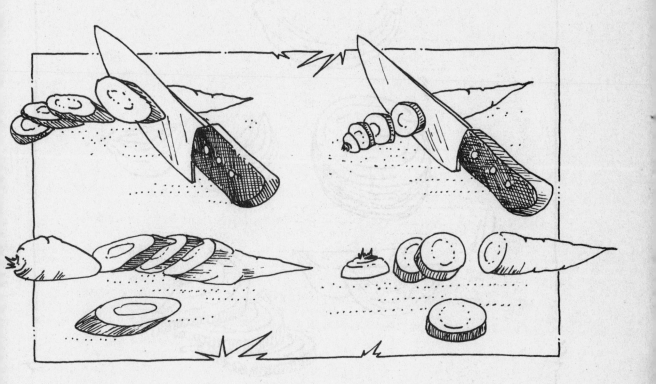

For hard vegetables such as pumpkin, use a heavier cleaver or knife. Please learn how not to cut yourself. Cut vegetables gently, and each type in a different manner or shape. A wooden chopping board, which is not too small, is a basic requirement. 'Opportunity' shops and second-hand stores usually have good wooden ones which have been rejected in favour of their modern-day plastic counterparts. If using a wooden chopping board for animal foods, be sure to clean it thoroughly after use. Salt and lemon rubbed into the board will remove dirt and bacteria. Wipe it well and dry carefully. It is easy to make a good board by cleaning a suitable piece of wood and sanding it to smoothness.

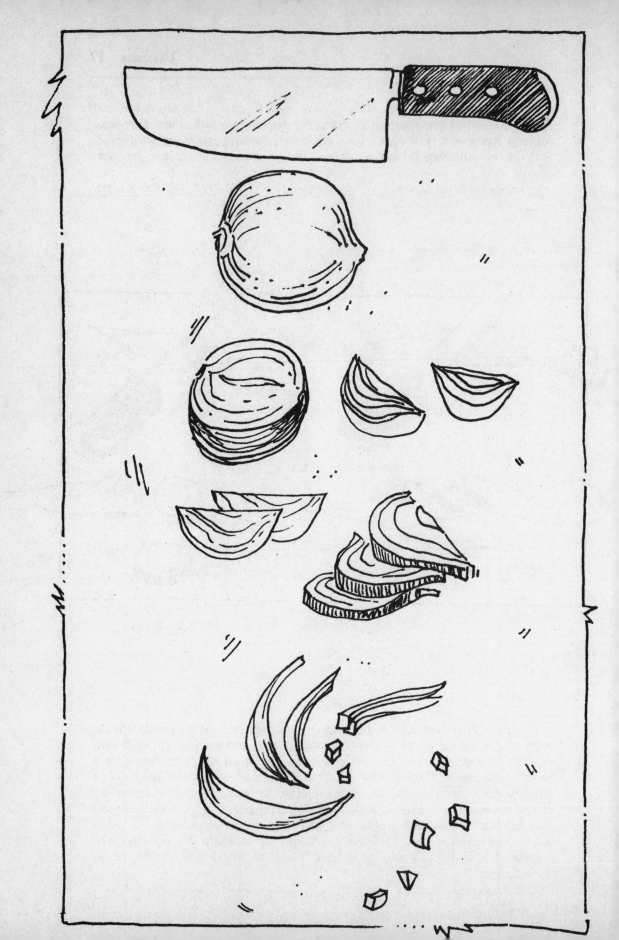

Cooking utensils should be earthenware, enamel or good quality metal such as cast-iron, rolled steel or stainless steel. Avoid Teflon and other technological gadgetry. Aluminium ruins the quality of good food and initiates stomach trouble. A potter would make baking pots or earthenware saucepans on request. Asian grocery stores and some natural food stores carry superb pottery rice cookers. These need a 'flame tamer' for cooking and care in handling. Soak in salted water for one hour before use.

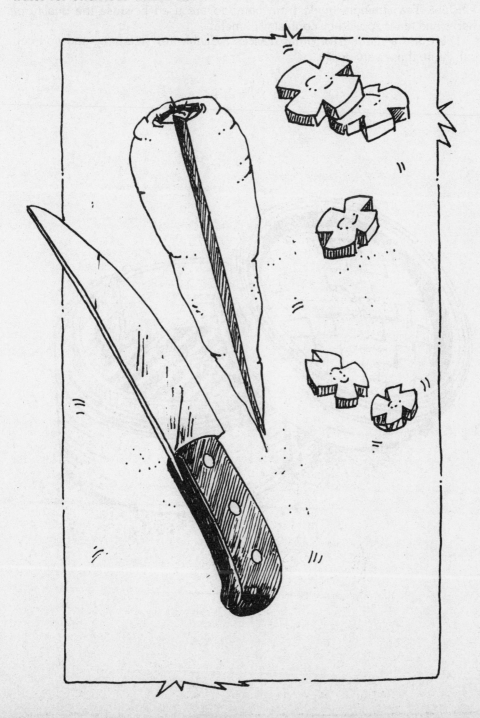

Heavy cast-iron skillets and saucepans are cheap and ideal for slow but thorough cooking, or toasting grains and seeds. Pyrex or heat-proof glass is very good for some cooking, especially pot-roast, casseroles or jelly. Use wooden and earthenware spoons rather than metal where practical. Bamboo paddles are useful with grains. Bamboo is used extensively in Asia for cooking. It requires thorough cleaning and drying. Bamboo steamers which can be obtained in Chinese groceries impart subtle fragrance to food, and are very efficient. Tea strainers made from bamboo are used because the quality of herbs and tea is spoiled by contact with metal.

There are a number of other devices available for steaming, and you can substitute these very easily.

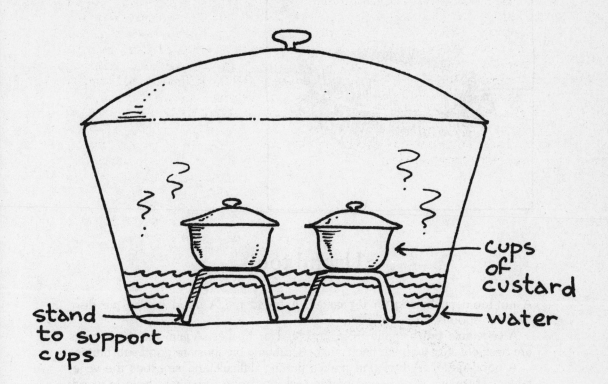

cups
of
custard

water

stand
to support
cups

Crockery mixing bowls are a basic necessity — try second-hand shops.

If pastry doesn't roll, it may just be your rolling pin — it's called rolling, so use an appropriate action, and an instrument which is practical.

A mortar and pestle of good size are essential. Japanese 'suribachi' grinders are very good. These are used for making sesame salt and grinding nuts, seeds, spices. By hand grinding, if practical, you impart energy to food.

A wok is a vital utensil. The cheap rolled steel ones from Chinese groceries are excellent. Copper bottom stainless steel woks are good but expensive. To season a wok: wash with hot soapy water. Rinse and dry thoroughly. Rub well with vegetable oil. Place the wok over medium heat and add 1 tablespoon freshly grated ginger root. Stir in the oil, adding more as necessary, for 5 minutes. Wipe clean with a rag and clean with hot water and a brush. Using a clean rag, rub the whole of the inner surface with vegetable oil for 10 minutes. Wipe clean with a rag.

Certain woks are good for deep frying, but need much oil to fill them. Use a selected saucepan or buy a special deep-fry pan which has enough depth and an efficient strainer. Spiral Foods distribute them.

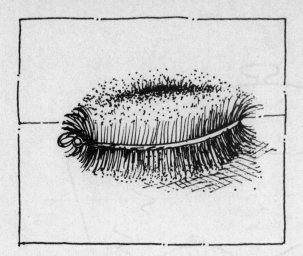

Useful tools

A not-too-deep baking tin for cakes. A bread tin. A good quality pie dish. Wooden spoons.

A vegetable brush made from fine reed or bristles. Again, the Asian ones are best; old-style wooden-back nail or scrubbing brushes are good substitutes.

A good grater. A bad one makes grating difficult and smashes the vegetables. To make a very good grater, tack tin around a square hole in wood. Turn over and punch nail holes in a downward direction so these are sharp from the grating angle, and present a diagonal face to the vegetable. Porcelain graters are now available through some natural food stores.

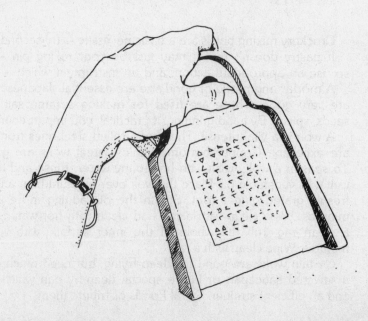

3

Preparing vegetables for cooking

Remember to sharpen your knives — blunt knives slip off the vegetables and will actually cut you more easily. Fix the point of the blade on the cutting board, and use the section of blade near the handle for cutting. This does not apply in all cases, but generally for fine chopping. If you have a Japanese style knife (page 16) with a special point, this enables you to insert the point and slice like a razor for making 'matchstick' shapes. With green vegetables, notably Chinese cabbage, spinach and mustard cabbage — slice off the root section on the above-ground side. Wash out grit and slice through the white fleshy stems and leaves in 1 cm strips.

For example, in a stir-fry using ginger, carrots, onions, parsnips, zucchini and cabbage: finely grate the ginger; cut the carrots into matchsticks or fine half moons; cut onions in half, and in half moons from top to bottom — these then fall into slivers; parsnips in matchsticks or half moons. Slice the zucchini in half from end to end, then slice through. This makes an 'oblique' shape. Cut cabbage in half. Slice from side to side in ½ cm strips.

Basic rules for chopping vegetables are: chop all of the same vegetables the same way. Cut in chunks for baking or pot roasting. Stir-fry requires finer cut vegetables. Each should be finely chopped in an individual fashion — but carrot or parsnip matchsticks are good together.

Cut vegetables in sizes according to their cooking qualities. For example, carrot and parsnip take longer to cook, so for stir-frying, cut them thin. For baking or pot roast, cut harder vegetables smaller than other fast-cooking ones such as zucchini. Always cook greens the least, and last.

Waste as little as possible. Carrot tops and especially radish and turnip tops are excellent and highly nutritious foods, which are very palatable when stir fried, or blanched for salads.

Wash vegetables in cold water and scrub off the dirt with a reed or bristle brush. Don't peel them unless absolutely necessary.

Orderly eating

To ensure correct digestion and optimum value from food, it is important to eat in an orderly and regular fashion. Generally, don't mix foods too much. To begin with soup, proceed through grains and vegetables and finish with salads, is a useful general rule, although soup often accompanies rather than precedes a meal in the Orient.

Authors such as Raymond Dextriet in *Our Earth, Our Cure* recommend beginning a meal with fruit, then proceeding to salad and on to cooked food. This suits some people admirably and can be a refreshing change, especially in summer. However, as long as you are aware of the need for orderly eating and do not eat refined foods, there is no need to be exclusive and dogmatic about your style of eating.

Yes, it takes longer to consume a real meal in an orderly fashion, just as it takes longer and costs more to produce whole foods. Try to eat three regular meals a day, and ensure you have eaten enough to satisfy the needs of your body and whatever form of work the food will be expended on. If you starve yourself, it is more than likely bingeing will result. It is better to eat good food till you are satisfied (not stuffed full).

Wait until you have been eating well for some time before being extreme about fasting or strict diet. Otherwise, you will run screaming for whatever you crave. In this respect, it is better to cook sweet foods and cake at home to satisfy cravings, rather than bingeing on shop-bought sweets. This way, you can gradually solve the sweet tooth cravings and the chocolates can stay in the stores, not in your system.

Oriental medicine teaches that the body craves that which is being eliminated, and sometimes the craving is too strong to resist. Don't resist unless you are very strong-willed or healing yourself. It is ridiculous to be neurotic and exclusive about food. This creates neuroses and bigotry, as well as secret bingeing, which is merely self-destructive. Most of us have plenty of time to overcome our past eating habits. Do it slowly and in a well thought out, orderly fashion. The results are smoother and more satisfying.

4

Basics: grains

Rice

Rice is the staple food of a large proportion of the world's population. Its preparation and variety are about as diversified as those who cook it. There are many varieties of rice. A few which are obtainable in Australia are long-grain, short-grain, black rice, glutinous rice, basmati. There are many individual varieties therein.

Brown rice (unpolished) is the best to use. White rice has been stripped of valuable nutrients and is an incomplete food. Beri-beri, or vitamin B deficiency, was unknown as a widespread complaint in Asia before the introduction of polished white rice. The brown germ and bran on the rice contains B vitamins and minerals; in fact the word vitamin arose from research on the polishings left after refining brown rice to white rice.

You should attempt to eat 'whole' foods. Polished rice is not whole, but incomplete and therefore cannot be wholesome.

Basic method
Use a ratio 1 cup brown rice to 2 cups water. Wash rice well under cold running water. Rub between your hands. This step is important, as it removes dust and impurities. Rinse clean. Place in anything but an aluminium pot, preferably an earthenware rice cooker or heavy saucepan, with a small pinch of sea salt or 1 umeboshi plum. Bring to the boil over a high heat with the lid on. When rice boils, cover and simmer slowly for approximately 40 minutes. Tilt the saucepan. If the rice doesn't move from the edge of the pan, it is ready. Do not stir at all; the bottom should be slightly scorched. If you intend to use the rice for fried rice, or if you prefer it chewier, use 1¾ cups of water. New season rice requires approximately ½ cup less water than rice which has been stored for some time. If using for cakes or pastry, add half a cup of extra water — i.e. 2½ cups. When cooking all grains, add an umeboshi plum. Break it up with your fingers and mix in. This provides necessary salt and makes inorganic grains more suitable. Use natural sea salt if umeboshi are not available.

Soft rice

Good for sweet dishes, breakfast, brilliant for children's and invalids' food.
> 1 cup brown rice
> 6 cups water
> 1 umeboshi plum (optional)

Bring to the boil over a high heat, cover and simmer over low heat for 4 hours. Stir once or twice every hour. Sprinkle with tekka and/or sesame salt. If you add vegetables while cooking this dish, it is called 'congee', a favourite Chinese breakfast. Left-over rice can be cooked in this manner. Add 1 cup of water per cup of rice and simmer over a medium heat for 40 minutes, stirring gently at 10 minute intervals.

Roasted and simmered rice

Wash 1 cup brown rice, then toast slowly over a low heat until light golden. This can be done in an oven or a pan. Add 2 cups of water and an 8 cm piece of kombu seaweed. Boil, then simmer covered for 40 minutes. Do not stir.

Baked rice

> 1 cup roasted brown rice (washed)
> 1 cup washed plain brown rice
> 4½ cups water
> 1 piece kombu seaweed

Place in a baking dish and bake for 1–1½ hours at 190°C (375°F). Remove when ready.

Rice cream

Wash the rice. Roast it gently until dry and golden. Grind into a slightly coarse flour meal. Fine-grind if you like it, or for a creamy texture. For each cup of rice meal use 3 cups of water. Place rice meal in pot. Add half water and a pinch of salt. Stir well to avoid lumps. Add the rest of the water. Put on fairly high heat, stir constantly — even vigorously — for about 10—15 minutes until thickening. Add more water if you think it necessary. When creamy-thick, put on low heat and simmer for 30—45 minutes. This is beautiful with sesame salt, tekka, seaweed powder, grain syrup, vegetables or fruit.

Rice milk

Follow directions for soft rice, using 1 extra cup of water. When cooked and cool, place all of the rice in a cheesecloth bag, or line a strainer with cheesecloth. Press and squeeze the bag until milky liquid comes out. Collect this rice milk. The leftover rice inside the bag is delicious mixed with sesame salt and deep fried — or used in bread. Rice milk is a good food for young children. Mix with finely mashed vegetables and well ground, toasted sesame seeds. Sieve the seeds to remove impurities.

Glutinous rice

Soak rice for at least 2 hours prior to cooking — preferably overnight. Use 1 cup rice with 1½ cups water. Add a pinch of sea salt or umeboshi plum, bring to boil over high heat, simmer covered for 45 minutes.

Red rice

Red rice grown in Sri Lanka is available in some natural food stores. It is supposedly a high protein rice. I have had little success in tracing the traditional method of cooking this rice. The Chinese seem to use it for fermenting rather than as a direct foodstuff. It has an unusual flavour when cooked which leads some to dislike it. In Asia a little of the red bran is removed by light polishing before cooking which seems to me to improve the flavour. Many people find red rice delicious and it can be cooked in the same way as brown rice or mixed in varying proportions with brown rice. Another method is to soak it overnight, two parts rice to one part water, and measure the volume of water left after soaking. Discard the water it has soaked in and replace with an equal volume of fresh water for cooking. Red rice requires more salt than usual, say 1 teaspoon of salt to 5 cups of rice.

Long grain rice

When cooking long grain brown rice, measure the volume of water and bring to the boil. Drop the washed rice into the boiling water. Bring to the boil again, cover and simmer slowly for 45 minutes. The best ratio for long grain rice is 1¾ water : 1 rice.

Black rice

Soak for 4 hours or overnight. Rinse well and discard soaking water. Use 2 cups water to 1 cup rice. This can be cooked using half brown rice. Cook as for glutinous rice.

Left-over rice or grains

If you have rice which has gone slightly tacky, and is unsuitable for direct consumption, don't throw it out. Break the rice up with a wooden spoon and add sufficient water to make a thick gruel. This can be made into a sweet or salty porridge or custard.

Salty: Bring the rice to the boil. Add your choice of chopped vegetables. Turn the heat down and simmer for 15 minutes. Add miso and chopped greens . . . serve.

Sweet: Add dried fruit such as raisins, a grated or chopped apple, a split vanilla pod and some toasted coconut or kinako. This is a delicious and quick custard. The more this is stirred the creamier the texture. If desired, add agar-agar (kanten), cook until the agar-agar dissolves and allow to cool and set. Similarly, add ground kuzu arrowroot dissolved in a little water or apple juice, place this in the rice mixture when it boils, and stir until the mixture thickens. Allow to cool and set. Another combination is ground, freshly roasted nuts and rice honey, maltose, or honey.

Mugwart rice

Eating-quality mugwart is hard to come by. The Japanese variety is slowly becoming available and is very good quality. Mugwart is excellent for the blood when eaten with rice, and is a traditional Asian food for lactating mothers. Soak two mugwart rounds in hot water for 10–15 minutes. Break up into strands with your fingers, and add to rice — cook as usual. A delicious treat. Two rounds are sufficient for four cups of rice. Mugwart noodles are available in some natural food stores.

Basmati rice

A delicious aromatic white rice grown in the Punjab. A refreshing dish eaten occasionally.

> 2½ cups basmati rice
> 4 cups water
> pinch salt or an umeboshi plum

Cook as brown rice, or bring water to a boil, add rice, let boil again. Turn down low and simmer covered for 30 minutes. This rice is delicious cooked with mung beans or lentils and vegetables in a pilau.

Wild rice

It is possible to buy North American wild rice in 'gourmet' stores. It is almost prohibitively expensive, but if you can afford it, try some. When cooking brown rice, use half wild rice, or place 1 cup wild rice in 2 cups boiling water. Allow to boil again, then turn down and simmer for 30–40 minutes. Use it in pilau form with rice, other grains and vegetables or beans.

Australia has two varieties of wild rice that I know of. One of these is a variety of our standard short-grain rice, which has seeds a little smaller than domestic rice. The other is a swamp grass variety, about which I know nothing. We hope to search these out in the near future.

Cooking rice with vegetables

By adding vegetables to brown rice as it is cooking, you can make a meal in itself.

> 1 cup washed brown rice
> 4 cups water
> 1 cup hard-sweet pumpkin, cubed
> pinch sea salt

Bring to the boil. Simmer slowly for 1½ hours. Replace the pumpkin with other vegetables such as carrots, squash, parsnip, onion, or with apple for sweets.

These mixtures are highly suitable as food for children. You can add a little kombu, hijiki or any seaweed or some slightly toasted sesame or sunflower seeds, crushed. Any grain can be cooked in such a way to make a very suitable infants' food. Add more water if you want it softer.

Soak wheat or barley overnight before cooking in this manner, and mash lightly before giving to children. This breaks the grains and makes them more digestible.

See pilaus on page 59 for other grain and vegetable combinations.

Ricecorn

> 2 cups washed brown rice
> 2 cups fresh corn kernels (cut from the cob)
> 5 cups water
> pinch sea salt or an umeboshi plum
> diced vegetables if you wish (and an extra cup of water). Pumpkin is good

Bring rice to a boil. Add corn (and vegetables if using). Simmer for 45 minutes. Barley-corn combination is delicious.

Chick pea rice

2 cups washed brown rice
1 cup cooked chick peas
1 small onion, diced
1 cup diced pumpkin *or* carrot *or* celery
1 piece kombu seaweed (or local dried seaweed)
5 cups water (or chick pea cooking water)
1 umeboshi plum

Bring rice to boil. Add chick peas and vegetables (if using). Simmer, covered, for 45 minutes.

Soya rice

4 cups washed brown rice
1 cup cooked soya beans
1 teaspoon kinako (dry-roasted, ground soya beans)
Pinch sea salt or 1 umeboshi plum
8½ cups water
15 cm piece kombu seaweed

Bring to the boil and then simmer covered for 45 minutes. Rolled into balls and deep fried it is delicious!

Sticky rice

1 cup sticky or glutinous rice (brown if you can get it) soaked overnight
2 cups brown rice, washed
1 cup washed red or mung beans
9 cups water (9½ with red beans)
½ teaspoon sea salt or 1 umeboshi plum

Bring to the boil and simmer covered for 1½ hours with red beans, 50 minutes with green beans.
Add:
vegetables and/or sea vegetables for variation, or ¾ cup dried currants, 1 star anise, 2 diced apples, and 1 extra cup of water for a sweet.

Or stir in fresh summer fruits 5 minutes before end of cooking time, or place them on top to steam.

Seafood rice

3 cups brown rice
6 cups water
15 cm piece kombu seaweed
1 cup diced raw fish or ⅓ cup shrimps or raw, diced green prawns
½ teaspoon grated ginger
1 bay leaf (optional)

Bring rice to boil with kombu and bay leaf. Cook as usual. Add seafood and ginger 10 minutes before completion of cooking. Stir in gently.

Wheat

Wheat groats or kernels

Soak 2 cups organic whole wheat overnight. Bring the wheat and 5 cups water (soaking liquid) to the boil over high heat with a pinch of sea salt. Cover and simmer slowly for 1½ hours.

Use more liquid and cook longer for softer groats. Serve with gomasio and baked vegetables. Whole wheat helps develop togetherness by its very nature. Mash it for young children, it is an excellent protein source.

Wheat cream

Very warming in cold climates, as are wheat groats. Roast whole wheat until golden. Cool. Grind to a coarse flour meal. Add water slowly to flour meal until you have a thick stirrable paste.

Slowly add all the water: 2½ cups per cup of meal, and a pinch of sea salt. Bring to near boiling, stirring constantly. Turn heat down to medium flame and continue stirring for 10 minutes. Turn heat to low, cover, and simmer for 20 minutes. Excellent with sesame or sunflower salt, warm maltose, or toasted nori seaweed.

Wheat porridge

Lightly toast coarsely crushed wheat. Place in a pot, add water — 2½ cups per cup of grain — a pinch of sea salt or umeboshi plum.

Bring to the boil over a medium heat, while stirring. Turn heat to low, cover and simmer for 30 minutes; or add to boiling water and stir for 10 minutes. Turn heat to low and simmer for 20–30 minutes. If adding to boiling water, make a thick cream with some cold water and add the rest of the water. This avoids lumps.

Soft wheat

Follow directions for wheat groats, but add 2 extra cups of water and cook for 3 hours.

Semolina

Lima Ohsawa's recipe for sweet semolina is an example of how to adapt foods to your needs. Semolina is often cooked with milk and sugar which gives it a creamy texture and sweet flavour. You can use sweet potato or parsnip with the same results.

Add 1 teaspoon light sesame oil to a skillet or heavy frying pan and toast 1 cup semolina for 10 minutes until fragrant. Cool.

Add 2½ cups water and a pinch of salt and bring to the boil. Turn heat down and simmer for 30 minutes, stirring occasionally.

Meanwhile, steam — or cook in a little water — one medium or 2 small sweet potatoes — the Golden variety are excellent. When cooked, mash and add to the cooked semolina. Stir for a few minutes and let stand over low heat for 5 minutes. Pour into a rinsed basin or baking tray.

This will become firm in 2 or 3 hours and you can remove it from the mould by inverting and tapping carefully, or by slipping a lifter under it.

Savoury semolina can also be made in this way. Add cooked onions and serve with a thick vegetable sauce.

You can cook dried fruit with the semolina too. I recommend raisins, sultanas or currants, which are sun-dried.

Barley

Delightful and satisfying, barley is a cooling grain. Cook in the same manner as whole wheat or wheat cream.

Whole barley is good with baked carrots and sesame salt, pressed parsley salad. Soft cooked barley with carrots is an excellent food for young children.

Unpearled barley makes a delicious soup with wakame, laver (nori) or dulse seaweed, vegetables, beancurd and miso.

Millet

Use hulled millet.
>1 cup millet
>2 cups water
>small pinch salt *or* 1 umeboshi plum

Wash millet and toast slowly until fragrant. Bring to a boil over high heat. Cover and simmer for 35 minutes. Alternatively, omit toasting and proceed as above. Make cream as for wheat, using more liquid.

Millet has a favourable effect on the spleen. It is good for singers or those who must project their voice.

Australia has quite a few native varieties of millet, harvested by the Aborigines. They are worth following up.

Buckwheat

You can use roasted or unroasted, whichever you prefer. I like to use it roasted.

>   1 cup buckwheat
>   2 cups water
>   1 strip kombu seaweed (optional) or pinch salt

Bring water and kombu to a boil. Add buckwheat. Turn heat to low and simmer covered for 25–30 minutes.

Buckwheat cream and porridge may be cooked in the same manner as wheat.

Buckwheat warms — lights an internal furnace.

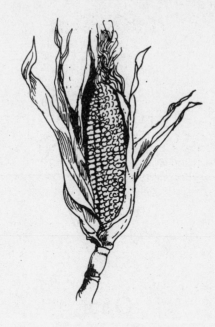

Corn

Corn can be steamed, baked, or simmered on the cob. It can be eaten from the cob sprinkled with shoyu or sesame salt, or cut off the kernels for further use. To cut from the cob, stand the corn on end and slice down, keeping the knife against the corn husk. My favourite way to eat corn is smeared with the flesh of an umeboshi plum. It is a sweet and sour delight.

Polenta (or Cornmeal)

Polenta is ground sweetcorn, used mainly in Italian cooking. Maize meal tastes quite different and should be lightly toasted before use.

 2 cups polenta or cornmeal
 7 cups water
 1 10 cm piece kombu seaweed
 1 teaspoon sea salt

Toast cornmeal over low heat in a heavy saucepan until fragrant and nutty. Slowly add water while stirring. Add kombu seaweed. Bring to the boil. Simmer over slow heat for 1 hour. Add a little water if necessary. Pour into a rinsed dish and allow to set. Alternatively, bring water and seaweed to a rolling boil. Add salt. Quickly add polenta to boiling water. Stir rapidly with a whisk until liquid boils again. Simmer with the lid on for 15 minutes, stirring occasionally.

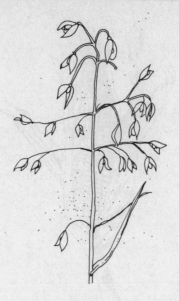

Oats

Oats are a good source of vegetable quality fat to keep you warm. Cook whole groats or kernels as for wheat. Or, if you can, cook oats overnight in the oven, on a wood stove or in a crock pot.

Rolled oats can be toasted before making porridge — ratio oats to water 1:2. Bring to the boil slowly while stirring. Simmer over low heat, stirring occasionally, for 30 minutes.

Rye

Protein and energy rich. Cook as for wheat. Very tasty cooked with $1/4$ teaspoon aniseed or caraway seeds per 2 cups grain. Excellent baked in a casserole with beans and vegetables.

Noodles

Wheat (udon), buckwheat (soba)

Put noodles in boiling, slightly salted water — enough to cover noodles adequately. When water returns to the boil, add 1 cup of cold water. Let water boil again, add another cup of water. Do this once more. Turn down and simmer for 10–15 minutes, stirring occasionally.

Test to see if done by tasting a noodle. Strain. Rinse noodles under cold water unless serving within 10 minutes. Keep warm in steamer, or pour boiling water over noodles in a strainer to heat up.

A good instant meal is noodles with soup made from the cooking water. After removing noodles, add miso or shoyu and green leafy vegetables while it is very hot. Add finely grated vegetables if you wish, and chopped spring onions.

Spaghetti

Drop into plenty of boiling water with a pinch of salt. Return to a rolling boil and simmer for 15–30 minutes depending on how coarse the spaghetti is. When it is cooked but firm and ready to eat it is called 'al dente'.

Brown rice noodles (bifun)

Boil water. Drop noodles into water and let stand for 10 minutes. Rinse under cold water.

When cooking noodles ensure there is plenty of water, or the noodles will stick together. Carefully place noodles into the boiling water and stir gently to eliminate adhesion.

Chinese white rice vermicelli

Drop into boiling water, turn off heat, let stand for 5 minutes. Remove, strain and serve, or rinse and keep for addition to a dish.

Transparent noodles (sometimes called vermicelli or pea-starch)

Drop into boiling water for 5–10 minutes. These cook quickly.

The Chinese have many varieties of noodles in sticks or bundles.

Most of these can be prepared in a similar manner to other noodles.

Making noodles

Use freshly-ground high gluten flour — all wholewheat or 40 per cent buck-wheat.

>   2 cups flour
>   pinch salt
>   ½–¾ cup water

Mix and knead for 10 minutes, adjusting water until you have a pastry-like dough. Let stand for 2 hours.

Knead and roll until thin. Cut out thin strips, or your choice of shapes. Drop into boiling, lightly salted water or broth. Boil for 10 minutes or until noodles are cooked thoroughly and floating — try them.

You can make unique noodles by adding bancha tea or clear soup to the flour instead of water.

Egg noodles — add one beaten egg to the above.

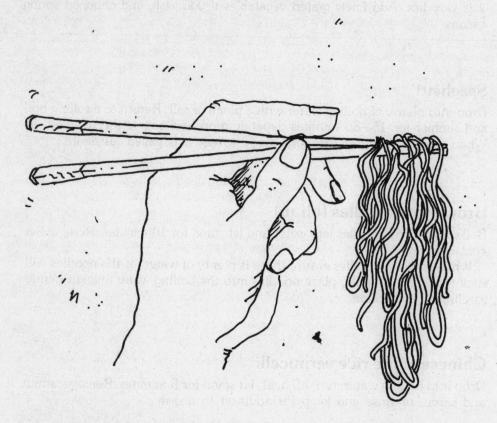

Cheong fun

Soak 2 cups brown rice overnight. Drain off water. Wash. Wet grind or use a blender to purée the rice with 6 cups water. Must be thoroughly ground. Add 5 tablespoons kuzu or 6 tablespoons arrowroot. Mix well.

Using a large Chinese bamboo steamer, set the water on rapid boil. Wet a close weave cotton cloth and place in the steamer. The steam must be pouring through the cloth. Mix the batter and rapidly ladle enough on to the cloth to cover it. Cover the steamer and steam for 20 minutes over high heat. Remove cloth and peel off the noodle sheet. Spread precooked green prawns, cooked hijiki seaweed and spring onions on the noodle. Roll it up. Cut into 10 cm lengths and douse with shoyu, dark sesame oil and rice vinegar in the proportions 5 : ½ : 2.

Serve immediately. If not using prawns, substitute tofu or fried tempeh.

Grain textures

In terms of dietary therapy, it is desirable to persevere through sensory demands for such foods as creamy dairy products and fruit such as avocados, even abstaining from creamed cereals which can be used as substitutes for the dairy drugs. This is because there is a direct relationship between creamy quality foods and mucus deposits which cause problems such as sinus complaints, vaginal discharge, sexual maladjustment and malfunctioning organs.

When water is mixed with crushed grains, the texture is similar to that of creamy dairy products such as milk, cream, yoghurt, cheese and butter. Continual consumption of these products undeniably causes deposits of fat and cholesterol in the body. Such build-ups cannot be removed even when these foods are avoided, if you still eat food of a similar texture. Grain creams will not cause harmful deposits, but along with other sloppy or creamy foods, such as nut butters and tahina, will inhibit the elimination of stored fats caused by consumption of animal food. Some complain that grain based diets cause mucus. My experience has been that this is transitory. Excess mucus is merely being discharged, especially from the lungs, where the bloodstream eliminates some waste matter.

Creamy consistencies are for the young of the species and should mainly be used as an introduction to firmer foods. Adults should eat more solid whole foods, because this is what they are designed for. The difference between eating whole grains and grain creams is important. Unbroken grains will still sprout even after years of storage. They still contain the life force. Broken grains, especially flour, rapidly lose their vitality after grinding.

It will tend to make you more mature to eat food which requires a mature type of chewing and digestion, i.e. adult food. This is particularly important for vegetarians.

For young children, cook whole grains with more liquid, and mash them before feeding.

5

Basics: vegetables, seaweed, beans

Vegetables

Wok or stir-frying

This is a brilliant Chinese technique. Hot oil and steam cook the vegetables very quickly, ensuring vitality and nutrition. For a small wok, use 1 teaspoon to 1 tablespoon oil depending on how much oil you want to eat or how many vegetables you have.

Heat oil, but don't burn it, and add vegetables. Cook onions first, with ginger or garlic, grated or crushed. You can slice ginger or garlic big, and remove it before you add other vegetables if you desire. If using dried spice, e.g. Chinese peppercorns, or ground cummin or coriander, add with the onions.

Cut vegetables so they will cook at the same rate. For example, small pieces of carrot (hard) and larger pieces of zucchini (soft). These will then cook at the same rate. When the onions are cooked, usually 20 seconds–1 minute, add the other vegetables, lifting and mixing with the oil and onions.

Cooking chopsticks are good here, or a special wok instrument.

After 2–3 minutes of stir-frying, add ⅓ cup water, stir and place lid on wok. If too dry, add more water, but not too much. Lift lid and stir frequently. After 5 minutes, add greens or sprouts, stir, replace lid, turn off heat, and let stand for 1 minute. Sprinkle with shoyu and a small amount of dark sesame oil, for a special taste. Stir and serve. Wok frying can be done using water or stock instead of oil.

Stir-frying becomes second nature in a matter of weeks. The process requires close attention, however, to ensure even cooking, no burning, and to eliminate under-cooking. Greens should be translucent and firm, not over-cooked and soggy. For a delicious touch, add ten or twelve dried salted black beans immediately before the onions.

Spices used can be Szechuan pepper, Chinese red pepper, cinnamon, chillies, star anise, cummin, mustard seeds or others. I think these are only for a special touch, however, because the vegetables taste so good anyway. Too many spices create a spicy temperament and interfere with good digestion.

Grains and beans can be stir-fried also. This requires more oil and less initial heat. Make sure the grains are not too soft and are as individual kernels. Cook grains with a little less water if preparing in order to fry. Heat oil with onions or garlic or ginger or spice as required. Add grain and stir quickly so as to cover all the grains with vegetables and add a little water as the wok gets dry, but don't make the grains soggy. Use some salt because beans contain oil which needs salt to balance its effect. If you want to fry rice or other grains with vegetables, it is best to cook the vegetables first and remove from wok. As soon as the grain is fried, add the vegetables, stir till hot, then serve.

If frying rice noodles, simply soak the noodles in hot water for 10 minutes, but do not cook them first as they are too glutinous to fry. When frying buckwheat (soba) or wheat noodles (udon) or Italian-style spaghetti, do not cook for as long as usual so they will be slightly firm. Wash in cold water before frying as this will make them less glutinous and sticky. Add noodles in the final stage of stir-frying vegetables.

Steaming

Bamboo steamers are best. Make sure your vegetables are sliced finely enough to steam. By putting herbs/roots such as ginger in the steaming water you can achieve delicious results. Steam grains or mixtures or cakes wrapped in or on cheese cloth.

Baking

Use glass or earthenware dishes and throw your aluminium foil away. 190°–200°C (375–400°F) is a good temperature for baking vegetables.

Place the chopped vegetables in the baking dish (don't chop too large) and add 1 cup of liquid (½ water, ½ shoyu), depending on the amount of vegetables and size of container. Use plain water if you like. Oil is unnecessary unless you really want the type of texture it produces. For this, rub the vegetables in a little oil and sprinkle lightly with salt. Use ½ cup water. Bake slowly at 175°C (350°F) for 1–2 hours.

Corn germ oil or dark sesame oil gives the vegetables a unique flavour, especially with a few salted black beans added.

Otherwise, cover and bake for 40 minutes–1 hour. A sprinkle of tekka is delicious for baking, or a handful of roasted rolled oats or barley mixed with the vegetables.

Cut the vegetables so they are attractive and not just lumps. You can remove the liquid and thicken it over heat with roasted flour or kuzu arrowroot, or starch from making seitan (wheat gluten), to make a delicious gravy.

If baking casseroles, it may be necessary to lightly oil the inside surface of the dish — especially if it is glass.

Pot roasting

Heat 1 tablespoon oil over medium heat in a heavy pot (½ corn germ oil is good) and add about 4 cups of vegetables cut in fairly large chunks — no bigger than a small egg. Stir with a wooden spoon until all are coated with oil and frying. Add ½ cup water and some shoyu (mixed), stir, cover and simmer for 40 minutes–1 hour.

Stir every 10 minutes. Add more liquid if necessary. Root vegetables and pumpkin are good done in this fashion. Serve them with corn pancakes or griddle cakes and red kidney beans.

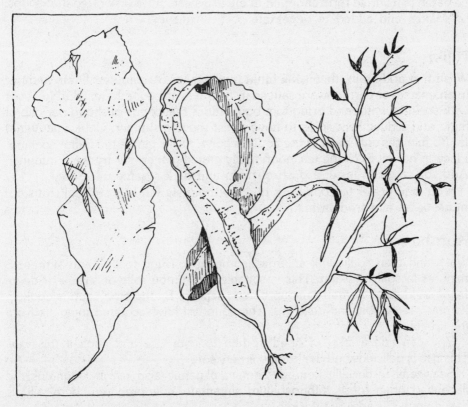

Seaweed (sea vegetables)

Basic preparation

Seaweeds are mineral-rich and a delicious accompaniment to any meal, especially fish dishes. Some remove metallic waste from the body and have a remarkable effect on people afflicted with radiation sicknesses.

They are a traditional food of all coastal Europeans, especially the English and Irish. Ever heard of Irish moss or carageen in an old cough mixture commercial? A traditional British Isles dish is laver (nori) oat cakes.

Australia's coast abounds in edible seaweeds. Go out and find them — only the very fine filament-type seaweeds are not edible. Australia's first settlers made jellies from agar seaweeds which abound. Agar and nori exist in the zone out from a low tide or even between low and high tide. Light green sea lettuce grows on rocky headlands and is easily collected. Wash it very well to remove grit, and add to soup or seafood dishes. Most are perfectly edible, but don't collect them from polluted places.

Dulse

Dulse is not widely available in Australia, but hopefully it will be harvested in the near future. This seaweed is red when in its dried form and broad leafed. Dulse is still used by many people from Alaska to Ireland in their traditional cooking. It is nutrient-rich, being a vegetarian source of vitamin B12. It can be eaten in its dried form chopped finely in a salad or incorporated into soups, or soaked and added to vegetable or bean dishes.

Hijiki

Wash first and drain, then soak hijiki in water for 30 minutes. Drain and put in an enamel or earthenware saucepan (metal is not good here). Barely cover with soaking water and bring to a boil. Add 2 teaspoons of shoyu per cup of hijiki and reduce heat so as to have a fast-moving simmer. Cook uncovered for 35 minutes until most of the liquid is gone. Hijiki can be fried after soaking. Place in hot oil with one teaspoon finely grated ginger, stir fry for 2 minutes. Add soy sauce to taste, a dash of mirin and dark sesame oil. Serve.

You may prefer to cook your hijiki without shoyu. It is still delicious but more of an acquired taste.

Kombu

Wash and then soak until enlarged completely. Bring to boil and simmer 5 minutes in soaking water. This is suitable for kombu rolls or salads or deep-frying. Add dried kombu to soup before heating. By the time soup is cooked, kombu will be soft and delicious. The soup will have acquired minerals from the kombu.

You can add a strip of dried kombu to your rice and cook it this way. This rice is delicious and the kombu is very soft.

Seaweeds (especially kombu) contain glutamic acid which heightens the flavour of other foods. Monosodium glutamate, now prepared chemically, is based upon this ancient principle.

Wakame

This has a slimy texture which offends some, but delights others. It is very good in salads, and best in miso soup.

Simply wash, then soak for 10 minutes. You can add it to any cooked dish — soups, stews, vegetables, for pie fillings, casseroles, deep-frying.

Nori

For nori rolls, lightly toast nori on one side over a flame or heat. Besides the nori available from Japan through macrobiotic outlets, there is Chinese laver available in all cities at Chinese stores. This is cheaper and not of as excellent quality, but is still delicious and nutritious, especially in soups, which is where the Chinese usually use it, not in rolls, as the Japanese do.

Nori can be roasted and crumbled into, or onto, many dishes. It has a strong but very endearing flavour. Great on sandwiches or in salads, in breads, pies, baked and with deep-fried foods.

Agar or kanten

It is possible to buy cheap, good quality agar from Chinese and Japanese stores. With agar you can make sweet or savoury jellies, amazing custards, mousses, soups, flans, and cold pies.

Simply add chopped or torn-up agar to liquid, boil then simmer till the agar dissolves. For example, for a savoury jelly, make your favourite soup and simply add agar before you cook. When it cools, it will be a jelly with chunks of vegetables or seafood. Great in summer and good for the intestines!

Or cook apples with added agar and when they cool — jello!

7.5 cm of Kanten stick is suitable for 1 cup liquid. Kanten sticks are usually 3 cm square. Powdered agar is not as good — add 1 teaspoon per 3 cups liquid. Dissolve it in cold water before adding. This can be added to a hot dish in this way and put away to set after five minutes' cooking.

Agar, when eaten in combination with a balanced diet, is good for high blood pressure and a heart which is enlarged. It has a noticeable cooling effect, so is especially good in hot weather and for 'hot heads'. There are other seaweeds with whose names I am not familiar, which can be purchased in Asian food stores. I have found them all delicious.

Calcium content of sea vegetables compared to animal products (per 100 g):

Dairy foods:	cow's milk	100 mg
	goat's milk	120 mg
	various cheeses	250–850 mg
Seaweeds:	kombu	800 mg
	hijiki	1400 mg
	wakame	1300 mg
	agar-agar	400 mg

Beans

Some of the beans more commonly used are: chick peas, brown beans, borlotti, navy, pinto, lima, kidney, soya, black soya, mung, azuki and blackeyed. There are basically two types of beans: those which require soaking and those which do not. Chick peas, brown beans, borlotti, navy, pinto, lima, kidney and soy beans need overnight soaking for them to be rendered digestible. Mung, azuki,

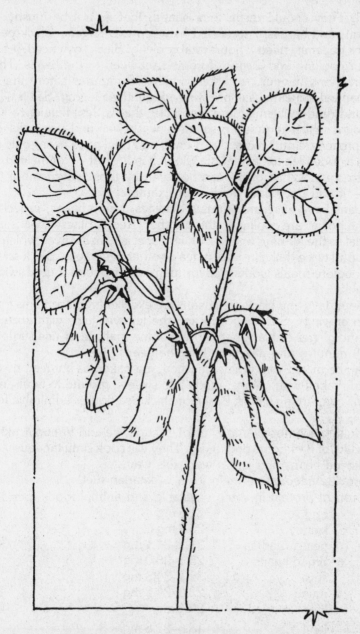

blackeyed beans and lentils can be cooked without soaking. Haricot beans can be cooked with 3-4 hours soaking but are best soaked overnight. Make sure to use plenty of soaking water as beans expand considerably when soaked. A ratio of 1 beans : 4 water is usually sufficient. Discard soaking water as it contains anti-nutritive factors, and wash beans well before proceeding with cooking.

For cooking beans use a 3 : 1 water : bean ratio and bring them to the boil over high heat with the lid off. When they reach boiling point, turn down and simmer rapidly for 15 minutes with the lid off. Give them a good stir. This allows gases to escape. Then turn heat to low, cover and simmer until the beans are cooked. They should retain their shape, that is, not be mushy (unless making dahl), and be easily squashed between two fingers. Chick peas and kidney beans generally need 2 hours total cooking. Black soya need 4–5 hours. After 1 hour cooking add a stick of kombu seaweed to the beans. This provides minerals and flavour. Add salt to beans 5 minutes before the end of cooking. If added too early, salt prevents adequate softening. Salt is a balancing factor and renders beans more digestible, that is, less flatulence causing! To cook beans which require no soaking, wash well and use a 4 : 1 ratio. Follow the procedure outlined above. Lentils and blackeyed beans only require 1 hour. It is a good idea to have a little juice left in the pot – for making a sauce or adding to soup. White beans can be eaten by those who cannot tolerate much oil – if you have liver trouble for example.

Some beans have excellent curative qualities. Mung beans, especially the black-green variety, are cooling in the summer. Red (Chinese) beans or azuki are beneficial to the kidneys and sex drive, especially azuki juice which can be drunk, 1 cupful twice daily, instead of tea or other beverages. Black soya bean juice drunk before meals works well for menstrual troubles if used twice daily for 5–6 weeks.

Red kidney, navy and blackeyed beans are excellent replacements for Heinz baked bean cravings. Strain and thicken the leftover juice with kuzu, add a little miso and ginger or black pepper and some maltose or rice syrup. Cook the sauce 5 minutes and mix back into the beans.

Beans can be mixed with grains, mashed and baked as burgers, rissoles, in loaves, fried, baked with onions, made into sweets, ground to flour and used as creams or deep-frying batter. Besan or chick pea flour is admirable for deep frying.

When cooking rice, for example, use 1½ cups rice and ½ cup azuki beans. Soak the azuki for 3–4 hours previously. They will cook simultaneously. Mung, urad, blackeyed beans and lentils work this way.

Beans provide adequate protein for a vegetarian diet.

Comparison of protein in some vegetable and animal foods (per 100 g):

Beans	azuki	21.5 mg
	kidney	20.2 mg
	peas (dried)	21.7–24.1 mg
	broad beans	25.1–26.0 mg
	soya	34.1–34.3 mg
	mung	23.0–24.2 mg
	lima	20.4 mg
Meat	beef	13.6–21.8 mg
	pork	9.1–21.5 mg
	chicken	14.5–23.4 mg
	eggs	12.9–13.9 mg
Dairy food	cheeses	13.6–27.5 mg
Sea food	fish	16.4–25.4 mg
	shellfish	10.6–24.8 mg

However, this chart does not indicate the balance of amino acids which is the key to getting enough protein from beans. By themselves, beans are deficient in some proteins and need to be supplemented with another source of complimentary proteins. These are found in cereal grains. So the traditional main-stays of diet are grains and beans; red beans with corn, quinoa or amaranth, rice and tofu, rice and dahl (lentils), millet and chick peas and so on. The correct ratio is approximately 3 parts cereal grain to 1 part beans. This provides what is called complete protein − at least the equivalent protein to meat. Keep this in mind when constructing a meal and you need not fear any form of protein deficiency − quite the contrary. This combination is extremely healthful with none of the side-effects of meat or meat products.

Beans seem to cause flatulence (stomach gas or wind) in many people. I think this is unavoidable and not harmful unless chronic. Ancient treatises on cooking beans mention this fact and make light of it:

> *Beans are such delicious fruit,*
> *The more you eat*
> *The more you toot.*

Stomach problems can be initiated by beans which are incorrectly prepared. Pay close attention to the cooking procedures outlined above.

Another good method of eating beans is to sprout them. Soak overnight. Keep the beans in a dark place (cupboard) and wash them well daily. A jar with gauze over the mouth is an excellent sprouting appliance. Most beans are ready in 4 days − make sure they are at least 3 days sprouted before eating. Sprouts are good in winter and spring in cold climates when there is not a great abundance of fresh raw produce.

Soya beans are a particular problem because they are highly indigestible unless cooked and prepared thoroughly. They contain a substance which prevents the excretion of protein-digesting enzymes in the stomach and this substance must be broken down through thorough preparation before the beans are eaten. Asians, who should know about soya beans because the beans originated in Asia, never eat plain soya beans. They learnt of their indigestibility thousands of years ago so they ferment them or make bean curd or bean milk from them. We should learn from their valuable experience. Many High Protein diets recommend eating masses of soya beans, but this seems to be a modern fad. There are much more delicious beans than soya beans available − leave them and try miso, tempe, tofu, soya milk and shoyu.

6

Soups

I have attempted to describe some soup making methods. Quantities vary with the amount of people to be served, the recipes given serve 6–8. Miso and shoyu are used 'to taste'. This means use them wisely; don't have everything tasting of miso or shoyu. They are nutritious additives which should be used to heighten soups, not dominate them.

I could have written a whole book on soups, and these are a small percentage of the soups we have used. So experiment, remembering to keep ingredients simple and complementary.

Miso soup

Chop 2 onions and 1 small piece of ginger (20 cent size) into fine matchsticks. Use 2 pieces of kombu or wakame seaweed (15 cm long). Add to 8 cups of water and bring to boil. Simmer for 10 minutes.

Take a cup of liquid from the soup and dissolve 6 teaspoons of your choice of miso, either barley, rice or all-soy (hatcho). Let stand or simmer for 5 minutes. This is a good time to add green vegetables sliced very thinly. They will be a beautiful colour when served. You can alter the amount of miso to suit your taste. Or use finely diced vegetables in this soup, or 4 or 5 shitake mushrooms, soaked (water added to soup) and sliced finely, to make this soup special. For climbing mountains, stir in a well beaten egg before serving.

Winter vegetable soup

Carrots, onions, swede, turnip, parsnip, and 3 bay leaves.

Chop all vegetables to a small size, such as cubes, matchsticks and half-moons. Cover well with water and bring to a boil. Turn down and simmer for 45 minutes. Remove half the vegetables and mash or blend them. Return to the pot and simmer. Add shoyu or miso to taste.

Creamed soups

To make a 'creamed soup' slowly roast or toast about ½ cup of fresh flour in a heavy pan. When this is lightly toasted and giving off a 'nutty' aroma, remove from heat and cool. Mix with 1 cup water and add to soup. Stir for 5 minutes and simmer for 20 minutes. This effect can also be achieved by adding toasted rolled barley or oats 20 minutes before completion of cooking.

Rice soup – Congee

A traditional Asian dish which keeps you coming back for more, this can be made while cooking the rice or from precooked or left-over rice.

 3 cups brown rice
 10 cups water (use soaking water from mushrooms)
 5 or 6 shitake mushrooms, presoaked
 6 pieces kombu seaweed, in hard form (not soaked) broken into small
  pieces
 1 umeboshi plum

Bring this to the boil over high heat. Turn heat to low and simmer for 3 hours. Stir every 20 minutes. The texture should be a thin glutinous 'gruel' – add more water if necessary. When cooked, dissolve 1½ tablespoons white, barley or rice miso in 2 tablespoons water and add to the soup, stirring in well. Or add 2 tablespoons of shoyu. Use more of these if required. For a more elaborate dish, add 1½ cups chopped fish fillet, prawns or squid (or other seafood), 15 minutes before the end of cooking. Or add 2 cups finely diced vegetables 30 minutes before completion.

This soup can be made with different varieties of rice. Black rice used in this way is extraordinary. Make sure to soak it overnight or at least 5 hours before cooking. The same applies to glutinous or sticky rice. A very good combination is two-thirds black rice, one-third basmati rice. Long-grain brown rice produces quite a different soup to the short-grain variety. North American wild rice is truly wild here. Buckwheat can be used half and half with rice, as can millet, oats, wheat, rye or cornmeal. Wheat or rye should be presoaked and cooked. Beans can be added if precooked or presoaked for the varieties which require less cooking. Short-grain brown rice and azuki beans make a wonderful soup for sick people. Basic rice soup is ideal for children and babies. To create a sweet soup, omit mushrooms and add grated or finely chopped fruit and a split vanilla pod 40 minutes before completion of cooking. When completed stir in 1 tablespoon of sesame purée or tahina. It is best to remove a cup of the gruel, stir the tahina into this and add back to the gruel.

Sea lettuce soup

Next time you visit the seaside, collect some sea lettuce from the rocks. This is bright yellow-green and has the appearance of small lettuce leaves. It usually grows between high and low water mark or in rock pools. There is a seaweed growing in similar locations with almost identical colours. It is more filament-like and slimy, but not what is wanted for this brew.

Wash the sea lettuce very well – 3 or 4 times – and remove any particles of rock from its root section. When washed, cover well with water. If using approximately 2 litres of water, add 2 onions sliced in half from top to root, then in slivers and 1 teaspoon finely grated ginger root. Bring to a boil over high heat. Turn down to low, cover and simmer for 30 minutes. Then add 1 tablespoon kome or mugi miso and a handful of bean sprouts. Make sure to dissolve the miso in a little of the stock before adding to the bulk of the soup, otherwise it will be difficult to dissolve. Serve immediately. This is excellent with a meal containing seafood.

Onion soup

>5 brown onions
>fresh or dried basil, oregano or caraway seeds

Chop the onion in slivers. Sauté for 3 minutes with 1 teaspoon olive oil. Add the basil and sufficient water to cover well. Bring to the boil and then simmer until the onions lose their sharp odour, about 45 minutes. Add one-third cup of roasted flour dissolved in water (or toasted rolled oats or barley) and shoyu to taste. Simmer for 20 minutes, stirring to ensure the flour does not lump. Chop half a bunch of fresh parsley into the soup before serving.

Green vegetable soup

Make a basic stock with water, one chopped onion and one teaspoon caraway seeds or 1 teaspoon finely grated ginger. Bring to a boil, then simmer for 30 minutes; 5 minutes before serving add finely chopped spring onion tops, Chinese cabbage, dandelion leaves, carrot tops, radish tops, celery leaves, broccoli — any combination of green vegetables you find desirable. Add miso or shoyu to taste and the juice of 1 lemon. Serve immediately, before the greens lose their brightness.

Sea vegetable soup

    2 15 cm strips kombu seaweed or wakame
    1 cup soaked hijiki
    3 sheets nori, lightly toasted on one side
    1 teaspoon kelp granules
    any seaweed from a fresh source
    1 teaspoon finely grated ginger
    2 onions cut in half-moons

Place all of the above in a pot and cover well with water. Bring to a boil and simmer for 30–45 minutes. Remove kombu and dice finely. Slice hijiki into 2 cm pieces if in large strands. Add shoyu or miso to taste. Serve with a fish dinner.

Pumpkin buckwheat soup

Cook chopped pumpkin with water (3 cups per litre) and one piece kombu seaweed. Purée pumpkin and return to simmer. Roast buckwheat flour lightly, cool and dissolve in a little water, being careful to remove the lumps. Add buckwheat batter to soup and stir for 5 minutes over medium heat. Simmer for 10 minutes. Add shoyu or miso to taste. Add finely chopped spring onion, including tops and roots, serve topped with a sprinkle of tekka. Alternatively use 3 cups of cooked buckwheat instead of the flour.

Bean soup

Use chick peas, kidney beans, azuki, brown but not soya beans. You will need 2 cups, cooked with 2 or 3 bay leaves. Bring to a boil 2 onions, 1 parsnip, 1 carrot and 2 sticks of celery finely chopped, cover and remove from heat. Purée half the beans and add to the soup with half a teaspoon salt. Add rest of beans, add 2 teaspoons kinako, and return to heat and simmer for 30 minutes. If using chick peas, dissolve or emulsify 1 tablespoon of natural tahina (sesame butter) with $1/2$ cup water and $1/2$ teaspoon sea salt. Add to soup but do not heat. Stir for 5 minutes. Top with chopped parsley and serve with crackers or cornbread.

Shitake mushroom soup

Wash 8 shitake mushrooms then soak them in water for 2 hours. Slice finely and discard stalks. Using soaking water and enough extra water to make 9 cups, bring to a boil: 1 onion, 1 parsnip, 1 carrot, 1 umeboshi plum, 1 cup diced pumpkin, 1 cup cauliflowerettes, 1 clove garlic, soaked in shoyu for 30 minutes (or 1 teaspoon grated ginger) and one piece of kombu seaweed. Simmer for 30–40 minutes. Add shoyu or miso to taste.

This soup is excellent for kidneys damaged by too much animal food and bad salt, especially if you use azuki bean juice for the stock.

Gojiru soup (a favourite winter regeneration broth)

> 1 onion, sliced thinly
> 2 carrots in half-moons
> ½ teaspoon finely grated ginger
> 1 small sweet potato, diced
> 5 soaked and sliced shitake mushrooms and 4 cups soaking water
> 1 finely chopped small daikon radish (keep top) or
>   1 cup diced red radish
> 2 cups thick gô purée (see page 120)
> 1 teaspoon miso per person

Sauté onion in 1 teaspoon oil. Add other ingredients and enough water to make a thick broth. Bring to a boil, simmer, stirring occasionally, for 30 minutes. Add kome or mugi miso or shoyu to 1 cup of broth, dissolve and return to soup. Finely chop radish tops, add and serve. Internal combustion!

Tofu broth

Make a clear broth with ½ teaspoon finely grated ginger, 3 shitake mushrooms and 6 cups soaking water, 1 cup finely sliced radish, 2 pieces kombu or ½ cup cooked hijiki or 3 sheets toasted nori seaweed, 2 chopped onions, ½ cup green peas and 3 cups water. Boil, then simmer. Add 6 thin half-moon slices of orange, shoyu to taste (about 3 tablespoons) or rice miso. Simmer slowly, add tofu in 2 cm dices and some finely chopped fresh greens. Serve immediately. Pour over noodles for a noodle soup.

Summer juice soup

Obtain juice from 2 cucumbers, 3 carrots, 1 onion, 2 sticks celery, small piece pumpkin and ½ daikon radish or 4 small radishes. Add as much water as juice. Add 1 umeboshi plum and slowly bring to high heat, but don't boil. Add finely sliced spring onions and 2 cm cubes of tofu if you have them. Shoyu to taste. Use the juice pulp by mixing some with rice and shoyu and kneading well. Form into small balls and deep-fry. This soup is good cooled or even with ice cubes in it if you prefer.

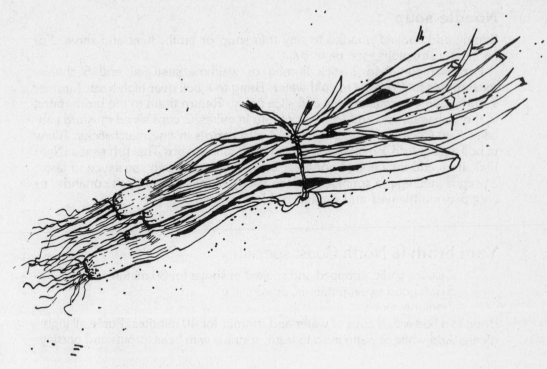

Cheese and greens soup

    2 onions in thin half-moons
    1 clove garlic, crushed
    1 teaspoon caraway seeds
    1 cup chopped cauliflower
    1 cup cottage cheese, ricotta or ½ cup grated natural matured cheese
       or fetta cheese in small cubes
    ½ cup finely sliced broccoli
    chopped parsley and radish tops

Sauté onions, garlic, caraway in 1 teaspoon oil for 3 minutes. Add cauliflower and 8 cups water. Slowly bring to a boil, then simmer for 20 minutes. Add cheese or tofu, greens, cover and let stand for 5 minutes. Add ¼ cup shoyu to taste and serve with sourdough bread.

Carrot and peanut soup

    3 cups finely diced carrot
    1 teaspoon finely grated ginger
    1 star anise, whole
    2 onions in thin half-moons
    ½ cup finely ground, freshly roasted peanuts

Combine all ingredients with 8 cups of water. Slowly bring to the boil and simmer, covered, for 40 minutes. Remove star anise and mash or purée vegetables. Add shoyu to taste. Reheat for 5 minutes. Sprinkle with parsley and finely chopped fennel greens.

Noodle soup

Simply add cooked noodles to any thin soup or broth, heat and serve. For cooking instructions, see page 37.

For example: Add 1 stick kombu or wakame seaweed and 5 shitake mushrooms to 1½ litres of cold water. Bring to a boil over high heat. Simmer 1 hour. Remove mushrooms and slice finely. Return them to the broth, bring to the boil again and add ½ block of tofu in cubes, 2 cups sliced mustard cabbage (Gai Choy) or Chinese green, 1 cup carrots in fine matchsticks. Allow to boil again. Add 1 tablespoon mirin and 2 tablespoons Thai fish sauce (Nam Pla), then add the cooked noodles. Serve into bowls with soy sauce to taste, a prepoached egg, a sprinkle of sliced spring onions, a few fresh coriander or chopped mint leaves and a grind of black pepper.

Yam broth (a North Coast special)

2 cloves garlic, chopped and soaked in shoyu for 30 minutes
5 or 6 good sweet potatoes, diced finely
2 onions, sliced

Bring to a boil with 8 cups of water and simmer for 40 minutes. Purée all ingredients. Add white or natto miso to taste, sprinkle with beansprouts and parsley.

Egg flower soup

2 15 cm strips kombu seaweed
4 pieces ginger, sliced to 20-cent size
½ teaspoon crushed Chinese red peppercorns (optional but delicious)
3 large or 6 small shitake mushrooms, washed, soaked and sliced
      (discard stems)

Bring these ingredients to the boil over high heat with 6 cups water and the soaking water from the mushrooms. Simmer covered for 30 minutes and add shoyu to taste. Remove ginger. Break 1 duck's egg or 2 hen's eggs into a bowl and stir with a fork. Little stirring produces yolk and big egg 'flowers'. If you stir constantly, the flowers will be tiny and of one colour. Mixing very finely chopped fresh coriander with the egg mixture is a delicious and unique variation. Slowly pour a thin stream of egg mixture into the hot soup while stirring gently. Add 1 cup of bean sprouts and serve immediately.

A type of bouillabaisse

3 brown onions, sliced to half-moons
4–5 cloves garlic, crushed and chopped
6 twigs fresh or ½ teaspoon dried basil and/or oregano
5 bay leaves
1 tablespoon olive oil
5 black peppercorns
pinch saffron or a few saffron threads (optional to all but the French!)

Sauté onions, garlic, bay leaves and peppercorns in olive oil, over medium heat for 2–3 minutes. Keep covered but stir frequently. Add 12 cups water, basil, saffron, one 15 cm piece kombu or some local fresh seaweed, 1 lightly toasted and crumbled piece of nori. Bring this to a boil and simmer for 10 minutes. Remove peppercorns and bay leaves if you desire. Add 10 small, deveined, green prawns, 8 2-cm cubes of fish (mackerel and flounder are excellent), and, if you want to create a bonza dish, some squid, cockles, octopus, oyster, mussel, crab claws or scallops. Simmer this very slowly for 30–40 minutes, until fish is cooked and very tender. It should still be in chunks. Add shoyu to taste. Serve with crusty leaven bread.

Follow bouillabaisse with brown rice, vegetable pie (pages 75–80) and a tossed lettuce salad (page 115) with parsley. Sweets could be strawberry jelly (page 153). Jasmine tea ensures a complete feast.

Thai seafood soup

> ½ kilo green prawns
> 3 cloves garlic
> 1 stalk of lemon grass (These are available in Oriental groceries. The 'stalk' consists of the top of the root section and the base of the stem.)
> 5 green chillies (more if you like it hot)
> 12 large basil leaves
> 5 spring onions
> 1 tablespoon palm sugar
> 1 litre coconut milk
>   fish sauce (Nam Pla)
>   fresh coriander leaves

Clean prawns – remove spinal cord. Skewer the garlic and toast it over a flame or in the oven till it softens slightly and becomes oily. In a mortar or blender, pound or grind to a fine paste, the garlic, lemon grass (chopped first), chillies, basil leaves, spring onions and palm sugar. Slowly bring the coconut milk to a boil. Add the prawns and paste. Allow to re-boil. Add fish sauce to taste (about 3 tablespoons) and stir in some broken (not chopped) coriander leaves.

Tofu can be substituted for prawns. Serve with long grain brown rice or basmati, blanched greens and a sprout salad. This is a way to enjoy a summer evening.

7

Vegetal dishes

Vegetal dishes, that is, dishes prepared from vegetables, grains, beans, seaweeds, fruit and nuts are almost endless. I have listed but a few which have passed through my kitchen. Where the text mentions mung beans, you could easily substitute blackeyed beans or lentils or any cooked beans such as navy or lima. Similarly, parsnip can be substituted for carrot, and pumpkin for sweet potato and so on. These recipes, then, are merely guidelines intended for inspiration. From these basic methods, you should be able to innovate extensively, remembering to keep the individual qualities of particular foods in mind so as to create balance in your meals.

Food should vary seasonally. This is only common sense. To eat the same foods in summer and winter precludes any adaptation to the change of weather and excludes you from the dynamics of natural change. It also creates inflexibility and physical discomfort from one season to the next. Those who cannot tolerate either hot or cold weather should look to their food intake. If you eat correctly according to the seasons, you can tolerate any weather.

Grains such as buckwheat, rye, oats and wholewheat are suitable for colder weather as is longer cooking, more baked food, less raw food, less liquid, some animal food and more salted food. Summer is the season of rice, corn, noodles, shorter cooking, more raw food, fruit and less salt. That is not to say that buckwheat, for example, cannot be consumed in summer — enjoy it occasionally in the cool of the evening. Similarly, rice is an all-year-round requirement.

The ability to adapt is endless and it is in your hands. You are free to eat any food at any time. The responsibility for physical discomfort or negative mentality is in your own hands, and so many of us are ready to put the blame elsewhere. By not eating, you will surely perish. Eating the correct foods will help to develop a clean bloodstream which will lead to clarity of thought and action. Food preparation is alchemy. From basic ingredients you create life.

If this seems to be 'codswallop' why not experiment? Try an easy fast, or eliminate all sugar, meat and dairy products from your diet for a week or two. Such experiments will have a strong effect, proving the power of food. By thinking on food and refining your intake, after two or three years it is impossible to return to past eating habits if a sensible, balanced diet is followed. This would be similar to having a beautiful piece of machinery which was found rusting in a paddock, restored to perfection and then returned to the paddock to rust. Changing eating habits should not simply be for 'spring cleaning', but permanent well-being. Such periodic 'tune ups' are only fooling yourself. Mao Tse-Tung says, 'Where the broom does not reach, the dust will gather'.

Bali Pilau (1)

Simple:

        1½ cups mung beans, washed
        ½ cup ground roasted peanuts
        2 onions, sliced fine
        1 sweet potato, diced
        1 carrot, diced
        celery leaves, whole
        1 tablespoon shoyu or 2 umeboshi plums
        5 cups liquid (coconut milk, water, or broth)

Mix ingredients and bring to the boil over medium-high heat. Simmer for 45 minutes with lid on. Stir gently twice, as the mung beans may rise to the surface.

   Serve with brown rice, pressed salad and deep-fried tofu or vegetable.

Bali Pilau (2)

To the above mixture, add:

        1 chilli (more if you prefer)
        ½ teaspoon Laos powder
        ½ cup extra peanuts
        1 tablespoon coriander seed
        1 tablespoon cummin seed

Pound or blend all ingredients to a paste. Serve with long grain brown rice, cucumber salad with umeboshi plum, and steamed pumpkin.

Azuki Pilau

        5 shitake mushrooms, soaked and sliced
        soaking water from mushrooms (4 cups)
        2 cups washed and soaked azuki beans
        1 cup washed brown rice or other grain, e.g. corn kernels, soaked wheat
        2 onions, chopped fine
        2 tablespoons shoyu
        1 cup chopped cauliflower
        4 cups water

Combine all ingredients. Bring to the boil slowly, then simmer covered for 1 hour. Add greens to the top of pot 5 minutes before completion of cooking. Serve with brown rice, greens and bean sprout salad (page 115), baked vegetables. For sweets, fruit tart (pages 159–60).

The method of pilau is very easy. Experiment with different beans, grains and vegetables.

Chick pea stew

2 cups cooked chick peas
4 sticks celery, sliced
2 onions, chopped fine
1 cup diced pumpkin
chopped fresh basil or oregano
2 cups water
1 teaspoon cummin seed
1 teaspoon crushed coriander seed

Sauté onions in ½ tablespoon oil. Add the other ingredients. Bring this slowly to the boil, then add ³/₄ tablespoon whole tahina and 1 tablespoon shoyu. Mix well. Simmer for 40 minutes with lid on.

Serve with steamed greens and vegetables; millet; crushed wheat-parsley-umeboshi salad. For sweets you could serve raisin halva (page 160) made with rice cream.

Baked beans

3 cups cooked red kidney, navy or blackeyed beans with 3 cups of cooking liquid from beans

Sauté 2 chopped onions in ½ tablespoon oil.

Add fresh oregano or basil, 1 tablespoon shoyu, juice and beans. Cook over medium heat for 20 minutes. Keep covered, stir gently, so as not to mash the beans.

OR

Strain the liquid from the beans. Add to it 1 teaspoon finely grated ginger, 2 tablespoons prepared natural mustard, 1 tablespoon maple syrup. Bring up to high heat. Dissolve 3 tablespoons of kuzu or arrowroot in a little water. Add to bean liquid stirring rapidly. Stir until thickened. Simmer 5 minutes, then add to beans.

Black bean potage

2 cups cooked black soya beans (pages 47–8)
1 teaspoon finely grated ginger
2 cups diced carrots
1 tablespoon shoyu
2 tablespoons water
2 onions, sliced
1 sheet toasted, crumbled nori seaweed

Mix all ingredients well and bake at 190°C (375°F) for 45 minutes. A very strengthening dish.

Serve with brown rice, hijiki seaweed and pumpkin pie.

Kuzu beans

4 cups cooked white beans — e.g. baby lima — cooked with 3 bay leaves
1½ cups cold liquid from bean cooking
1 tablespoon kuzu or 1½ tablespoons arrowroot
3 tablespoons white miso

Dissolve kuzu in bean liquid. Place in a saucepan over medium heat and stir until kuzu clears. Add beans and miso, stir with sauce for 5 minutes, but don't mash them. Top with finely chopped parsley or herbs when serving.

Flavoured shoyu sauce

Put 6 or 7 star aniseeds, cracked but not broken, into a bottle of shoyu. Set aside for one week — a delicious topping for noodles. It imparts an exotic flavour to dishes, especially chilli sauce.

Dahl or dal

This is an Indian preparation which can vary endlessly.

Dahl can be hot, spicy, savoury, sweet or all of these. It is based upon lentils or split peas and is usually of a texture between soup and mash, whichever suits the occasion. You can use any beans really, but in India, chana (skinned chick peas) or mung (split skinned mung beans) or toor (yellow split peas) or urad (dark blue-green beans) are most commonly used. My favourite is quite un-Indian:

3 cups hot, cooked, brown lentils
1 teaspoon finely powdered anise seeds
1 tablespoon shoyu

Mix well and place on low heat, stirring constantly for 5 minutes

Hot dahl

2 cups mung dahl (without skin preferably, but if you can't get them, cook mung beans with skins on and mash very finely)
1 teaspoon salt
2 cloves garlic, crushed
½ teaspoon finely grated ginger
1½ teaspoons garam masala (make this by finely grinding ½ teaspoon each of cloves, cardamom seeds, cummin and coriander)
1 red chilli pepper, crushed
¼ cup ground, roasted peanuts
½ teaspoon turmeric powder

Cook mung dahl in 2½ times volume of water. bring water to the boil with whole beans, or add split beans to boiling water.

Simmer over medium heat until water is absorbed and beans are quite soft but not sloppy. Sauté the spices, garlic and ginger in 1 tablespoon coconut oil and 1 tablespoon mustard seed oil, or 2 tablespoons vegetable oil or ghee for 5 minutes over medium heat.

Add peanuts and cooked beans. Cook till hot. Serve with chapatti.

You can sauté finely chopped vegetables with the spices and oil and cook until done. Mix with dahl, heat and serve.

Adding some tamarind softened in hot water before cooking gives a pleasant sour taste (1 tablespoon tamarind without seeds in 2 tablespoons hot water). This taste can also be achieved by adding 1 tablespoon yoghurt to the dahl 5 minutes before serving — cook over low heat while stirring.

Hommos

6 cups cooked chick peas (cooked with bay leaf)
4 cups cooking water from chick peas
¾ cup natural tahina (½ sesame purée and ½ water)
2 teaspoons sea salt
3 teaspoons finely ground cummin seed
2 teaspoons finely ground coriander seed
1 cup lemon juice (or cook 4 umeboshi plums in 1 cup water and cool)
2 teaspoons very finely chopped and crushed garlic soaked in 1 tablespoon shoyu for 30 minutes.

Blend or vitamise chick peas with tahina, lemon juice, cooking water and garlic shoyu until very smooth. Some Lebanese add extra olive oil to make this a fairly thin, oily paste. I prefer it less oily and quite thick. Adjust liquid proportions to suit yourself. Stir in spices and salt and beat well.

Serve with felafel, tabboule and flat bread, or as a dip with cracker biscuits.

Hommos is very strong food so don't overindulge or you will be as quarrelsome as the Middle East.

Vegetable Hommos

1 cup cooked sweet pumpkin
½ cup each cooked parsnip and fried onion
4 cups cooked chick peas
2 cups cooking liquid from peas and vegetables
1 tablespoon shoyu
½ tablespoon natural tahina

Blend all ingredients.

Sweet potato or pumpkin bhaji

> 6–8 small sweet potatoes (or 4 cups diced pumpkin)
> 3 cloves garlic, crushed
> 1 teaspoon finely grated ginger root
> 2 onions, sliced
> 1 red chilli pepper, chopped (or ¼ teaspoon chilli oil)
> 2 whole cloves, crushed
> 1 teaspoon coriander seeds, finely ground
> 1 tablespoon coconut oil (or ½ with ½ vegetable oil)
> 1 teaspoon salt (if using pumpkin use ½ teaspoon salt and add 2 teaspoons shoyu at the end of cooking)
> 1 teaspoon honey

Sauté onions, garlic, spices, ginger and honey for 5 minutes over medium heat — stir well.

Add sweet potato and salt, stir for 3 minutes. Add 1 cup water, cover and simmer for 35 minutes. Add shoyu if you like; this makes the dish a darker colour.

This is delicious using goat's milk instead of water. A teaspoon of butter or ghee stirred in at the end is very tasty.

Serve with dahl, chapatti, brown rice and green salad dressed with salted plum or yoghurt.

Vegetable kebbe

This Lebanese dish is based on ground beef. Substitute minced seitan and brown lentils or just lentils.

> 2 cloves garlic soaked in 1 tablespoon shoyu or salted water for 30 minutes, and crushed
> 1 cup finely minced or very finely chopped seitan (see page 122)
> 2 cups finely chopped onions
> 2 cups brown rice, cooked
> 2 cups lentils, cooked and strained
> 1 cup roasted pine nuts or almonds, chopped
> ½ cup chopped parsley
> 1 teaspoon crushed cummin seeds
> ½ teaspoon crushed coriander seed (or ½ cup freshly chopped leaves)
> 1 teaspoon salt or 1 tablespoon shoyu
> 1 tablespoon kome miso
> ½ tablespoon natural tahina
> 1 tablespoon zaatar (a Lebanese spice made from sesame seeds and coriander)
> spinach or comfrey leaves

Mix tahina with lentils, seitan and spices. Mix garlic and onions and shoyu. Mix rice and miso. Layer ingredients and separate layers with leaves or nori sheets for a special variation.

Bake at 170°C (350°F) for 20 minutes in a covered baking tray. Uncover, sprinkle with zaatar and bake 10 minutes.

Serves 4.

Turnip slice

This requires daikon radish to be perfect. You can use any selection of root vegetables or pumpkin.

>3 sheets nori seaweed, toasted and torn up
>1 cup diced daikon radish
>1 cup diced white turnip
>½ cup diced carrot
>2 onions, sliced fine
>6 shitake mushrooms, soaked and sliced fine
>2 cups soaking water from mushrooms
>5 tablespoons arrowroot or kuzu
>¾ cup brown rice flour
>2 tablespoons shoyu or kome miso
>1 teaspoon grated ginger (and garlic if desired)

Cook vegetables, ginger and mushrooms in shoyu and mushroom water until soft. Strain. Mix well – almost mash. Bring 3 cups strained liquid (make it up with water or mushroom soaking water if you haven't enough left) to high heat, but don't boil. Quickly add the rice flour, stirring with a whisk.

Dissolve 5 tablespoons kuzu in a little cold water. Mix well and add to hot stock. Stir over medium heat until quite thick. Add vegetables and nori, stirring over heat for 10 mintues. Pour into a rinsed dish and cool. When cold, cut with a wet knife. The slices can be dipped in batter and deep-fried, or fried in a pan without batter.

Nut roast

>1 cup roasted ground peanuts
>½ cup roasted chopped almonds
>2 cups cooked brown rice, or wheat or buckwheat
>1 cup cooked brown lentils, or azuki or other beans
>1 cup grated pumpkin
>½ cup roasted whole hazelnuts
>10 spring onions chopped
>3 tablespoons shoyu or 2 of mugi miso

Mix nuts with shoyu or miso. Start with a layer of brown rice. Then a layer of pumpkin, onions, lentils etc. as you like, or separate the layers with nori seaweed. Even mix all of the above together. Whatever the outcome, bake covered at 170°C (350°F) for 30 minutes, then uncovered for 10 minutes.

Stuffed capsicums/cabbage/pumpkin

>1 cup cooked azuki, or other beans (e.g. lentils)
>2 cups cooked brown rice
>½ cup cooked hijiki seaweed *or* 3 sheets nori toasted and crumbled
>   *or* 1 cup soaked wakame
>6 finely chopped spring onions
>chopped parsley or fresh or dried herbs (not too many as these can
>   be overpowering, especially don't use too much sage)
>½ cup chopped roasted nuts
>1 tablespoon shoyu or miso (not hatcho)

Mix ingredients well. Mash the beans for a change or add a beaten egg for a firm stuffing. Finely chopped seitan and vegetables is an excellent stuffing, or use mashed tofu, grains and vegetables.

Cabbage leaves should be soaked in a bowl of boiling water for 10 minutes to make them flexible. Place mixture on cabbage leaf and roll up as a spring roll. After stuffing, steam or simmer cabbage rolls with 1 cup water and 1 tablespoon of shoyu. Cut the stalks out of mushrooms and stuff the tops with such a mixture. Bake at 160°C (325°F) for 25 minutes in an open tray containing 1 cup water and 1 tablespoon shoyu. Slice a round from the cap of a red (preferably) capsicum and spoon out the seeds. Replace top after stuffing. Slowly cook capsicums in a sealed, heavy pot, standing on their bases, with 1 cup water.

Make a small hole in one end of several small pumpkins, hollow out, then stuff. Slice larger pumpkins in half and scoop out the seeds. Bake pumpkins at 170°C (350°F) for 1 hour or steam in a bamboo steamer. Stuff and bake the half. Dry and roast the pumpkin seeds then grind them with salt and use as a garnish — don't waste them.

Fried rice

　　4 cups hard cooked brown rice (cooked with less water than usual)
　　¾ tablespoon light sesame oil
　　1 teaspoon grated ginger
　　4 spring onions in 2 cm pieces including tops and roots
　　1 cup mung bean sprouts
　　½ cup chopped greens — Chinese cabbage or broccoli or 1 tablespoon
　　　　fresh coriander
　　1 cup 2 cm seitan cubes — if you have them

Sauté ginger in oil over medium heat for 3 minutes. Add spring onions, rice and seitan. Lift and stir continuously for 2 minutes.

　　Add sprouts and greens and 1 tablespoon shoyu. Stir, cover and heat for 1 minute.

　　Serve with pumpkin-bean burgers, corn-on-the-cob, pressed salad (page 114). For dessert: grain halva (page 160) or almond mousse (page 156), followed by dandelion coffee.

　　Wholewheat or barley or rye can be used instead of rice in this recipe. Omit the ginger and use one brown onion instead of shallots. Half a cup of fresh-roasted and ground peanuts makes this dish very tasty.

Buckwheat and millet hash

　　2 cups cooked millet
　　1 cup cooked buckwheat
　　1 onion, finely chopped
　　1 cup grated pumpkin or zucchini
　　1 tablespoon oil
　　1 tablespoon shoyu
　　2 tablespoons finely chopped parsley *or*
　　1 tablespoon fresh coriander

Sauté onion in oil over medium heat for 3 minutes. Add pumpkin, shoyu and $1/2$ cup water. Cook for 5 minutes at medium heat, stir frequently. Add grains and parsley. Stir and cook for 5 minutes. Serve for breakfast with wholewheat toast or put inside a nori roll for lunch.

Corn off the cob

　　1 clove garlic soaked in shoyu for ½ hour
　　3 cups fresh corn off the cob
　　6 spring onions in 2 cm lengths, including tops and roots
　　½ cup carrot juice
　　½ tablespoon olive oil
　　3 bay leaves

Sauté bay leaves and crushed garlic in oil. Add corn and stir-fry for 5 minutes. Add carrot juice and onions, cover and cook over low heat for 10 minutes.

　　As an accompaniment, collect the carrot pulp from the juicing, knead for 5 minutes with rice and miso, roll into balls and steam till hot, or bake.

　　Serve with vegetable pie and steamed greens. For sweets: tofu custard (page 172).

Moughrabia — a Lebanese dish

2 cups cooked chick peas
1 cup cooked wholewheat or barley
½ cup roasted pine nuts
1 tablespoon walnut pieces
2 onions, sliced
2 cloves garlic, crushed
2 sticks celery, sliced thin
2 teaspoons crushed coriander seed
1 teaspoon crushed cummin seed
1 teaspoon ghee or clarified butter
1 teaspoon sea salt
2 tablespoons olive oil

Fry onions, garlic and spices in ghee and olive oil over medium heat. Add nuts, salt, peas, grain and celery. Fry slowly for 15 minutes with lid on. Add a little water to prevent sticking, but keep it fairly dry. When cooked, sprinkle with 2 teaspoons natural tahina and some fresh ground black pepper. At this stage you can add strips of omelette if you desire. The Lebanese use chicken pieces.

Mix and serve. Enjoy it with stir-fried ginger and cabbage; steamed vegetables; salad with parsley, lettuce, radish and salt plum; brown rice (page 74) or millet burgers and flat bread.

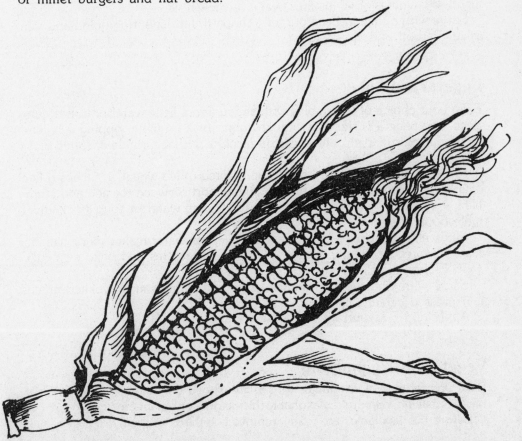

Wholewheat curry

> 6 cups cooked wholewheat (or barley, millet, rice, etc.)
> 2 onions, finely chopped
> ½ cup crushed, roasted peanuts *or* 1 tablespoon natural peanut butter
> ½ teaspoon sea salt
> 2 teaspoons grated ginger
> 1 cup finely diced carrots
> ½ cup roasted coarse coconut
> 1 teaspoon to 1 tablespoon dark curry powder (preferably from Sri Lanka)
>
> *or* for curry powder substitute:
> 2 teaspoons cummin seeds
> 2 teaspoons coriander seeds
> 3 whole cloves
> 1 red chilli
> ½ teaspoon aniseeds
> 1 tablespoon lemon grass, chopped finely
> 1 tablespoon curry leaves

Sauté onions, ginger and curry in 1 tablespoon vegetable oil for 3 minutes. Add peanuts, carrots, coconut, salt and whole wheat. Sauté for 5 minutes over medium heat. Add 1 cup water or soup stock or coconut milk and simmer for 15–20 minutes or 40 minutes over a very low heat.

Serve with pumpkin-bean burgers, chapatti, lettuce/spring onion and tofu salad. Parboil and cream tofu.

Vegetal crumble

Bake your choice of vegetables with shoyu and a little water until not quite done (see page 42), leaving enough room for a crumble-topping. I recommend pumpkin-parsnip-onion-carrot-zucchini with a sprinkle of salted black beans.

Make a crumble mixture from 1 cup roasted rolled wheat, 1½ cups rolled oats, ½ cup ground roasted nuts, 3 sheets nori seaweed toasted and crumbled, 1 teaspoon grated orange rind. Add ½ cup water or soup stock and 1 tablespoon shoyu.

Mix well, add more water if necessary — less water makes more crumbly texture, spread carefully on top of baked vegetables and bake at 170°C (350°F) for 10–15 minutes.

Serve with wholewheat noodles (page 37), satay sauce, wokked greens and pressed celery salad.

Apple and blackcurrant for dessert (pages 159–60).

Vegetal-barley pudding

Bake your choice of vegetables with a little shoyu until almost cooked. While they are baking, prepare a reasonably thick barley or oat cream.

Before the vegetables are ready, remove two-thirds of them. Pour in a layer of barley cream. Layer more vegetables, then barley cream until complete. Top with the cream. Return to the oven and bake uncovered for 15 minutes.

Make oat cream by toasting rolled oats and stirring into a porridge over medium heat with water and some salt. Add toasted, crushed nori to the oats. Barley needs to be toasted and ground, then made into a cream with water — see pages 31–2.

Polenta (Italian method)

>   1 cup cornmeal (polenta)
>   ¼ teaspoon salt
>   1 teaspoon olive oil
>   3–4 cups boiling water

Sauté the cornmeal lightly in oil until fragrant. Add salt and boiling water, stirring to avoid lumps. Place on medium heat, stirring constantly. When this boils, cook over low heat for 30 minutes, stirring occasionally. Pour into a rinsed tray or dish and cool till it sets. Cut into cubes.

Vegetables for polenta:

>   2 diced or sliced carrots
>   3 chopped brown onions
>   1 clove garlic, crushed
>   2 teaspoons fresh or ½ teaspoon dried oregano

Sauté onion, garlic and oregano in 1 tablespoon olive oil for 3 minutes. Add carrots and garlic-shoyu and ¹/₂ cup white wine. Cover and simmer for 15 minutes.

Add chopped broccoli and ½ cup natural matured cheese or parmesan if you like it, or cottage cheese or 1 tablespoon fetta cheese. (For an interesting substitute cheese, soak 1 cup rice in 3 cups water for 3–5 days, until sour. Strain rice and discard water. Roast the rice in an oven until brown. Cool and grind finely. Cook as rice cream, adding 1 teaspoon salt. You will be surprised — add where cheese is mentioned). Cook for an extra 5 minutes with greens such as celery or capsicum.

Pour over chunks of polenta. Serve with noodles sprinkled with sesame salt or a warm mixture of 1 tablespoon shoyu with 1 teaspoon lemon/orange juice, and a green salad.

Ginger pears for dessert.

Cous cous

For this you need bulghur wheat or cracked steamed hard wheat, known as cous cous. The idea of cous cous is to use a large, flat steamer and layer it with wheat then chick peas then vegetables. This is served with a chick pea sauce and flat bread.

Soak the cous cous or bulghur wheat for two hours in plenty of water. Strain and use any water left over as a soup base. Rub this soaked wheat with olive oil, 1 teaspoon per 2 cups. Mix with ¹/₂ tablespoon roasted pine nuts per cup and steam for 20 minutes, lifting with a fork or chopsticks regularly, to separate the grains.

Some cous cous has cummin for spiciness. When wheat is almost done, place cooked chick peas and chopped vegetables (thin enough to steam) on top of wheat — or prepare separately if you have to. In this case, steam the vegetables and serve on top of cous cous on the plate. Otherwise, steam cous cous and vegetables for 10 minutes.

Good vegetable combinations are onion, greens (especially celery), pumpkin, carrot, parsnip; or onions, greens, cooked artichokes, pumpkin with a goat's cheese dressing even. Serve the cous cous and vegetables together, preferably vegetables on top of cous cous, and a bowl of chick pea sauce. This can be made using chick pea cooking water, coriander greens and shoyu. Thicken with kuzu arrowroot. Don't forget the chapattis or flat bread, parsley and lettuce, string beans, blanched and dressed with plenty of lemon juice, cucumber and mint.

Tabboule — Lebanese crushed wheat salad

Wash first and then soak bulghur (or crushed hard wheat) for 1 hour in plenty of water — 1 cup wheat: 3 cups water. Strain. Use water for soup. Rub wheat with a little olive oil. Add very finely chopped parsley, cucumber and red (only red) capsicum. Mix these and use 1 cup for each cup of wheat. The Lebanese use tomato and not capsicum; this makes it more suitable as a meat side-dish.

Sprinkle with 1 teaspoon salt, 1 teaspoon sommaque (semak) — a Lebanese spice made from crushed, dried pomegranate — and ½ cup lemon juice or flesh from 4 salt plums mashed in ½ cup water. Serve with hommos and felafel, all rolled in flat bread. If you are using salt plums, do not add salt.

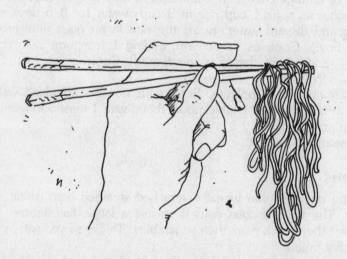

Noodles

Generally, serve noodles as a side dish seasoned with shoyu or some broth. They can be added to a variety of dishes, such as stir-fried dishes, to make fried noodles. Be careful not to cook too long or burn them. They can stick together and become soggy very easily. Noodles are excellent served cold in summer or in salads.

Red bean noodles

Cook azuki beans (or beans of your choice) so as to have some liquid left over. While hot, mix 4 cups beans with about the same quantity of cooked buckwheat or wholewheat noodles or macaroni. Season with 1 tablespoon shoyu or miso, add finely chopped shallots, pour in 1 cup bean liquid. Thicken bean liquid with kuzu or arrowroot for a variation.

Peanut-miso noodles

    1 tablespoon rice or barley miso, or natural soy sauce
    1 tablespoon ground roasted peanuts
      a few thin slivers of orange rind
    1/2 cup water or bean cooking liquid or clear soup stock

Mix and heat these ingredients; pour over noodles. Cover with fresh coriander, mint or watercress.

Noodles and greens

Use Italian rye noodles — or your choice. Tagliatelli (flat) noodles make this dish attractive.

Stir-fry a selection of green vegetables (see page 41). When these are cooked, add an equal volume of cooked noodles. Mix gently. Sprinkle with anise-shoyu and place in a covered pot to keep them hot during the meal. Serve with brown rice, vegetable salad and flat bread. For sweets — orange sesame jelly. Yannoh grain coffee.

Kuzu noodle rolls

    1 1/2 cups of liquid
    4 tablespoons kuzu arrowroot

The liquid can be strained left-over soup, vegetable juice or the strainings from cooking a pie filling. Mix the cold liquid and kuzu until well dissolved and place in a heavy saucepan. Stir continuously over medium heat until the mixture thickens and begins to clear. Turn heat to low and continue stirring; this gets a little hectic as the kuzu becomes very thick. After 4-5 minutes, spoon out onto a rinsed pie tray or dish with low sides. Spread with a wet spoon so the mixture is quite thin. Allow to cool slightly and then refrigerate until cool and firm.

Meanwhile, bake several small squash, parsnip or other sweet vegetables. These must be well chosen, tasty vegetables. When ready, mash the vegetables. You should have 3-4 cups. Add chopped shallots or spring onions and 1 tablespoon of mugi (barley) miso. Mix well.

Remove kuzu sheet from the tray by carefully tapping the bottom of the tray and inverting it. Spread the vegetable mixture onto the kuzu sheet to within 2-3 cm of the folding edges. That is, the edges closest and farthest from you. Carefully lift and roll the sheet over the mixture to form a roll. Slice with a sharp knife and serve immediately.

Accompaniments — brown rice, tempura and salad. This can also be a sweet dish with a cooked fruit or nut filling.

Kuzu noodles

Follow the directions for kuzu roll, but when the sheet of kuzu is firm and cool, cut into thin strips and serve with your favourite sauce.

One-pot noodles

1 packet udon (wholewheat) noodles, soba (buckwheat)
　　　or whole rye vermicelli
approximately 8 cups of water, or sufficient to cook noodles
chopped daikon
sliced cauliflower
2 sliced onions or 5 spring onions
green vegetables such as daikon tops or kale (not silver beet),
　　true spinach or mugi miso
1 teaspoon grated raw ginger

Cook noodles by method described (page 37). After the last cup of water is added and the noodles are simmering, add the vegetables, except for the greens.

After 10 minutes, when the noodles are cooked, add greens, miso to taste and 1 teaspoon grated raw ginger.

Serve as soup followed by steamed vegetables and grilled marinated tofu.

Noodle nori rolls

Soak bifun (brown rice noodles) or Chinese rice vermicelli in boiling water for 10 minutes. Drain well. Spread 1 cm thick on a sheet of toasted nori seaweed, leaving a 2 cm gap at the end farthest from you, and 1 cm gap at either side. On the closest edge, spread a layer of bean or seed sprouts 5 cm wide. Moisten the three available edges with water and roll it up, tucking under the edge nearest you, and rolling from there.

Neatly fold in the edges so as to seal, and let stand on the seam for a few minutes. Cut into three with a sharp clean knife.

Serve with Bali pilau, sweet potato pie (page 75) and green salad.

Nori and pumpkin rolls

5 cups cooked mashed pumpkin (preferably baked with shoyu, or
　　cooked in a saucepan with shoyu)
10 cups cooked brown rice
6 sheets nori, lightly toasted on one side.

Lay out the sheet of nori. Spread with cooked rice, leaving a 2 cm border at farthest edge and 1 cm border at the sides. Rice should not be too thick (about ½ - 1 cm). Cover thinly with cooked pumpkin up to 5 cm from farthest edge. Moisten the edges of the nori and roll up. Tuck in edges. Leave to stand on seam. Slice into three pieces, wiping and moistening the knife after each cut. Knife must be sharp. Simple and delightful.

Ume-nori rolls

　　　8 cups cooked brown rice
　　　mashed flesh of 4 or 5 umeboshi plums

Mix rice with mashed plum flesh. Spread on toasted sheets of nori, as with other nori rolls.

　　　Makes 6 rolls.

Peanut nori rolls

　　　8 cups cooked brown rice
　　　½ cup ground, freshly roasted peanuts
　　　6 spring onions or shallots finely chopped
　　　¾ tablespoon ginger juice squeezed from freshly grated ginger root
　　　2 tablespoons rice or barley miso

Mix miso with ginger juice. Mix this with other ingredients. Roll up in nori which has been toasted on one side.

　　　Slice into four pieces, stand each piece on end, and serve.

　　　Makes 6 rolls.

Popia

These are served in Singapore, notably Bugis Street, and have many variations. They are a mixture of Malay and Chinese cooking. This is my version.

　　　Skins: *see* savoury steamed buns. Instead of forming steamed bun jackets, roll this pastry into very thin rounds about 17 cm in diameter. Dust lightly with flour, stack on top of each other and cover with a cotton towel. Meanwhile, prepare the filling, which you can make spicy if you like, by adding freshly chopped chilli, freshly ground cummin and coriander whilst sautéing.

　　　Fresh chopped coriander leaves can be sprinkled on the mixture just before the popia is rolled up, for a delightful flavour.

　　　Prepare the filling as follows —
　　　　　1 tablespoon sesame oil
　　　　　1 tablespoon finely grated ginger
　　　　　3 cloves garlic chopped fine or crushed
　　　　　2 onions finely chopped
　　　　　1 tablespoon maltose or rice honey
　　　　　1 cup shredded cabbage
　　　　　2 cups fresh bean sprouts
　　　　　½ cup finely ground, freshly roasted peanuts
　　　　　2 tablespoons barley or rice miso

Sauté ginger, garlic, and onions in oil for 5 minutes over medium heat. Add maltose then cabbage and cook until cabbage is tender. Add bean sprouts, stir, cover and let stand for 5 minutes. Remove any liquid from the pan, and mix with peanuts and miso. Stir this into the cabbage.

In Singapore the popia has an omelette filling. If you want this, soak 1½ tablespoons of shitake mushrooms in 1 cup of water for 30 minutes. Add 4 eggs to the water with 1 teaspoon shoyu (tamari) and beat well. Cook in an oiled pan slowly to make thin omelettes.

The popia skins are cooked two at a time so they are flexible enough to be rolled. Place one on top of the other and drop into a medium hot pan. When one side is just cooked, flip over to cook the other side. When done, allow to cool briefly, then carefully separate by peeling them apart. Lay the omelette on the pastry skin, and spread the vegetable filling on this.

Then roll up and stand on its seam. You can tuck in the edges and roll them up like a spring roll if you desire.

Pumpkin bean burgers

> 6 cups cooked mung beans, strained and mashed
> 4 cups cooked mashed pumpkin or carrot or parsnip
> 8 spring onions, finely chopped
> ½ cup roasted crushed pine nuts or almonds
> 1 tablespoon kome miso

Mix all ingredients. Form into large balls (burgers–rissoles). Bake at 170°C (350°F) for 15 minutes.

Serve with crusty leaven bread, pressed salad and wokked vegetables.

Rice Burgers

> 2 cups cooked vegetables
> 4 cups cooked rice
> 1 tablespoon ground roasted nuts (optional — peanuts are the best)
>   or
> 1 teaspoon kinako
> 1 tablespoon shoyu

Knead all these ingredients together for 5 minutes. The vegetables may need chopping. Form into balls which resemble rissoles. Bake for 15 minutes at 190°C (375°F). Serve with baked or steamed vegetables, hijiki seaweed, cauliflower tart and salad.

Gô burgers

> 2 cups very thick gô purée or okara (*see* page 120)
> 2 cups cooked brown rice
> 1 cup mashed baked vegetables
> 2 sheets nori seaweed, toasted and crumbled
> 1 tablespoon shoyu or miso
> ½ cup finely diced celery

Knead together, bake at 170°C (350°F) for 15 minutes.

Pies

Use any of these pie fillings with the pastry recipe in the Bread and Pastry section (page 130). There are a thousand more fillings — be sure to decoratively cut a small hole(s) in the top of pies to allow steam to escape.

Bake pies at 250°C (400°F) for 15 – 20 minutes.

Pumpkin pie

> 6 cups pumpkin, finely diced
> ½ cup water
> 1 tablespoon shoyu
> ½ teaspoon cummin seeds

Cook over medium heat, covered, until soft. Use more water if necessary. Strain well before filling pie. Add toasted nori for a change. Omit shoyu and add 2 teaspoons mugi miso after cooking for pumpkin miso pie. Add azuki beans for azuki pumpkin pie.

or

Chop 2 onions finely. Sauté a little oil with 10 salted black beans. Add pumpkin, sauté for 5 minutes. Add water and shoyu. Cook until soft.

Substitute sweet potato and mix with buckwheat for another filling.

Vegetal slice — A 'Goodness Gracious' special

> 2 cups diced carrots
> 2 cups diced pumpkin
> 1 cup diced swede or white turnip
> 1 stick celery, chopped
> 1 onion, chopped
> 2 cloves garlic finely chopped
> 1 tablespoon shoyu

Sauté onion and garlic in a little oil. Add vegetables, shoyu and ½ cup of water. Cook over medium heat until soft. Strain and bake in pie shell. Use liquid for soup. Add ½ mashed and ½ whole chick peas to this for chick pea vegetable pie.

'Hunza' pie

> 3 onions, chopped
> 3 cups cooked rice
> 1 cup fetta or ricotta or cottage cheese (fetta or ricotta make a very
>   rich pie)
> 1 tablespoon crushed coriander seeds
> 1 tablespoon shoyu
> 4 cups greens (turnip or daikon greens are best) placed in boiling water
>   for 5 minutes

Sauté onions (and garlic if you want) with 1 tablespoon olive oil and coriander seeds. Mix all of the ingredients and bake in pie shell. Add ground roasted peanuts for a variation.

Carrot and hijiki pie

> 1 cup soaked chopped hijiki seaweed
> 3 cups diced carrot
> 1 teaspoon finely grated ginger
> 2 chopped onions
> 1 teaspoon dried salted blackbeans

Sauté onions, ginger and blackbeans in 1 tablespoon white sesame or corn oil. Add carrot and hijiki; sauté for 5 minutes.

Add 1 cup hijiki soaking water, being careful not to add any grit which may have collected at the bottom of the bowl. Add 2 tablespoons shoyu, cover and cook for at least 30 minutes, until carrot is soft. Add more liquid if necessary.

When cooked, strain off liquid and place ingredients in a pie shell and bake.

For a special pie, soak 6 pieces of dried lotus root for 3 hours. Bring to a boil in soaking liquid and simmer rapidly, covered, until lotus has softened. Dice and add to pie mix before cooking.

Pumpkin, parsnip, daikon or onion can be substituted in this recipe.

Summer vegetable pie

> 2 red capsicum sliced
> 2 brown onions
> 1 clove of garlic *or* 1 teaspoon of finely grated ginger
> 1 tablespoon olive oil
> 4 cups finely chopped cabbage
> 4 cups grated pumpkin
> 2 tablespoons shoyu
> 2 tablespoons chopped parsley

Slice onions and finely chop garlic. Sauté in olive oil for 2–3 minutes over medium heat. Add cabbage, pumpkin and capsicum and stir-fry for 5 minutes. Turn heat to low and cover. If you have a thick-bottomed pot there is no need to add water, simply stir vegetables every 2 minutes for about 10 minutes — they will cook in their own juices. Otherwise, add 2 tablespoons of water, cover and cook.

Just before completion of cooking, add shoyu.

Drain well, add parsley and place in a pastry-lined pie dish. Cover with pastry or a criss-cross of pastry strips and bake.

Soba pie

> 1 packet cooked soba (buckwheat) noodles
> 2 onions
> ½ teaspoon finely chopped garlic
> 2 bay leaves
> 1 tablespoon kome miso
> 2 tablespoons toasted flour

Sauté onions, garlic and bay leaves in 1 tablespoon oil over medium heat. Add ½ cup water when onion absorbs all oil. Cook over medium heat for 5 minutes, covered. Dissolve flour in ¼ cup water with miso and add to other ingredients.

Cook while stirring until a thick gravy is formed. Remove from heat; pour in noodles and mix gently so as not to break them.

Place in a pie shell, cover with ½ cup chopped parsley; or lay comfrey, spinach or borage leaves over the filling.

Cover with three sheets toasted nori, seal with pastry top and bake.

Hokkaido pie

Filling:

> 2 cups cooked, partly mashed azuki beans
> 2 cups cooked (preferably baked) strained and mashed pumpkin
> 1 teaspoon shoyu
> 4 sheets lightly toasted nori seaweed
> 2 cups cooked buckwheat

Mix shoyu with azuki beans.

Pastry:

> 3 cups soft cooked rice
> ½ cup kokkoh or toasted flour
> 1 tablespoon sesame salt

Knead the pastry ingredients together — add a little water if necessary. It should be pliable but together.

Press this out into an oiled baking dish. Place a layer of nori on the rice pastry at the bottom of the pot, then a layer of buckwheat, a sheet of nori, a layer of azuki beans, nori, pumpkin, then nori.

Cover this with a thin layer of the 'pastry' (this is not easy). Top with a crumble mixture if you prefer. Bake at 150°C (300°F) for 40 minutes.

Serve with sautéed greens, baked carrot, parsnip and onion, or pressed salad.

Zucchini pie

> 6 – 8 medium zucchini chopped in large pieces
> 1 clove garlic soaked in shoyu for 30 minutes, then crushed
> ¾ teaspoon basil or oregano
> 1 tablespoon shoyu
> 1 onion chopped finely

Sauté onion and garlic in a little oil for 3 minutes. Add zucchini and basil and sauté for 3 more minutes. Add shoyu, cover and cook slowly for 5 minutes until zucchini is barely soft.

Drain well — zucchini seems to be mainly liquid! Bake in pie. Zucchini reduces in volume considerably when cooked, so be careful to use enough or add another harder vegetable.

Other pie fillings

Cook similarly to pumpkin filling:

> parsnip and onion
> carrot and onion with 1 tablespoon soaked fermented blackbeans
> cauliflower and onion
> turnip and onion with miso (add miso at completion of cooking)
> raw grated pumpkin and bean sprouts
> scallopini, onion, garlic and oregano
> chick pea, celery and vegetable
> azuki bean, pumpkin and kombu seaweed
> swede, turnip and onion cooked with 2–3 umeboshi plums
> pumpkin and tofu (add tofu at completion of cooking)
> kohl rabi, onion, greens
> celery, Chinese greens, broccoli, thyme, parsley and onion
> soft cooked wheat and vegetables
> lentil and vegetable
> spicy lentils
> rice and carrot (or vegetables)
> buckwheat and vegetable
> millet and vegetable (parsnip and greens)

Any pie filling can be created in this way. Use your choice of vegetable and add beans, noodles or seaweed as you like.

Cooking with shoyu gives a richer flavour. Use spices or curry powder to make a hot or spicy pie, but don't make it overbearingly spicy or hot. Curry and spices are best used in summer.

Flans

A flan is a pie without a pastry top, or with a lattice of thin pastry strips.

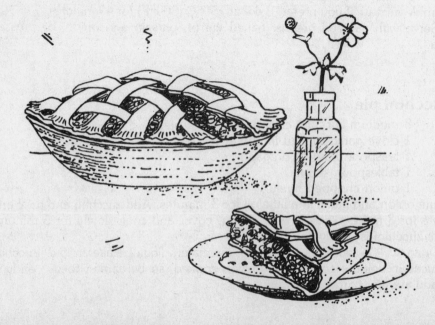

Cheese or Tofu and blackbean flan

1 cup cooked carrot (steamed is best − put 2 star anise into the steaming water)
3 onions in thin half moons
½ teaspoon finely grated ginger
2 teaspoons salted blackbeans
1 tablespoon shoyu
½ teaspoon dark sesame oil
½ cup grated, mature cheese

Sauté carrots, onions, ginger, blackbeans in a little oil for 3 minutes. Add shoyu and 1 tablespoon water. Cover and cook for 5 minutes. Remove from heat, add cheese and sesame oil, mix well and place in a pre-baked flan bottom (careful not to overbake the bottom or it will be rock hard). Cover thinly with grated cheese and bake for 5 minutes.

As an extra add ½ cup chopped fresh mushrooms and stir-fry with onions; or use cooked shitake mushrooms for a delicacy.

If using tofu, purée 1 cup diced tofu in a blender with 1 tablespoon mirin. Spread over the surface of the flan with a spatula. Bake 10 minutes.

Carrot tart

5 medium carrots, finely diced (2 − 3 cups)
1 star anise
1 teaspoon grated ginger
2 teaspoons rice or barley miso
1 onion, chopped finely
fresh coriander, parsley, watercress

Sauté onion, anise and ginger for 3 minutes in 1 tablespoon oil. Add carrot and sauté for 3 minutes. Add ½ cup water or stock and cook covered over medium heat until carrots are just soft. Strain. Remove anise. Add miso and mix well. Mash the mixture lightly and spread on a baked flan base. Sprinkle with greens and serve.

Parsnip flan prepared in the same manner is delightful. Use white miso.

Cauliflower tart

2 onions in thin slivers
2–3 cauliflowers, broken into small flowers, stalk chopped fine
½ cup grated parsnip
1 tablespoon oil
1 tablespoon shoyu

Sauté onions in oil for 3 minutes. Add parsnip and cauliflower, sauté for 1 minute then add 1 cup water. Cover and cook over medium heat until cauliflower is barely soft. Sprinkle with shoyu.

Strain liquid and thicken with 2 tablespoons roasted flour or kuzu (see Glossary) thickening. Should be quite thick. Place the vegetables in a prebaked flan base, pour sauce on top. Sprinkle with tekka.

Serve with rice burgers and tofu salad.

Buckwheat-tofu 'quiche'

    3 cups cooked buckwheat
    1 cup mashed tofu
    1 cup finely chopped seitan (optional but desirable)
    8 spring onions or shallots finely chopped
3–4 sprigs of oregano or basil, chopped
    ½ cup chopped parsley

either

    3 teaspoons rice or barley miso dissolved in 1 – 2 tablespoons orange or lemon juice

or

    flesh from 2 umeboshi plums with 1 tablespoon shoyu (soy sauce);
    ½ cup fine cut, blanched cauliflowerettes, or your choice of grated vegetable

Gently mix these ingredients so as not to mash them. Place in a lightly baked flan base, 5 cm deep, and bake for 10 minutes at 170°C (350°F).

Usually quiche is made with eggs and cheese. Add either of these to the above if you require a richer food.

Four flavours tempeh flan

    3 chillies
    3 tablespoons tamari (not shoyu) or natural Indonesian Kechap (soy sauce)
    3 tablespoons rice vinegar or 5 of lemon juice
    3 tablespoons of maltose, rice syrup or palm sugar
    1 tablespoon ground coriander seeds
    1 teaspoon Laos powder
    1 teaspoon ground cummin seeds
    3 garlic cloves
    1 brown onion, finely diced
    3 tablespoons peanut oil
    ¾ block tempeh, finely diced
    3 cups sweet pumpkin, finely diced

Grind together chillies, tamari, lemon juice, palm sugar, aromatics and garlic. Fry onion briefly in oil. Add chilli mix, sauté 1 minute. Add tempeh, sauté 2 minutes. Add pumpkin, sauté, and add ½ cup water or 1 cup coconut or soy milk. Cook covered over medium heat until pumpkin is barely soft. Put in a pre-baked flan base and smooth out. Sprinkle with ground roasted peanuts.

Serve with cucumber and mint salad, steamed sweet potato and long grain brown rice.

8

Deep-frying or tempura

Tempura, a Japanese word, is deep-frying vegetables, fish or other foods in hot vegetable oil. This process requires at least a 5 cm depth of vegetable oil. The oil should be 170°C (350°F). To test this, drop a tiny amount of batter into the oil. It should drop halfway into the oil and immediately rise to the top.

Be sure to have adequate implements before deep-frying. You need a safe instrument for removing items from hot oil. If vegetables drop back into the hot oil as you are lifting them, burns and oil spillage can result. Chinese stores sell cheap mesh spoons for deep-frying.

Gently lower the vegetable or parcel into the hot oil. If it splatters a lot, the oil is too hot. Don't add too many pieces of vegetable or items at a time, as this lowers the temperature of the oil and makes gluggy tempura. Avoid playing with the objects as they are deep-frying, but turn them once to ensure even cooking. When done, remove with a strainer and drain on something absorbent, like left-over cardboard or paper towels, or a bamboo plate. Serve as soon as possible to ensure crispness.

Batter for deep-frying

Batter is a mixture of any type of flour and water.

The most basic batter is wholewheat flour and water with some natural sea salt. You must practise to gain the right texture. If you fail, you will learn, by adding more flour or less water, what is the best consistency of batter. Place the wholewheat flour in a bowl and slowly add *cold* water. Mix with a wooden spoon and aim for a stirrable paste. When you have such a paste, this means the flour and water are well mixed. Now the addition of extra water can be done without lumps forming in the batter. The batter should eventually be liquid with a glutinous (sticky) quality — when you dip in a piece of vegetable which has been dusted with flour, the batter should coat it evenly and slowly drip off. If it is too thick, you will have, after cooking, a mass of half-cooked batter with a tiny piece of vegetable inside. If too thin, you will have no batter after frying. Keep this in mind as you experiment with different flours. Wholewheat flour seems to be the best overall base for mixing with other flours. Brown rice, corn or maize meal, buckwheat, millet, lentil flours and chick pea flour (besan) all require a base such as wholewheat flour to ensure the glutinous quality of the batter and proper adherence to the vegetable. Glutinous rice, white rice, barley, rye, water-chestnut, arrowroot or kuzu, azuki or red bean are some of the flours which make varied batter. Chick pea flour (besan) produces a deep red batter. Fermented soya bean flour with wholewheat produces a savoury golden batter. Kokkoh cereal with wholewheat flour is a delicate batter. Kuzu arrowroot forms the finest textured batter of all — truly a delicacy. Glutinous rice flour is also delightful and crisp. If you wish to be spicy, add ground cummin or cardamom or some curry powder to the batter. Sesame seeds are attractive and tasty in batter, especially black ones.

Sourdough batter

For a unique batter on deep-fried foods, allow a batter mixture to stand for a few days, covered; or overnight in a warmer climate. The batter is ready when it contains bubbles. Use as a standard tempura batter. It will be very crisp and light. A wholewheat flour-water mixture is best. Alternatively if you keep a leaven or starter, add some of this to the batter 4 – 5 hours before use.

Vegetables

Almost all vegetables can be deep-fried. Hard vegetables, such as carrot and parsnip, should be sliced thinly to ensure even cooking, or blanched beforehand.

Break or slice cauliflower or broccoli into flowers. Comfrey, borage leaves, parsley clusters, and herbs can be deep-fried whole. Be careful with sweetcorn — it can explode. Zucchini is a meany. Cut soft, juicy vegetables, such as cucumber into larger pieces, not bigger than half a matchbox. Pumpkin chips leave potatoes for dead. Sweet potato chips are delicious. When you can deep-fry properly, you will wonder what those things they sell in fish and chip shops are! I still can't see how they do it! Wrap vegetables in pieces of nori, using wet hands, then proceed as with other vegetables — a real treat.

Because tempura or deep-frying is a process involving large amounts of oil, you should attempt to balance out the effect of such an amount of oil. Salt in correct quantity will achieve this. A salt-pressed salad is a light way of attaining the balance. Dips are important, especially grated radish (daikon where possible) and shoyu or radish and salt plum.

Radish dip for tempura

This dip makes tempura more digestible.

½ cup grated radish
flesh from 2 umeboshi plums or a few drops of shoyu

Mix well and serve with deep-fried food. Add 1 teaspoon brown rice vinegar as a variation.

Marinating

For an exotic taste, marinate vegetables (soak in a sauce). Our favourites are shoyu and orange juice in equal parts. This is best for seafood, but beautiful anyway. Use lemon or lime juice instead of orange. Use shoyu and maltose or a little honey for a sweet marinade. Add rice vinegar to this for sweet and sour. Shoyu alone makes an excellent soak.

Teriyaki marinade

2 tablespoons rice or barley miso
1 teaspoon mirin (sweet cooking saké) or saké
½ teaspoon dark sesame oil
1 teaspoon grated ginger
1 clove crushed garlic
1 tablespoon shoyu
1 teaspoon honey or 3 teaspoons maltose or rice syrup

Blend together with 1 cup water. Marinate vegetables for an hour or two. Use the leftover marinating liquid as a dip for the finished article. Heat it up and add arrowroot dissolved in a tiny amount of water — thicken and dip; or just heat and dip; or just dip. You can use wines for rich marinades but keep them for special occasions.

Rice Balls

Rice balls are an everlasting treat. Knead rice until sticky, form into balls with wet hands — 3 cm in diameter — deep-fry then sprinkle with sesame or sunflower salt and enjoy. This is the most basic method.

Add to the plain rice: ¼ teaspoon shoyu for each ball, finely chopped spring onions and ground peanuts. Deep-fry with or without batter. To this mixture of plain rice, you could also add fresh ground chilli pepper and crushed garlic, fried in a very small amount of sesame oil and shoyu. Knead all together with rice until sticky. Roll into balls with wet hands and deep-fry with or without batter. This is for those who need the heat, but better in hotter climates or on special occasions. From this you can see a basic method to rice balls and varying ingredients. Experiment and you will learn. Visit Indian and Chinese restaurants and understand the basics of deep-fried foods. The Chinese variety of deep-frieds is delightful. It's a pity they have succumbed to western influence, by adding white sugar and chemicals such as monosodium glutamate to their food. If you can imagine the culinary delights of the Chinese stripped of their richness and oil and excess of meats, but rather emphasising the flavours of vegetables and bean curd, fish and prawns, then you have discovered an avenue of inspiration.

The Chinese have been vegetarian cooks with the most basic of ingredients for over 4000 years. Chinese cuisine is one of the few surviving intact today with a direct link to early history. Theirs has been an attempt to gain maximum nutrition from their available foods. Chinese knowledge of food preserving techniques BC surpasses ours today because they employed natural fermentation methods which preserve the foodstuff, and through enzyme processes create a nutritive broth. Such food is high in B vitamins, enzymes and all scientific extras.

All grains can be deep-fried in a similar manner to rice balls. You can use rice as a basis with other grains, and add vegetables in endless variation.

Millet croquettes

> 2 cups cooked, hulled millet
> 1 onion
> 1 tablespoon shoyu

Chop onion very finely and add this to the millet. Add shoyu. Mix well and knead it with your fingers, if this is necessary to make it hang together. Roll into balls and flatten slightly. Deep-fry with or without batter until light gold.

Carrot balls

> 1 teaspoon finely grated ginger
> 1 star anise
> 3 medium carrots, diced finely

Sauté ginger and anise in a little oil (1 teaspoon). Add carrots and sauté for a few minutes until carrots are coated with ginger and oil. Add 1 tablespoon shoyu and ½ cup water. Cook over medium heat until carrots are soft. Remove anise, strain and mash carrots. Roll into balls. Make a batter with wholewheat and rice flour, some coarse coconut or sesame seeds. Deep-fry until golden. Serves 3–4.

Wheat balls/berries

Instead of 2 cups of millet in the above, use 2 cups of cooked wholewheat. It may be necessary to use 1 tablespoon of rice or flour to make this hold together — it depends on your wheat. Add 1 teaspoon crushed cummin seeds and fry a clove of crushed garlic with the onions and cummin seed if you want it spicy. Proceed as above.

Hijiki rice balls

> 3 cups cooked brown rice
> ½ cup cooked hijiki
> 1 tablespoon shoyu
> ½ cup cooked vegetables
> 1 tablespoon roasted sunflower seeds

Chop hijiki finely, add shoyu, rice and vegetables (preferably cooked with a little ginger and chopped or mashed). Add sunflower seeds and mix or knead with fingers. Deep-fry with or without batter. I suggest a cornmeal/wholewheat batter if you use one.

Buckwheat balls

3 cups cooked buckwheat
1 tablespoon shoyu or 2 teaspoons sesame salt
1 cup cooked carrots
2 spring onions, shallots or chives

Add shoyu or sesame salt to buckwheat. Mash carrots (steamed with ginger) and add finely chopped spring onions. Mix together well. For deep-frying it is best to use buckwheat which is cooked with a little less water than usual — just make sure it is not sloppy or it will not form balls. Deep-fry with or without batter (besan and wholewheat perhaps). Serve with lettuce.

Cornball

2 cups cooked brown rice
1 cup cooked or raw corn kernels
2 spring onions, finely chopped
1 tablespoon shoyu or some sesame salt
1 tablespoon ground roasted hazelnuts or peanuts (optional)
1 teaspoon chopped fresh basil

Mix together, form into balls and deep-fry with or without batter. Be careful, as some of the corn may explode, depending on its quality. This is good with buckwheat batter.
or
Cook polenta (coarse Italian cornmeal) with your rice. Use 1:4 polenta to rice. When cooked, proceed as above, using 2 cups of polenta rice instead of plain rice. This is beautiful inside nori rolls (page 72).

Okara balls

1 cup okara (see pages 120–1)
2 sheets nori, toasted and crumbled
1 cup brown rice
1 finely chopped onion
1 tablespoon shoyu

Knead well with your hands and form into balls (using wet hands). Deep-fry until golden. Again, you may need a batter, depending on how dry the okara is.

Tofu balls

3 cubes tofu (about 1½ cups mashed)
2½ cups cooked brown rice or glutinous rice
½ cup fresh corn kernels
1½ tablespoons shoyu
3 spring onions, finely chopped
½ cup cooked hijiki seaweed, drained and chopped fine
black sesame seeds (white will do)

Tofu should be pressed first to expel excess water. Place it under a tilted wooden chopping board with a weight on top. Leave this for 1 hour, ensuring the water can drain away.

Mix all ingredients well until firm and able to be rolled into balls. Add more rice if necessary. Roll balls in sesame seeds. Dip in batter and deep-fry. Serve with baked or wokked vegetables, cooked hulled millet and pressed salad.

Azuki balls

> 2 cups mashed azuki beans
> 1 cup brown rice
> 3 teaspoons shoyu
> 2 spring onions, finely chopped

Deep-fry with batter.

Miso rice balls

> 2 cups cooked rice
> 3 teaspoons barley or rice miso

Knead well together, form into balls with wet hands and deep-fry.

Millet nori croquettes

> 2 cups cooked, hulled millet
> 2 sheets nori, toasted lightly and broken up into small pieces
> 2 spring onions, chopped finely
> 2 tablespoons roasted sunflower seeds, coarsely crushed
> 2 teaspoons shoyu or 1 tablespoon white miso

Mix well, form into balls and deep-fry with batter.

Mugwarts

Use rice which has been cooked with eating quality mugwart. Roll into balls and deep-fry with or without batter. Delicious!

Peanut rice balls

> 2 cups cooked rice
> 1/2 cup freshly roasted and crushed peanuts
> 3 spring onions, chopped
> 1 tablespoon shoyu

Knead well with hands. Roll into balls and deep-fry.

Balls of fire

This method can be expanded in many directions, using rice as the base.
Basically:

> 3 cups cooked brown rice
> 1 cup cooked mashed chick peas or mung beans (optional)
> 1/2 cup roasted ground peanuts
> 1 onion, grated or chopped finely
> 1 teaspoon grated ginger
> 1 teaspoon crushed cummin seeds
> 1 red chilli pepper, chopped (or 2 teaspoons curry powder)

Add other ingredients to rice, peas and nuts. Knead well, make into balls with wet hands, dip in batter and deep-fry.

Drained, left-over curry mixed with rice can be made into these fiery treats.

A type of felafel

1½ cups mashed cooked chick peas
1 cup soaked bulghur (or kibble) wheat (rolled wheat works too)
½ cup finely chopped onions
2 teaspoons crushed garlic
1 teaspoon ground cummin seeds (grind them yourself)
1 teaspoon ground coriander seeds
½ teaspoon sea salt

Fry onion, garlic, coriander and cummin together in a little olive oil. Add the wheat and chick peas. Mix well. Best to leave it for an hour or two, covered. Roll into balls and flatten, then dip in a thin besan/wholewheat flour batter and deep-fry until golden. Serve with hommos and tabboule or roll them up in flatbread with lettuce, tomato, cucumber and hommos. The Lebanese use soaked but uncooked chick peas, a lot of finely chopped parsley and no batter.

Vegetable pakora

Pakora is an Indian food, consisting of mashed or finely chopped vegetables, spiced usually, rolled into balls, dipped in batter and deep-fried.

1 onion, chopped finely
2 cups pumpkin in small dices
1 small parsnip, chopped finely
1 small carrot, chopped finely

Fry onion over medium-high heat in 1 tablespoon sesame oil, then add vegetables. Stir for 1 minute, cover and let cook for 3 minutes over medium heat. Then add ½ cup liquid, which consists of equal proportions of water and shoyu. Cover and cook until vegetables are tender. When vegetables are cooked, strain, chop them finely. Mix a sufficient quantity of wholewheat and besan flour (chick pea) to form a thick batter. Form vegetables into a ball quickly, roll in flour, dip in batter and drop into hot oil with a spoon.

If you want them spicy, add the following to the onions at the beginning:

½ teaspoon crushed coriander seed
1 teaspoon crushed cummin seed
seeds from 1 cardomom pod, finely crushed
1 clove garlic, crushed
1 chilli, finely chopped

Use herbs and other combinations of vegetables in the pakoras. For example, zucchini, basil and sweet potato; lentils, uncooked finely chopped spring onions; buckwheat and carrot; hijiki seaweed, carrot and onion; carrot and onion and ginger — really delicious; parsnip, onion and sweet potato. It depends on what vegetables your climate produces. Use these in preference to ones which come from other states. This recipe is suitable for seafood also.

Other deep-fried dishes

Samosa

Another Indian delight with many Asian equivalents, samosa is deep-fried small 'pasties' for those of you who know what 'pasties' are.

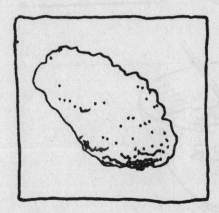 

Make thin pastry (see pastry, page 130). Cook a vegetable mixture as for the pakora. Roll out the pastry. Cut into squares 12 cm x 12 cm. Place the vegetable mixture in the middle. Roll as in diagram. Seal with a fork or other instrument. Deep-fry until golden.

Good mixtures: Mashed mung beans, onions, shoyu, ground peanuts; sweet potato; brown rice and onions; black beans cooked with vegetables; pumpkin; mashed chick peas, onions and shoyu; well-cooked seitan and green vegetables; tofu (drained) and vegetables; hijiki seaweed or wakame with bean or seed sprouts.

Buddha sticks

I think these are made in Laos. Cook brown rice and when cooked, knead it with your hands until sticky. Form into a tight cylinder 8 cm long and 2 cm in diameter. Slide a bamboo skewer or satay stick through the middle of the cylinder, end to end. Carefully roll in sesame seeds and deep-fry. Serve with sauce or sprinkle with sesame salt. Satay sauce is excellent for a hot, spicy accompaniment. Miso sauce is also good on these.

Shaslick

These are typical shaslicks. Slice your vegetables thinly. Carefully thread onto bamboo skewer. Dust with flour. Dip in batter then deep-fry until golden. Pieces of seitan on the skewer are very delicious and would fool any 'dyed in the wool' meat eater!

Spring rolls

These can be made with or without seafood. The filling is basically ginger, onions, garlic, mung bean sprouts and cabbage with an arrowroot sauce. To this you can add vegetables such as carrot, cauliflower and radish; or grains, beans, seaweeds, nuts, seeds and seafood — chopped prawns, fish, squid, crab — or chicken if you eat it.

Vegetable spring rolls

 1 cup bean or seed sprouts
 6 cooked shitake mushrooms, finely sliced
 4 spring onions, finely sliced
 2 tablespoons shoyu
 2 teaspoons chopped fresh basil
 3 cups blanched sliced cabbage
 1 cup blanched daikon or carrot, coarsely grated

Mix all ingredients thoroughly and place in spring roll skin. Roll up as in illustration. These can have any number of fillings, e.g. chick peas or lentils or mung beans instead of azuki beans. Good results can be achieved by concentrating on one vegetable, e.g. pumpkin rolls or zucchini rolls. My favourite is hijiki and onion. Left-over pastry rolled thin can be used instead of spring roll skins.

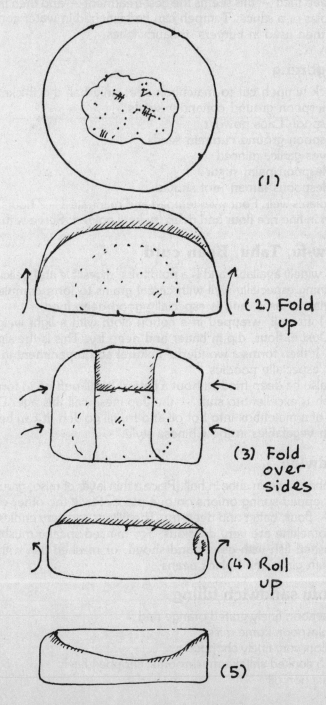

(1)

(2) Fold up

(3) Fold over sides

(4) Roll up

(5)

Tempeh

Tempeh is an Indonesian soybean cake. The soybeans are fermented with a special culture, which grows into a white mycelium binding the beans together. The mycelium and other ferments render the soybeans highly digestible, and enrich its vitamin content – notably of vitamin B12. Usually tempeh is fried, especially deep fried – this seems the best treatment – and then incorporated with vegetables or a sauce. Tempeh can be blanched in water containing soy sauce, and then used in burgers or sandwiches.

Tempeh goreng

1 block tempeh cut to matchbox size, only half the thickness
1 tablespoon ground coriander seeds
1 teaspoon Laos powder
1 teaspoon ground cummin seeds
3 cloves garlic, minced
1 tablespoon palm sugar
5 tablespoons tamari (not shoyu)

Mix all ingredients well. Pour over tempeh and marinate 1 – 2 hours. Mix often. Dust tempeh in fine rice flour and deep fry until golden. Serve with cucumber.

Tofu, Dow-fu, Tahu, Bean curd

Bean curd is widely available and is a nutritious, digestible and delicious protein food, combining especially well with cereal grains to form complete protein. It has a myriad of uses, and is especially good deep fried.

Press the tofu well, wrapped in a cotton cloth with a light weight on top, to drain it. Dust in flour, dip in batter and deep fry. This is the simplest fried preparation. It then forms a wonderful textural accompaniment to vegetables and cereals, especially noodles.

Tofu can also be deep-fried without a batter. It will puff up to form a golden 'pouch' which is excellent to stuff – the Japanese call this agé. Drop pieces half the size of a matchbox into hot oil and fry till golden. It can be sliced and stir-fried with vegetables in the Chinese style.

Tofu sandwich

Slice a matchbox size tofu cube in half. Place a thin layer of miso, ground peanuts and finely chopped spring onions on one piece. Place the other on top as in a sandwich – flour, batter and deep-fry. The fillings can vary endlessly. Layers of nori and omelette are very delicious. Try minced shitake mushrooms and miso; or mashed fish with ginger and shoyu; or mashed fish with seaweed; or prawns with ginger and black beans.

Special tofu sandwich filling

¾ teaspoon finely grated orange rind
1 tablespoon kome miso
1 onion, very finely chopped
4 or 5 cooked shitake mushrooms, chopped finely
1 teaspoon oil

Sauté onion in oil with orange rind. When done, add miso, mushrooms and ¼ cup soup stock or water. Cover and cook for 10 minutes. Cool. Strain off excess liquid and spread between layers of tofu. Then wrap tofu in nori, roll in flour, dip in batter and deep-fry. This is a tricky operation!

Fritter aways

    1 egg
    2 teaspoons shoyu
    1 spring onion, finely chopped
    2 cups cooked vegetables, strained well
    ½ cup cooked corn kernels or green peas
    1 tablespoon wholewheat flour

Beat egg. Mix with flour. Add other ingredients and mix well. Form into patties and deep-fry with or without batter. These can be fried in a pan.

Zucchini fritter aways

    1 cup finely grated zucchini
    1 tablespoon shoyu
    1 beaten egg
    3 finely chopped spring onions
    ½ cup wholewheat flour

When grating the zucchini, be sure not to lose the juice. Mix all ingredients thoroughly. Drop a spoonful into hot oil and deep-fry until golden brown.
or
Without using eggs, 2 cups zucchini, cooked with 2 tablespoons shoyu and ½ teaspoon basil. Chop zucchini and add basil, shoyu and ½ cup water. Bring to the boil over a medium heat and simmer till soft. Mix in $1/4$ cup buckwheat flour, $1/2$ cup wholewheat flour and 3 finely chopped spring onions. Add more flour or liquid if necessary. The texture should be stiff. Deep-fry until golden brown.

    This method can be followed using pumpkin, daikon radish, carrot or parsnip.

Lotus root tempura

Lotus root is available in dried form from Chinese grocery stores. Because lotus root is a water plant, it is excellent for eliminating excess water and mucus from the body. It has a favourable effect on the respiratory system. For this purpose it should be soaked, then boiled till tender, and eaten plain with vegetables. Deep-fried it is really a treat.

    Wash, then soak the root slices in plenty of cold water overnight. Slice the pieces into thin ovals, place in cold water and bring to the boil. Cover and simmer for 1 hour until it softens. The best way to establish whether it is cooked, is to break off a small piece and taste. It should be crunchy but chewable. When ready, slice the root into thin pieces (see page 23). Dust with flour, dip in batter and drop into hot oil. Brown rice flour and wheat flour is an excellent crisp batter.

Kombu seaweed

Soak kombu seaweed in water until reconstituted. Dry very well. Drop into hot oil. Remove when crisp. Careful, as this splatters! The kombu can be formed into decorative shapes.

Make a slit in the middle of kombu and fold it through the slit or simply drop dry kombu pieces in hot oil.

Orange crisps

Slice orange, including skin, into thin rounds with flour. Dust, dip in batter and deep-fry until crisp. Marinate them in brandy for a heavy hit, in shoyu and wrapped in nori for a delight. Buckwheat and wholewheat batter is recommended.

Nori rolls

These are not usually deep-fried, but are delicious treated in this manner. This recipe need not be deep-fried. Nori tastes very much like seafood. You can use a number of fillings. Plain brown rice is great, as is plain glutinous rice. Millet and cooked vegetables is a favourite.

Nori-millet rolls (deep-fried)

        2 cups cooked hulled millet
        1 onion
        3 small parsnips, finely chopped
        ½ cup roasted, chopped almonds
        1 small sweet potato, finely chopped
        ¾ cup water and 1 tablespoon shoyu

Place all vegetables in a pot, add the liquid, cover and cook over a medium heat until tender. Cool, strain well and mix together firmly so as to mash lightly. Add to millet and almonds. Mix in ½ cup bean sprouts or alfalfa sprouts.

Place in nori. Roll up. Seal ends (see nori rolls, pages 72 –3). Leave the roll standing on its seam for a few minutes. Slice into 5 pieces, dip in batter then deep-fry. Corn or rice flour, with wholewheat flour are good batters.

Stuffed cucumbers

        6 small apple cucumbers
        arrowroot or kuzu
        2 cups cooked hulled millet
        ½ cup roasted almonds or peanuts
        2 teaspoons kome miso
        3 sheets nori seaweed
        1 teaspoon shoyu
        1 onion finely chopped
        1 teaspoon crushed coriander seeds

Cut cucumbers in half. Scoop out seeds and pulp. Fry onion in a little sesame oil. Add about 1 tablespoon cucumber pulp and coriander seeds. Cook over medium heat for 2–3 minutes. Add a little water if too dry. Add almonds, finely chopped, miso and a little more water. Cook for 3–5 minutes. Remove from heat, add millet, shoyu. Roast the nori sheets over a flame on one side only. Crumble into small pieces. Mix with other ingredients. Stuff the cucumbers with this mixture. Mix a very thick paste of arrowroot and water. Spread on top of the mixture in the cucumber so as to cover the top completely. Carefully slide into oil and deep-fry until the top is slightly golden, the cucumber wrinkled and transparent looking. When they are cooked and drained, arrange in a steamer, preferably a Chinese bamboo steamer and steam for 10 – 15 mins. Serve with noodles or spaghetti, stir-fried vegetables with greens, and salad.

Sauces for deep-fried items

Satay sauce

1 cup ground roasted or boiled peanuts, in 1 cup water
1 tablespoon ground cummin seeds
2 tablespoons ground coriander seeds
1 teaspoon Laos powder
1-5 chillies
2 brown onions
5 cloves garlic
3 tablespoons tamari (not shoyu) or natural kechap
2 tablespoons palm sugar
3 tablespoons peanut oil
4 cups coconut milk
1 tablespoon lemon juice

Grind or blend the peanuts with 1 cup water. Combine the rest of the ingredients except coconut milk and grind or blend into a coarse paste. Heat 3 tablespoons peanut oil in a wok. Add the paste and stir fry for 2 – 3 minutes. Add the peanuts and coconut milk, mix well and slowly bring to the boil. Simmer 20 minutes. Add the lemon juice, stir and serve. Is even better the next day. If you require a thinner sauce, add extra coconut milk or blend the peanuts with more water.

Miso sauce

2 onions
1 cup finely ground roasted peanuts
2 tablespoons rice or barley miso

Chop onions finely. Fry these in 2 teaspoons sesame oil. Mix with miso and peanuts. Add 1 cup water, heat and stir until creamy; or use 1 teaspoon natural tahina and fresh chopped basil instead of peanuts, or dissolve the miso in some fish broth instead of water.

Serve on buddha sticks (see page 89) with bean sprout salad. Serve hot.

Teriyaki sauce

  2 tablespoons rice or barley miso
  1 teaspoon mirin (sweet cooking saké) or saké
  ½ teaspoon dark sesame oil
  1 teaspoon grated ginger
  1 teaspoon crushed garlic
  1 tablespoon shoyu
  1 teaspoon honey or 3 teaspoons maltose or rice syrup
  pinch Chinese wild red pepper or Japanese sansho pepper

Mix or blend all ingredients. Heat but do not boil for 10–15 minutes. Preferably prepare 1 week before use. The wait is well worthwhile.

Keeping oil

Try not to burn your deep-fry oil. Strain after use and store in a sealed jar with an umeboshi plum. You can re-use this for 3–4 weeks if consistent and thorough about straining and sealing.

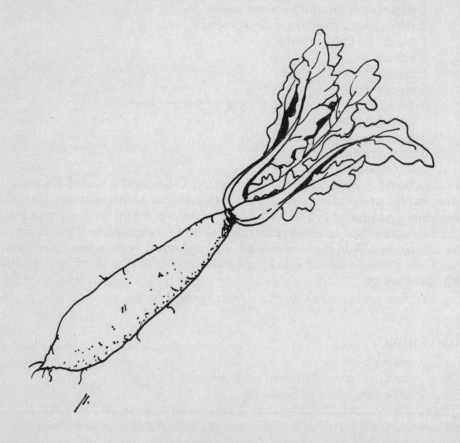

Menus containing deep-fried items

Miso soup
Tempura cauliflower
Brown rice with sunflower salt
Baked pumpkin, onion, parsnip, carrot
Spring onion, lettuce and celery salad
Stir-fried Chinese cabbage with ginger

Pumpkin buckwheat soup
Tofu sandwich with dip
Brown rice
Baked vegetables
Salad or wokked greens
Apple and strawberry crumble (page 144)

Zucchini soup
Azuki balls
Millet
Cracked wheat salad with parsley
Stir-fried vegetables with greens

Gojiru soup
Nori (fish) rolls
Cucumber-umeboshi plum salad
Steamed vegetables
Brown rice
Gingernut snaps

Seafood spring rolls
Bali pilau
Steamed broccoli
Sea vegetable salad with lettuce, celery and radish
Dried fruit tart

Keep in mind that a radish or daikon dip is a valuable digestive, palate cleansing and flavourful accompaniment to deep-fried foods.

9

Egg dishes

French omelette

    ½ cup finely diced carrot
    1 onion, sliced
    1 stick celery or fennel, chopped fine
    1 teaspoon thyme (preferably fresh)
    1 teaspoon olive oil
    4 eggs

Sauté onion in olive oil for 2 minutes. Add carrot and thyme and sauté for 5 minutes. Add celery, cover and remove from heat.

    Break 4 eggs into 1 cup soup stock, or water with shoyu added. (Mushroom soup stock is excellent, especially shitake.) Beat well. Add carrots, onion, celery. Pour this back into the pan. Cook over low-medium heat until slightly firm. Place under a griller and toast the top.

Serve with toasted wholewheat bread and tossed lettuce salad.

Variation: Add 3 – 4 teaspoons white wine to egg mixture for a rich omelette.

Steamed omelette or egg custard — called Chawan-Mushi in Japan

    4 eggs, well beaten
    1 cup shitake mushroom soaking juice or soup stock (use water and
        shoyu if you don't have stock)
    ¼ cup cooked hijiki seaweed *or* 2 sheets toasted nori, crumbled
    6 spring onions, finely chopped
    3 soaked, sliced shitake mushrooms (discard stalks)

Mix all the ingredients with 3 teaspoons shoyu or miso, a few slivers of mandarin or orange peel and 1 teaspoon mirin (sweet cooking saké).

Place mixture in individual cups, cover with a leaf from a green vegetable (spinach, comfrey or radish top). Place in a cooking pot and add water until half-way up the sides of the cup. Cover cups with a lid. Cover pot and bring to a boil. Simmer for about 15 minutes.

Serve hot or cold. Use seafood in this custard if you wish.

Egg foo yung — a variety

    ½ teaspoon finely grated ginger
    8–10 salted black beans
    3 soaked and sliced shitake mushrooms
    soaking water from mushrooms
    3 spring onions in 2 cm lengths, including tops and roots
    fresh coriander leaves
    ¼ teaspoon Chinese red peppercorns
    ½ cup bean sprouts
    6 eggs
    ½ teaspoon shoyu
    1 teaspoon maltose

Sauté black beans and ginger in 1 tablespoon oil for 1 minute. Add mushrooms and peppercorns if using (these are for a very fiery taste) and maltose. Stir for 2–3 minutes over medium heat. Beat eggs very lightly in 1 cup mushroom stock. Pour egg-mix into wok, stir, cover and heat until bottom is firm.

Add bean sprouts, coriander and shoyu. Stir and mix gently and cook for 2 minutes. Lift out and serve as a whole. You can simply add bean sprouts (etc.) and flip omelette over in half so it is 'stuffed' with bean sprouts. With sprouts you can use crabmeat, diced prawns, fish or free-range chicken for a most fulfilling dish.

With blackbean sauce, this is masterful. (See blackbean fish tempura, page 106 — omit garlic when using eggs as this combination causes internal fermentation.)

Rolled omelette — (Datemaki in Japan)

    6 eggs
    2 teaspoons shoyu
    1 tablespoon wholewheat flour
    ½ cup water or soup

Mix ingredients well. Lightly oil a pan and pour in egg mixture. This should be quite thin.

Cook over low-medium heat until done. Meanwhile, cut a carrot into large but thin matchsticks and place in boiling water. (These should be 10 cm long if possible.)

Finely chop parsley or fresh coriander or watercress. Remove omelette from pan and place on board. Sprinkle with greens. Place carrot on edge of omelette nearest you so it will roll easily.

Roll up the omelette, letting it sit on the rolled edge. Cool, slice and serve. Pour on sauce if using. I recommend sweet and sour (page 106).

Noodles, eggs and seafood

    2 cups cooked, strained wholewheat noodles
    4 eggs
    1 cup chopped, 'deveined' green prawns (or raw fish cubes)
    1 tablespoon shoyu
    6 chopped spring onions
    ½ cup finely diced celery
    fresh coriander if possible
    2 teaspoons vegetable oil
    ½ teaspoon grated ginger
    ¼ teaspoon dark sesame oil

Sauté prawns in vegetable oil with ginger until cooked (5–7 minutes). Add ½ cup water after 1 minute.

In a bowl, mix the rest of the ingredients. Place in a baking dish, cover and bake for 10–15 minutes at 160°C (325°F).

Serve with steamed green vegetables, millet pilau and pressed salad. ('Deveined' means to remove the prawn's spinal cord — rip his spine out.)

Egg noodles — deep fried

Preferably make noodles yourself, using the noodle recipe on page 38.

Cook the egg noodles as per directions. Drain very well and cool. Place in a deep-fry basket or large spoon with holes. Put in hot oil for 2 minutes. Remove and drain.

Nori roll with omelette and rice — A variety of nori maki sushi

    6 fresh eggs
    1 cup water
    1 tablespoon flour
    1 tablespoon shoyu
    rice 'sushi' mixture
    6 sheets nori seaweed

Thoroughly mix eggs, water, flour and shoyu and make 6 thin omelettes. Preheat oiled pan over medium heat, pour in egg mixture and cook over low heat — preferably in a square pan about the size of the nori sheets. Allow to cool.

Lightly toast nori and place the omelette (or strips of it if it's the wrong shape) on the nori.

Moisten edges and roll up. Stand on seam.

Slice into 5 pieces. Stand them up and place slivers of pickled red ginger on top. Serve with noodles and baked or steamed vegetables.

Andusaad (whole egg curry)

       3 onions
       5 cloves garlic
       1 tablespoon ginger root, chopped
       1 tablespoon tumeric
    2 – 5 chillies
       4 tablespoons peanut oil or ghee
       1 teaspoon mustard seeds
       1 tablespoon ground cummin seeds
       2 teaspoons garam masala
       3 cups water
       2 teaspoons sea salt
      12 hard boiled eggs
       1 cup raisins

Grind or blend together onions, garlic, ginger, tumeric, chillies. Heat oil, add mustard seeds and fry this mixture for 2 – 3 minutes. Add cummin and garam masala, water and salt. Mix well. Add the eggs and raisins and slowly bring to the boil. Simmer 30 minutes. Serve on long grain brown rice with cos lettuce and radishes.

10

Flesh, fish and seafood

Many people who have changed their food are not at all interested in eating any type of flesh — well and good. Others eat some fish or some dairy products. There are no rules about what you should eat, only your intuition and well-judged personal needs. I know of vegetarians who eat some fish because they feel the need. This is often because the change from carnivore to vegetarian is more than their bodies can cope with. I think this is far more sensible than rejecting all flesh and becoming sick through fanatical vegetarianism. It depends on your individual constitution. Fish and properly cooked poultry are light and relatively easily digested as compared to red meats, which you can safely avoid completely. If eating poultry, make sure the hens have been allowed to free range and fed on scraps and grain. Better still, raise your own. Then the act of slaughter requires you to do justice to the animal by preparing and cooking it with care and respect.

Commercial chicken are fed rubbish and are injected with hormones. There are a large number of cases where the consumption of commercial poultry has led to hormonal imbalances in the consumer as evidenced by the development of breasts on men. Similarly, commercial eggs with yolks which are almost indistinguishable from the whites, are the product of battery-tortured, chemically fed chickens, raised under lights in totally alien circumstances. Eggs from your own chickens or ducks, which you have raised on wholegrains, have orange yolks and do not seem to cause the foul smelling stomach fermentation and gas which I had associated with egg consumption.

Just a final word about flesh consumption. After you have been a vegetarian for some months, you may crave some animal food. This often means you are eliminating stored animal protein or fats. If you lash out on a hamburger, it simply means that your past months of vegetarianism have been wasted, and you will not eliminate stored animal salt, fats or protein. This is an old maxim of oriental medicine, that you usually crave what is being eliminated from your body. On fasts, you can experience cravings for ice cream or chocolates which you may not have eaten for years. Well, this is why I was horrified to read of a well-respected Australian herbalist who broke a fast with a piece of steak. She argued that her intuition told her to eat it because this was what she needed. Intuition can easily be confused with sensory impulses or eliminatory cravings. Heroin addicts still crave the drug for years after they stop consuming, and sugar is far more powerful than heroin in lots of ways — it certainly has a larger following and is almost as difficult to kick. Who would believe an ex-heroin addict when he claimed his intuition was telling him to use it again. I realise that this is a somewhat radical comparison but I believe it is useful from what I have observed. Rather than break a fast with steak, wait two days, and see if you still crave. Chances are, these cravings will have passed, especially if you resume eating a balanced, vegetal quality diet. I have found that many such cravings can be banished completely by carefully selecting alternative foods, e.g. miso and shitake mushrooms and/or beans, such as mung, lentils, can help overcome meat cravings, as can deep-fried tofu or seitan.

Fruit, dried fruit, baked sweet pumpkin and parsnip and grain honeys such as maltose or rice syrup can help you through withdrawals. Cooked rolled oats made creamy, grain creams and tofu can help you through dairy product craving. This is only if you want to get through the cravings, of course!

Seafood: fish

When you are buying fish, ensure that they are fresh. Fresh fish have clear eyes which bulge and are not sunken. The flesh should be moist rather than dry and, of course, should not smell in any way stale. Buy from somebody reputable, who gets regular fresh supplies. Buy whole fish rather than fillets, as fillets can be frozen and kept for ages, unbeknown to the innocent consumer. Good fillets are not soft or broken and should be of good colour and odour. Learn to fillet and scale your own fish as this involves you in the preparation more fully. Better still, catch your own fish from a clean place.

Scaling

Use a small sharp knife. Wet the fish first and then scrape its surface from tail towards the head, being careful to avoid being pricked by the sharp fins. The scales almost fall from fresh fish — so, the harder it is to scale, often the older or drier the fish is. The scales should not be soft and loose, however, as this also means old fish.

Filleting

Use a very sharp knife. Begin cutting at the tail. Try to keep the knife based on the backbone, and slide it gently towards the fish head. You are trying to remove all the flesh and leave the backbone. Make sure to cut close to the top and bottom of the fish to avoid leaving big pieces on the bone. This requires practice more than anything, so practise.

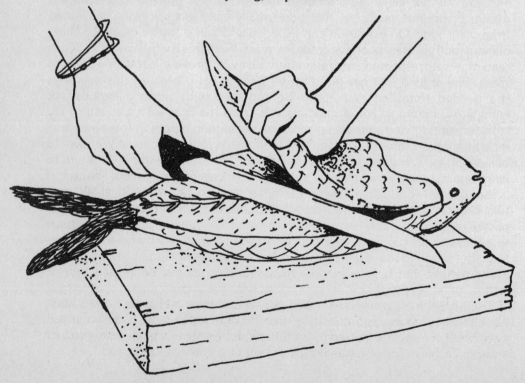

Baked fish

Scale, clean and wash fish. Bake at 160°C (320°F) or less — i.e. a slow oven, so as to ensure tender fish. I think it is important always to cook fish slowly. Oil the bottom of the baking dish. Add a little water and shoyu to prevent burning and sticking, or place fish on a layer of vegetables. Pieces of orange, lemon or lime cooked with the fish and removed before serving make good flavour and aroma.

Simmered fish

Make a soup broth with water, ginger, onions and seaweed. When this boils, remove from heat. Place fish in broth. Simmer *very* slowly until fish is tender (about 10–15 minutes). Add shoyu to taste.

Fried fish

Use a heavy pan and prewarm it over low heat. Add a little oil, increase heat to medium and add the fish. Cook slowly, but not so slowly that it is flabby. The oil must be medium-hot or oily 'flabfish' will result. Add a little water and shoyu or miso (kome) and use a well-fitting lid. This is almost steam-frying. These directions apply to most sea and freshwater fish.

Wokked fish

Slice the fish into bite-size pieces and stir-fry in a wok over medium heat with 1 tablespoon oil and 1 teaspoon finely grated ginger. Add 2 cups bean sprouts and ¹/₂ tablespoon shoyu when fish is cooked. (*See* page 41 for wok technique.) Or add sliced fish to vegetables which are being stir-fried in a wok. Add fish 5 minutes before completion of cooking vegetables. Be sure to slice fish small enough for this short cooking.

Steamed fish

Chinese bamboo steamers are ideal for this. Place 5 or 6 pieces of ginger the size of a 20 cent piece in the steaming water. Clean and scale the fish. Lay in the bamboo steamer and steam away! Turn to cook the other side. 1 minute before the completion of cooking, add 6 spring onions chopped in 5 cm lengths. Serve with the fish. A clear ginger sauce completes this light, delicate process.

Fish tempura

Corn, wholewheat and rice batters are suited to fish deep-frying. (*See* page 82.) Fish may be deep-fried whole, in fillets, or in pieces. You can wrap nori (seaweed) around the fish prior to dusting, battering and deep-frying (as in vegetables). Add roasted sesame seeds to the batter for a delicious change, or marinate fish in orange or lemon shoyu.

Black bean fish tempura

Chop fish into 5 cm squares or pieces. Place fish in a bowl. For every 10 pieces, sprinkle with 2–3 tablespoons shoyu, and a few squeezes of orange or lemon juice. Turn and mix every 3 minutes. Soak 1 strip kombu seaweed in cold water. Meanwhile, prepare sauce.

Wash first and then soak 1 tablespoon salted fermented black beans in 2 cups water. Chop 1 onion finely. Fry with 1 teaspoon finely grated fresh ginger and 3 cloves crushed garlic in 2 tablespoons sesame oil for 2 – 3 minutes. Add 1 star anise, black beans with water and ½ cup water or stock. Bring this to a boil while stirring and then simmer slowly. Add 1 dessertspoon arrowroot or ground kuzu, dissolved in ¼ cup water with 1 tablespoon shoyu. Make sure you dissolve the arrowroot or kuzu well and begin stirring as it enters the main body of liquid or it will lump. Increase the heat and stir until arrowroot clears. Add pieces of finely chopped spring onion or other greens, such as thinly sliced broccoli tips or bean sprouts. For a hearty black bean sauce, make a bechamel: i.e. use flour as the thickener. Dust, batter and deep-fry fish until golden. Drain the pieces of fish well and place in a bowl. Pour hot black bean sauce over them and enjoy a delight.

Sweet and sour sauce

The best sweet and sour sauce is a simple combination of umeboshi vinegar (the red juice or brine from umeboshi plums) and maltose (wheat syrup) or rice syrup. This is the perfect colour, texture and flavour. I wouldn't be surprised if this mixture was the original sauce which would explain why sweet and sour sauces are dyed red in oriental restaurants — all that is remembered about the original recipe is the colour! Apart from this, sweet and sour sauce can be made from any combination of the sweet (honey, maple syrup, palm sugar (gula malacca), or grape juice) and the sour (umeboshi, vinegar, lemon or lime juice, sauerkraut). Simply mix a small quantity of a sweet and a sour and taste until it has the right balance — heat and thicken with kuzu arrowroot if desired.

> 1 tablespoon umeboshi vinegar
> 2 tablespoons rice or wheat syrup (maltose)
> ¼ teaspoon crushed garlic (optional)
> ¼ teaspoon juice squeezed from finely grated ginger (optional)
> ⅛ teaspoon finely chopped fresh chilli pepper (optional)

Place the maltose container in hot water until the syrup can be spooned out. Mix with other ingredients and heat gently until quite liquid. Mix with vegetables or pour onto deep fried items such as fish.

Bali fish tempura

Sauce:

>   3 cloves crushed garlic
>   2 onions, finely chopped
>   1 teaspoon finely chopped ginger
>   large pinch coarse lemongrass
>   1 chilli, finely chopped
>   1 teaspoon roasted Ceylon or Malay curry powder (brown)
>   1 tablespoon vegetable oil
>   1 cup finely ground peanuts
>   3 cups coconut milk
>   1 cup water
>   chopped fresh coriander
>   3 tablespoons natural soy sauce (shoyu)

Sauté garlic, onions, ginger, lemongrass, chilli and curry powder in 1 tablespoon vegetable oil for 2-3 minutes. Then add peanuts, coconut milk and water. Bring to the boil, and simmer till quite thick. Add fresh chopped coriander or basil and shoyu. Place fish chunks in hot sauce and very slowly simmer. Or mix through deep-fried pieces.

Fish fingers

>   3 cups raw, deboned fish, ground or mashed finely
>   1 cup cooked brown rice
>   2 sheets nori seaweed, toasted and broken up or ½ cup cooked hijiki
>   6 finely chopped spring onions
>   1 tablespoon shoyu

Mix well together and form into rectangular pieces the size of your largest finger, dust with arrowroot and fry in a little oil until well cooked.

Or slip a bamboo skewer through the 'finger' and deep-fry.

Seafood shaslick

Place prawns and fish pieces, onions, sweet potato, or your choice of vegetables on a bamboo skewer as in vegetable shaslick. Dust with flour, coat in batter and deep-fry.

Sauce:

>   3 teaspoons finely grated ginger
>   ½ tablespoon kuzu arrowroot
>   4 spring onions, finely chopped
>   1 tablespoon shoyu

Fry ginger in 2 teaspoons vegetable oil until lightly cooked. Add spring onions, shoyu and 1 cup water. Continue to cook over low heat. Dissolve arrowroot in ½ cup cold water — add to simmering mixture and stir carefully. Increase the heat to nearly boiling and stir until the arrowroot has cleared.

Seafood spring rolls

      spring roll skins (*see* page 133)
      2 cups mung bean sprouts
      sesame oil
      6 shitake mushrooms, soaked in 3 cups water
      sheets of nori seaweed
      6 medium green prawns
      cooked crab meat – half of the meat from a Queensland mud crab
      fresh ginger – 1 teaspoon finely grated
      4 spring onions, cut in very thin slices
      1 clove garlic, crushed and chopped
      1 teaspoon black beans
      2 tablespoons arrowroot or kuzu

Fry ginger, garlic and black beans over medium heat in 1 tablespoon sesame oil. Stir for 2 – 3 minutes and cover. Turn down heat, add mushrooms, destalked and finely sliced, and chopped prawns. Add a little mushroom soaking liquid. Cook over medium heat for 5 minutes. Add 1 dessertspoon shoyu, crab, and a little more liquid from the mushrooms to keep the cooking quite moist. Cook over medium heat for 5 minutes. Strain off liquid – put in a saucepan, add kuzu dissolved in ¼ cup cooled prawn liquid. Stir over high heat until thickening. Add this to prawns, stir well. Add bean sprouts and spring onions. Place a sheet of nori over a rectangular spring roll skin. This should be smaller than the skin. Spread prawns, vegetables and bean sprouts. Roll up, seal edges with flour paste and deep-fry. Serve with lettuce, brown rice, wokked greens and vegetables (radish tops, Chinese cabbage, celery, cabbage – any good green – avoid silver beet and spinach here). As a side dish for a dip or smear, use finely grated radish and umeboshi plums. Pastry, rolled very thin, makes substitute spring roll skins if you aren't inclined to make the real thing.

    Alternatively, add the seafood of your choice to the vegetable spring roll mix.

Seafood balls

      ½ cup chopped cooked prawns *or* ½ cup finely chopped cooked fish
      3 cups cooked brown rice
      2 pieces nori seaweed
      ½ teaspoon ginger, finely grated
      1 onion, finely chopped
      1 small clove garlic, crushed
      1 tablespoon chopped fresh basil
      ¼ teaspoon grated orange rind
      1 tablespoon shoyu

Fry onion, garlic, ginger and orange rind over medium heat for 5 minutes. Mix with other ingredients and knead together. Deep-fry. Serve with steamed vegetables, hijiki seaweed and green salad.

Prawns can be substituted for fish in any of the above recipes.

Tempura prawns

Prepare in the same manner as other seafood. It is best to use green (uncooked) prawns. Remember to remove the veinous spinal column — like a thread in the spine.

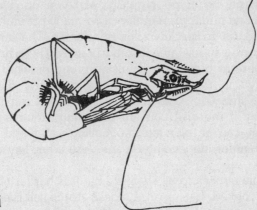

Prawns teriyaki

See Teriyaki Marinade for the sauce (page 83). This can be made hot or cold. Wrap the prawns in nori seaweed. Deep-fry, using a rice flour and whole-wheat flour batter. When done, toss with teriyaki sauce (not too much), sprinkle with chopped lettuce, cucumber, bean sprouts, fresh corn kernels and spring onions — toss again and serve immediately.

Scallops, Moreton Bay bugs or Balmain bugs, crayfish, squid and yabbies (freshwater crayfish) can all be treated in a similar manner. Use less salty sauces with seafood to create lightless. I loathe seafood smothered in rich flour and cheese or cream sauces. These create no balance with the seafood; and that feeling of never being able to eat again — blerk! You reach for volumes of liquid to relieve the heaviness and become a swill inside. The correct sauces make deep-fried food light and digestible. My favourite dip for deep-fried food, especially seafood, is radish and umeboshi plum, see page 83. It eliminates indigestion and that deep-fried feeling. Ordinary radish will do but daikon is best. White icicle (long white) radish comes closest. I do not recommend eating tempura or other deep-fried food every day — or if so, in small quantities — it depends on how much other oily food you eat.

Thai prawns

    1 cup deveined green prawns
    3 cups coconut milk (see glossary)
    1 tablespoon coarse lemongrass
    2 tablespoons fish sauce (Nam Pla)
    1 slivered onion
    1 chilli
    1 teaspoon of Laos powder

Bring coconut milk, Laos powder, chilli and lemongrass to a boil with 1 cup water. Simmer for 30 minutes. Add green prawns and fish sauce. Simmer slowly until prawns are cooked (10-15 minutes). Strain out lemongrass and serve prawns in this liquid, with sculptured spring onions and lots of chopped fresh basil leaves.

Crabs, crays, bugs and yabbies, oysters and scallops

Shellfish can easily be of poor quality, and you don't discover it until they are unwrapped and under preparation. Too many prawn heads separated from bodies is a good way to quickly pick a poor batch. The safest and most tasteful way to buy prawns is to use green or raw prawns. These aren't sold everywhere, so find out where to buy them. By using green prawns, you know they have not been boiled in muck. They can be delicately flavoured and cooked tenderly. Make sure you wash them well and pull out the spinal column — called deveining. If the dish you are preparing requires them to be cooked, e.g. salads, they can be plunged into boiling water and then simmered very slowly for 10 minutes, depending on size. Add a bay leaf or three for delicious cooked prawns.

The same rule applies to all shellfish, but it is harder to get crabs and crays which are not cooked. In season, Chinese stores sell live mudcrabs which are quite delicious. Balmain or Moreton Bay bugs are an uncommon delicacy and cheap! Be sure the yabbies (freshwater crayfish) you use do not come from the superphosphate and pesticide soup broth, which many of our waterholes or billabongs have become.

If you eat oysters, make sure they don't come from one of our many polluted bays or harbours, and that they are fresh.

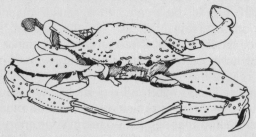

Mud crab with black bean sauce

> 1 mud crab (preferably live and 1.5–2 kilos)
> 1 cup black bean sauce (see recipe for black bean fish tempura)
> 1 cup bean sprouts

Drop the mud crab in a large pot of boiling salted water, preferably seawater. Simmer over medium heat for 15–20 minutes. Remove and cool. Keep all the claws, remove the meat from the body, being careful not to break the outer shell. This can be arduous at first, but becomes easier with practice. Clean all the celluloid matter out of the shell. Heat the black bean sauce and add half the crab meat. Strain the sauce, reserving the liquid. Stuff the shell with the meat and strainings from the sauce. Place the shell over the claws to simulate a live crab viewed from above! Gently fracture with one break, the larger claws (nippers) so the meat can be easily removed. Mix bean sprouts with the sauce and pour over the crab. Serve with noodles, stir-fried vegetables, sliced nori rolls and salad. For dessert — apple and strawberry jelly.

Oyster soup

      2 dozen fresh oysters, washed
      2 onions, finely chopped
      1 cup diced raw fish
      2 sheets nori, toasted on one side and torn up
      2 tablespoons shoyu
    4—5 pieces ginger, 5 cent size
      8 or so salted black beans

Sauté onions, black beans and ginger briefly in a little oil. Add raw fish, and cover with 6 cups water. Add nori. Simmer over medium-low heat until fish is cooked. Add oysters and shoyu and serve. Place a sliver of orange in each bowl. Don't serve out the ginger unless you particularly want it.

Scallops are rich and tasty. Use instead of oysters in the previous recipe, but add earlier as they require more cooking. Best of all, deep-fry them in corn-meal/wholewheat batter. Serve with a sweet and sour dip. Also excellent stir-fried with onions, ginger, Chinese cabbage and beansprouts.

Squid, octopus and other denizens of the deep

You may be repulsed by the thought of eating octopus or squid — I used to be but, take my word for it, you are missing out if you enjoy seafood and have not tried these. Remove the intestines from squid and octopus. Rub with salt and peel off the thin outer layer of transparent film or skin. Rubbing with salt makes it easier to remove the skin. Slice them very finely, so as to ensure tenderness, and cook slowly. Greek people call squid kalamari, and relish it! Deep-fried, stir-fried, simmered and in soups — enjoy them any way. Don't be afraid to ask an immigrant how to clean and prepare these sea-monsters.

Simmered squid

Use the smallest squid available, whole or larger ones sliced. After cleaning and removing the skin, you are left with an 'envelope' and tentacles. Slice into thin strips. Drop into lightly salted boiling water, remove from heat. Cover and allow this to cool. When cooled, remove squid, heat 2 cups of the water to near boiling. Add 1 tablespoon shoyu and 1 tablespoon mirin (sweet cooking saké). Place the squid into this hot liquid and allow to cool.

Serve after 1 hour – very tender! Or, thicken some of the liquid with kuzu, dissolved in a little water. Heat until clear. Add sliced and cooked hijiki seaweed and mustard cabbage (gai choy) one minute before serving, then add the squid, stir and serve onto a good sized dish.

Accompaniments could be mugwart rice balls deep-fried, page 87, vegetables steamed over ginger, and lettuce salad. Sourdough cake, page 139, for dessert.

Spaghetti or macaroni marinara

    2 medium onions, finely chopped
    2 cloves garlic, crushed
    2 tablespoons olive oil
    1 teaspoon chopped fresh basil
    1 medium carrot, diced finely
    2 stalks fennel, sliced
    10 cm dulse seaweed (wakame will do)
    400 gm tomatoes, peeled and seeded
    5 whole olives
    freshly ground black pepper
    cooked spaghetti or macaroni
    200 gm squid, cuttlefish or octopus
    200 gm fish
    1 tablespoon chopped parsley

Drop tomatoes into boiling salted water. Remove and peel off skins. Chop finely. Over medium heat sauté onions and garlic in olive oil for 2-3 minutes. Add the carrot, fennel, seaweed and tomatoes and sauté for 10 minutes then add the olives. Cook at same heat, with lid on, for 30 minutes. Clean and debone fish, wash squid in salted water, rub off the skin. Cut the fish and squid into large pieces and add them to the vegetables with basil and pepper. Turn off the heat, replace the lid and let the dish stand for 20 minutes, then slowly heat until almost boiling.

Meanwhile cook the spaghetti, strain, place in a heated serving dish. Pour the sauce and seafood onto the spaghetti, mix and serve immediately garnished with 1 tablespoon of chopped parsley and freshly ground black pepper.

11

Salads

Very little can be said about the preparation of salads. You can make an excellent salad with a lettuce, nothing more. Salads vary in importance with the season, with your own needs and with what else you eat. Obviously, salads are more desirable and satisfying in hot weather and therefore in warmer climates. Some people require more salad than others. This is often due to consumption of animal food, either in the past or currently. I find that eating as a vegetarian, I require less salad, especially less acid food such as tomatoes.

People who eat steak usually need to eat lots of salads in an attempt to balance out the strong effect of meat. Steak and tomatoes are often combined and this is an attempt to maintain some form of balance. Vegetarian food is much lighter than animal food and balance is easier to achieve, so I believe less raw food is required.

Some vegetarians believe in eating large proportions of raw food because nutrients are not destroyed by cooking. This is not really a traditional practice, and I believe it is too scientific an approach to food. Simply because the nutrients are identifiable in raw foods under laboratory analysis does not mean that all of these nutrients are in their most available form for us. Lots of things happen between the test tube and the final absorption into the body, and I think it is too simplistic to say that we get more nutrients from raw food simply because the nutrients are present in the raw state.

Man has evolved methods of food preparation which have proved the most efficient for him. The word 'salad' developed from the Latin root *sal*, meaning salt. Traditional peoples usually salted raw foods, or blanched them with hot water before consuming. This makes the nutrients more available and the food more digestible.

I think the idea of consuming large quantities of raw foods is a by-product of our leisure-filled scientific age. To me, less evolved animals eat raw products and we are an evolved species because we have learned to use fire and salt with our foods. My experiments with raw foods have led me to believe that they are conducive to a very 'laid back' or 'spaced out' mentality, which is fine if that is your desire. The ideal environment for raw food consumption is the distant countryside, free from much contact with the rest of humanity.

Traditionally, raw food or fruit consuming peoples have practised a minimum of agriculture (e.g. fruit orchards) and are interested in space, and the pursuit of ethereal ideals. People who live in extreme tropical areas have eaten much fruit and raw food and I think their simple mentality (not simplistic!) has resulted from this. Personally, I am much more active and purposeful with only a small proportion of raw food. But each to his own, and here are my salads:

Basic pressed salad with greens

Vary the ingredients depending on availability and season.

> ¼ cabbage, sliced very finely
> 4 spring onions in slivers
> 1 cup wild greens (e.g. young dandelion, Australian dandelion, or Cat's ear, chickweed)
> *or* radish tops
> *or* herbs such as sorrel, borage, comfrey, mustard
> a few sprigs of fresh oregano or basil
> 1 cup finely grated (not coarse) carrot, daikon, turnip or sweet pumpkin
> ½ cup chopped celery and its leaves

Mix well together in a bowl. Pour 3 cups boiling water over ingredients and let stand for 1 minute. Strain (keep the water for soup) and press between two bowls. Press on the top bowl to express most of the liquid.

Toss, cool and serve sprinkled with toasted sesame seeds.

Pressed vegetable salad

     1 cucumber, chopped in triangles
     1 cup grated radish
     1 brown onion, finely chopped
     1 cup grated sweet pumpkin
     1 zucchini, finely chopped
     ½ cup alfalfa, mung or lentil sprouts
     flesh from 3 umeboshi plums

Mix raw vegetables with the plum flesh. Pour boiling water onto the vegetables. Let stand for 1 minute, strain and press.

Sprout salad

     1 cup mung bean sprouts
     1 cup azuki bean sprouts
     ½ cup alfalfa sprouts
     ½ cup lentil sprouts
     ½ cup chick pea sprouts
     ½ cup buckwheat sprouts
     ½ lettuce, sliced finely

Mix and toss with dressing. Press, or simply blanch, if you prefer. Avocado and shoyu dressing is very tasty on this salad.

Sea vegetable salad

     ½ cup cooked hijiki seaweed
     ½ cup soaked chopped wakame seaweed
     ½ cup sliced radish
     ½ cup finely grated carrot
     ½ cup ground roasted peanuts
     ½ cup cooked brown rice
     ½ cup chopped greens
     6 chopped spring onions

Mix, sprinkle with a squeeze of orange juice, shoyu and serve.

Tossed lettuce

     1 lettuce, leaves whole
     3 spring onions in 5 cm pieces
Dressing:
     ½ tablespoon olive oil
     ¼ teaspoon brown rice vinegar

Mix dressing thoroughly. Do not toss salad with dressing until it is on the table ready to serve. Use walnut or corn germ oil for variation.

Garlic rice salad

    3 cloves finely chopped or crushed garlic
    6 cups cooked brown rice
    4 spring onions or shallots, chopped
    1 piece kombu seaweed, pre-soaked and diced, *or*
    2 sheets nori seaweed toasted on one side, and crumbled
    1 tablespoon chopped parsley, *or*
    fresh herb such as thyme or basil
    ½ cup toasted sunflower seeds
    1 tablespoon of shoyu

Soak garlic in shoyu for 10 minutes. Mix other ingredients gently so as not to mash the rice, then pour in the garlic and shoyu.

This salad is best left for an hour before serving.

Lemon-vegetable salad

    2 cups grated pumpkin
    1 stick finely chopped celery
    1 small cucumber, diced
    finely grated rind from ½ a lemon, and the juice of a whole lemon
    2 teaspoons of olive oil
    2 spring onions or shallots, chopped
    ½ cup shredded red or green cabbage
    1 capsicum, chopped

Mix lemon rind, juice and olive oil. Gently blend into other ingredients. Toss and serve garnished with strips of pre-soaked kombu seaweed.

Miso pickles as salad

If you have enough miso, bury some sliced, washed and well dried vegetables in it. They will be ready in three days, depending on how hard the vegetables are. Carrot takes two weeks. Remove from miso, wash well and serve with meal as a pickle. Bury whole onions or spring onions, radish, celery, broccoli, cauliflower etc.

Lark's tongue in aspic

    1 cup cooked wholewheat noodles, strained
    ½ cup bean sprouts
    ½ cup toasted whole almonds
    6–8 thin slices orange
    cucumber in thin half-moons
    radish in thin rounds
    whole celery leaves and parsley (or coriander or mint)
    ½ cup green peas
    one bar or ½ cup strand agar (kanten), chopped
    ½ teaspoon finely grated ginger
    ½ teaspoon dark sesame oil
    1 tablespoon orange juice
    2 onions in thin half-moons

Put agar in 3 cups water and gently bring to the boil. When agar has dissolv-ed, add peas and let stand while you prepare the other ingredients. Be careful it does not set! Sauté ginger and onion in oil being careful not to break up the onion too much. Sauté for 3 minutes over medium heat. Add 1 tablespoon water and much steam should result. Quickly add remaining ingredients, sprinkle with dark sesame oil, 1 tablespoon shoyu and orange juice. Stir gently, cover and remove from heat. This is to mingle the flavour and very slightly steam the ingredients. It is important that they do not become too sloppy.

Mix with the agar, stir gently and place in a rinsed, cool bowl. Allow to set — tap out of the bowl when set and cut with a very sharp knife.

Similar salads can be made with carrot juice as the liquid. Add agar to water, boil and dissolve, then add 1 cup carrot juice or cucumber juice. Proceed as above. Chopped cooked seafood can be added to this salad.

Dressings

Tahina (sesame purée)

Use only reputable tahina which does not have emulsifying agents. Dilute sesame purée with quarter its volume of water to make tahina.

    1 tablespoon tahina
    flesh from 3 umeboshi plums
    a little water

Mix very well and toss into salad. Use lemon juice and ½ teaspoon of sea salt instead of plums if you prefer.

Yoghurt or tofu

    ½ cup yoghurt or creamed tofu
    pinch salt
    chopped herbs or onions

To make spicy, add ½ teaspoon finely-ground coriander seeds.

Indian people mix this yoghurt dressing with banana or cucumber, as an accompaniment to curry it is called raita.

Ginger and sesame

    1 teaspoon ginger juice (grate ginger finely and squeeze out juice)
    1 teaspoon black sesame oil
    small pinch salt

Mix very thoroughly. Toss with lettuce.

Citrus:

    ½ cup lemon, orange, lime or mandarin juice
     1 tablespoon good quality vegetable oil, preferably olive
    salt to taste
    rind from half a lemon

Mix well — toss with greens. You can substitute carrot or cucumber juice for citrus.

Sprouts

The Chinese grow the best bean sprouts, having perfected the technique over many years. The secret is to grow sprouts under a rock or piece of wood. This makes for long and juicy, sweet white sprouts, commonly seen in Chinese meals. Soak beans overnight. Next day wrap loosely in a damp tea towel or cloth, put in a non-metal tray, a flat rock or a piece of wood with a weight, on top of the beans and cloth. Flush well with water daily. These take 6 days, and you can use any type of bean; azuki (red beans) take longer. This method can be applied to seeds as well.

Ingredients in salads will vary, as I have mentioned, so I have described three methods of preparation — pressing, pressing with a salt plum — use salt or shoyu if you wish — and tossing raw with a dressing.

Mix raw or pressed vegetables with a grain such as rice or buckwheat, and include some nuts if you wish. Avoid fruit and dried fruit in salads as this combination produces fermentation and gas in the intestines.

12

Tofu and Kofu

Tofu, dow-fu or soya bean curd

This is a soyabean product which has been prepared in the orient for thousands of years. It is a high quality protein source for people who do not eat animal products. The protein in tofu is readily available to the body, with no complex digestion required. This is certainly not true of most animal products which require long and complex digestion, which means your body must work harder for its due returns.

Tofu could be an excellent source of protein in all countries, because it is so energy efficient. Growing soya beans and producing tofu is far less wasteful in terms of energy consumption, than rearing livestock for protein and, in my opinion, it is a far more humane and evolved way of gaining nourishment.

Basically, making tofu involves grinding soya beans, making soya milk by heating and straining, and curdling the soya milk with a solidifier. You can use Epsom salts, magnesium chloride or calcium sulphate. Natural nigari, which is the product left from refining sea salt, or sea water itself, produce the best-tasting tofu. Natural gypsum produces the best texture.

Tofu is prepared for eating in a myriad of ways in the east, and I recommend you to read *The Book of Tofu* by William Shurtleff and Akiko Aoyagi for illumination.

To gain sufficient tofu for one week's consumption, use 6 cups soaked soya beans in the recipe below. Making tofu requires perseverance but it is a great centreing activity for all involved. The by-products, namely soya milk, okara and gô, can all be used in further cooking.

By making tofu with, say, 10 cups of soaked soya beans, you can extract some gô and set aside. Keep some soya milk, and of course the lees, or okara. Gô makes superb foods — custards, sauces, soups — and you should experiment with it.

Okara can be incorporated into baked loaves, or deep-fried balls, burgers or crumble toppings. It really comes into its own when added to bread mixtures!

Soya milk is great to have on hand for drinking, sweetened with maltose, or for making cakes, bread, sauces, etc. If you are resourceful, one session a week making tofu is quite sufficient.

Making tofu

Making tofu or soya bean curd is no more difficult than making bread. Most people simply assume it is complex. At first it is time-consuming and messy, but after four of five attempts you can reduce this time to one hour. The proper equipment is absolutely essential, or a mess and confusion can result.

Basically, you need a large pot, 2 big bowls, a vitamiser, a cloth sack (flour bag), cheese cloth and a settling container.

Use good quality, organic soya beans if possible. Soak them in plenty of water overnight. After soaking, strain off the liquid and wash the beans. The following measurements are for 1 cup soaked soya beans. Multiply as necessary.

Place 5 cups water in a large pot over high heat. Meanwhile purée (vitamise) the beans with 2½ cups water, until well ground and milky. The blended beans are called raw gô purée. Add this purée to the 5 cups of hot water. Stir continuously over medium heat until the mixture is well cooked, and foam rises in the pot. The product at this stage is called gô, and can be used in other recipes. Pour the purée into the moistened cloth sack, set in a bowl.

Strain the liquid and press sack very firmly to extract all the soy-milk.

Place the sack in 1 or 2 cups heated water in a saucepan, and squeeze or press again to ensure that all the milk is extracted. The grounds left in the sack are called okara. Remove and keep for other cooking. Place all the soya milk back into the cooking pot and bring to a boil over high heat. Stir often so the milk does not burn on the bottom of the pot. When the soya milk reaches boiling point, turn down heat and simmer slowly for 5 minutes.

Now curdle the soya milk to produce tofu. This is done by using nigari or clean seawater. These produce the best quality tofu. Use 1 cup seawater for each cup of soaked soya beans used, or $1\frac{1}{2}$ teaspoons finely ground nigari dissolved in 1 cup water. Remove soya milk from heat. Stir it vigorously a few times and carefully pour in two-thirds of the solidifier. Stir gently to ensure even distribution. Pour the remaining $\frac{1}{3}$ cup of solidifier over the surface of the milk. Cover and wait for a few minutes — or gleefully watch the delicate curds forming.

Give the curdling mixture a very gentle stir. By now you should have a lattice of curds floating in clear liquid. Put a large strainer into the pot to enable you to gently ladle out as much of the clear liquid (whey) as possible — you should be careful not to break up the curds.

Next, carefully pour the curds and remaining liquid into the settling container which is lined with moistened cheesecloth. The curds will remain on the cloth and the liquid will drain off. Fold the cloth over the top of the tofu and place the top of the settling container on this, then a weight, and leave for 2–3 hours.

Remove weight, unwrap tofu under cold water and there it is. What could be simpler for a once-a-week exercise which will keep you healthy and fulfilled?

Tofu making equipment

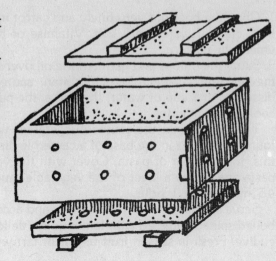

Settling Container

We made this type of settling container from wood. It is efficient and easy to make.

The large box should fit on the base.

Tofu lasagna

This is an adaption of an excellent recipe which appeared in the *East-West Journal*:

> 12 pieces of wholemeal lasagna pasta
> $1/2$ teaspoon salt
> 3 beetroot diced
> 20 medium sized carrots
> 1 tablespoon of umeboshi plum paste
> 3 cups of diced onions
> 5 cloves of garlic finely chopped or crushed
> 4 tablespoons of olive oil
> 3 cups of diced capsicum
> 3 cups of sliced mushrooms
> 3 cups of diced or minced seitan
> $1/2$ cup hatcho or mame miso
> 1 teaspoon of dried or 1 tablespoon of chopped fresh basil
> 2 teaspoons of dried oregano
>> (The Greek variety is sold tied in bundles and wrapped in cellophane or plastic; it is definitely worth hunting for.),
>> or 2 tablespoons of fresh chopped oregano or marjoram
> 1 teaspoon of freshly ground black pepper
> 20 stoned black olives, chopped

Tofu cheese

> 4 cakes of tofu, 5cm (2 inches) square
> 1 cup of lightly toasted, ground pine nuts
> $1/2$ cup of natto miso or $1/4$ cup shoyu
> 1 cup of preferably sourdough breadcrumbs, soaked in $1 1/2$ cups of water or soyamilk

Mash and stir the ingredients of the tofu cheese until smooth.

Boil the pasta in plenty of water with $1/2$ teaspoon of salt. The pasta must be firm or 'al dente'.

Chop the beetroot very finely and carrot into medium sized dices and boil in 2 cups of water until soft. Vitamise or blend until smooth. Mix in the umeboshi paste.

Sauté the onions and garlic in the oil over medium heat for 1 minute. Add the remaining vegetables and seitan, sauté for 1 minute. Add the miso dissolved in 1 cup of water, the herbs, the pepper and the olives. Cover and cook for 5 minutes.

Thoroughly mix the sautéed vegetables with the carrot mixture. Spread four of the pasta in the base of a casserole dish. Put a layer of tofu cheese on this, then a layer of pasta. Cover with the vegetable mixture, more cheese, pasta and finally a layer of the vegetable sauce. Bake at 170°C (350°F) for 45 minutes to 1 hour.

Serve sprinkled with fresh parsley and accompanied by steamed or lightly boiled spinach dressed with lemon juice, delicious bread for mopping up and endive. Fresh in season fruit or a fruit tart would conclude this meal nicely.

Kofu, fu, wheat gluten or seitan

Kofu sounds 'far-out' or unusual but is an easily prepared, tremendously satisfying, protein-rich food. It is traditional, having been prepared in Europe and Asia. Fu has a tremendously satisfying texture which is undoubtedly similar to types of meat. It thus provides psycho-satisfaction to meat-eaters who are changing to vegetal quality food, and gives immense pleasure and nutrition to people who eat wholly vegetal foods. Once prepared, it has many uses — as steamed or boiled cutlets; as seitan; cooked in ginger and shoyu; deep-fried, minced or finely chopped as stuffing.

14 cups of unbleached or 80% wholemeal flour
2 teaspoons sea salt dissolved in 5 cups cold, clean water

Slowly mix water into flour and form a dough. Knead for 20 minutes until a smooth dough is formed. Let stand for 30 minutes. In a large bowl, cover the dough with 9 cups of cold water. Knead under water until the liquid becomes very cloudy (about 10 minutes). Leave the dough on the bottom of the bowl and knead with your fists. Don't worry if it seems the dough is disintegrating. Strain off the liquid and keep it for baking, soups or sauces. Knead dough in bottom of bowl to remove excess liquid. Cover dough with 10 cups water and knead for 10 minutes. Discard water. Repeat. By this time the water should be much less cloudy. Knead dough to expel excess water. Rinse briefly. You will have a mass of brown gluten strands. Break off, or cut small pieces of this dough into 2 cm cubes. Drop into plenty of boiling water until these rise to the surface. Cool thoroughly or wrap the gluten in a damp cloth and steam over high heat for 30 minutes. It can be cooled under running water.

Now you have it — fu, kofu or wheat gluten. This can be added to soups, stir-fried with vegetables, deep-fried, finely chopped and stuffed into vegetables for baking, put in nori rolls, etc.

With the liquid reserved from kneading under water, you can make sauces and creams for pies or vegetables, or for dipping fu. When cooking vegetables for a pie, strain them and keep the strained liquid. Mix it half and half with the starch water. Slowly bring to medium-high heat, stirring all the time. This will thicken and become clearer — an excellent sauce texture. Make sure you cook it for long enough. Or try adding it to apple juice and proceed as above. If the starch is left to stand for a day, the water can gradually be spooned off and almost pure wheat starch remains, which can be used in place of arrowroot. This also works on shirt collars!

Seitan — a delicious variety

This is best made in a heavy cast iron pot, for low-intensity, even simmering.

> 1 tablespoon white sesame oil
> 1 teaspoon finely grated ginger
> ¾ cup shoyu
> 3 cups cold kofu, in pieces
> ¾ cup water or kombu stock

Sauté ginger in oil over medium heat, add gluten pieces and sauté for 3 minutes, stirring. Pour in shoyu and bring to a boil. Stir and reduce heat. Cover, stirring frequently, and simmer over very low heat for 2 hours. Uncover and stir often till all or most of the liquid is absorbed. This will keep for decades in a sealed jar, kept refrigerated.

This is quite a salty dish, so water down the shoyu if it's too salty. Use a tiny bit of garlic with ginger for a speciality, and mix the shoyu with water in which shitake mushrooms have been cooked.

Kofu sandwich

> rectangular strips of kofu 8 cm x 5 cm and ½ cm thick
> 2 finely minced cooked shitake mushrooms
> thin pieces of spring onion
> very thin strips of carrot, daikon or turnip, the size of kofu strips. Blanch
> these in boiling water.

Wrap moistened nori around the outside of the sandwich.

Sprinkle with flour, dip in batter and deep-fry until golden. A thin layer of tofu in this sandwich is smashing. If you have steamed the kofu as a whole, you will have something like a loaf. This is delicious sliced and eaten as is, or, simply dipped. For a dip, use one-third orange or mandarin juice and two-thirds shoyu … or a miso spread.

Kofu loaf

> 2 cups wheat gluten
> 1 cup kokkoh
> 1 cup wholewheat flour (fine or sifted)

Knead these together to form a smooth dough. Make into a rectangular loaf, approximately 10 cm x 12 cm and 2–3 cm thick. Drop gently into a large pot of boiling water. Allow to boil again, reduce heat and simmer for 40 minutes. Drain and cool well. Or steam over high heat for 30–40 minutes. This 'loaf' can be sliced and enjoyed with a spread, deep-fried, stir-fried, etc.

I was introduced to this process through Lima Ohsawa's cook book *The Art of Just Cooking*.

13

Bread and pastry

Bread

Use sourdough bread as a staple. It does not require the strenuous digestion of yeasted breads, and is chewier with a pleasant flavour. This bread may give you certain strengths because of its vitamin B content (from fermentation) and because it is a good way to introduce environment bacteria into your system so as to create strong immunity. When moving to a new location, sourdough bread acclimatises you to the neighbourhood bacteria.

Liquid and flour

All measurements for liquids used in this book are close, but only approximate! This is because different quality flours absorb varying amounts of liquid. Hard wheat tends to absorb more liquid than soft wheat, and kneading or mixing thoroughly causes more liquid absorption. Freshly ground flour tends to

absorb more liquid than flour which has been ground for some time. Finely ground flour needs more liquid initially than more coarsely ground flour.

Such problems do not concern those who use only commercially available bleached and refined white flour ... it is of one grade usually. It is essential that you, as cook, use your intuition and learn to gauge the correct textures. Bread texture should be elastic. Bun texture is slightly wet, and cake texture is wet or tacky. Bread dough should not stick to the kneading board, or only slightly. Bun dough will stick a little, and cake mix would have to be scraped off!

Sourdough

Mix 2 cups of flour in three cups of water and leave it in a protected, preferably warm, place. Cover with cheese cloth or muslin. After two to three days, depending on the location, the mixture smells sour and will have a few bubbles in it. This is the basic sourdough mixture.

Another method is to add ¼ teaspoon of miso to the flour and water mixture. This will be ready sooner than the flour and water mix, and is rich in nutrients.

Making sourdough varies considerably with the climate. A hot climate, especially in summer, produces sourdough overnight. In colder climates and during winter, fermentation can take up to 4 days. It is essential to have a warm place for making sourdough in a cold winter. A yoghurt-maker or a wood stove are ideal warm spots.

Sourdough bread

Place in a bowl 8 cups of wholewheat flour, preferably freshly ground, or use a mixture such as wheat and barley, or wheat and rye. Use 70 per cent wholewheat in each case, as this ensures a lighter bread. Rub 1½ cups of the sourdough into the flour for a few minutes. Use a smooth rubbing technique as though rubbing your hands in expectation.

Add approximately 1½ cups water. Add the water slowly to ensure you do not add too much. If too much water has been added, simply add a little more flour until a smooth, kneadable texture is obtained. Mix well with a wooden spoon, using strokes which lift the dough from the outside edge, and roll it over to the centre. This creates strength and elasticity. Rotate the bowl slowly.

When the dough begins to cling together, knead by hand. Lift the outside edge of the dough and gently press it into the centre. Then begin to knead on a low table, which will enable you to create a rhythm, and press the dough together with the whole of your torso — lift, then bring forward towards you, press down and roll away from yourself. Rotate the dough and repeat this procedure — what more can I say?

Knead this bread gently so it is elastic rather than a heavy dough. Form this dough into one shape and place in an oiled bread baking tin. Put in a protected, warm place. Depending on the quality of the sourdough used, this should double in size overnight, so be sure your tin is large enough.

Alternatively, if you desire a round loaf, use a round tin, or for rolls a gem scone iron which is made of cast iron. Aluminium gem scone irons are not suitable.

Bake at 205°C (400°F) for one hour. Tap the bottom of the loaf. If it sounds hollow it is ready. Sometimes it is necessary to take the loaf out of the tin, and let it sit in the oven for about 10 minutes to complete baking.

Another method of baking sourdough which results in quite a different textured bread is to make a dough with flour and water which has 1 teaspoon of miso dissolved in it. Knead and leave in a ceramic bowl overnight, covered with cheesecloth or muslin. Take it out in the morning and re-knead. Do this again before retiring in the evening, and again the following morning. Then place the dough in an oiled bread tin and allow to rise for 10–12 hours. Bake at 190°C (375°F) for one hour.

Sourdough accumulates rich ferments which aid in the development of intestinal flora, and good blood.

Apple sourdough bread

> fresh juice from three apples, or from cooked apples
> 1 tablespoon wholewheat flour
> 2 tablespoons sultanas
> 1 teaspoon miso

Set this mixture aside for 2–4 days or as long as it takes to smell sour and contain bubbles. Cover with cheesecloth.

Add this soured mixture to 6–8 cups of flour, one grated apple, 2 tablespoons sultanas, and mix well. Add more flour as necessary.

Knead and place in an oiled bread tin or tins, cover and set aside to rise. This may mean overnight. When risen sufficiently, brush the top with a beaten egg and sprinkle with sesame seeds.

Bake at 205°C (400°F) for one hour. Tap the bottom – if it sounds hollow it is ready. Don't be afraid to leave it in the oven for longer if necessary – bread is better overdone than doughy and uncooked.

For savoury sourdough use left-over soups as liquid, or add grated vegetables and nuts. Left-over tempura batter makes a good sourdough starter.

Rice and wholegrain bread

> 4 cups cooked rice or wholewheat/barley/millet/rye/buckwheat/oats
> 3 cups wheat flour
> 1½ cups buckwheat flour or kokkoh
> 1 tablespoon shoyu
> 2–2½ cups water

This is a no-knead bread. Mix the wholegrain with water. Break up the grain into individual kernels. Add the shoyu and flours. Mix with a slow turning motion, don't be violent. Sometimes it is slightly wet. Bake in a pan 3 cm deep – any deeper and the centre will not cook – 170°C (350°F) for 1 hour.

Usually surprising and perfect, sometimes crumbly and just as enjoyable. This bread is best left overnight before eating.

Buddha bread

> 8 cups fresh flour (at least 70 per cent wholewheat — use buckwheat/
> barley/rye, only 25 per cent)
> 1 tablespoon natural oil (optional)
> ½ teaspoon salt
> 1–2 cups water

Add salt to flour, rub in oil for 5 minutes. Add water slowly, mixing with a wooden spoon.

When the dough leaves the side of the bowl, knead for 15–20 minutes — meditation. Form into a round, flat shape 3 cm high. Lightly oil the surface and leave overnight.

The following morning prick holes in the top and bake at 170°C (350°F) for 1–2 hours. Superb bread, especially if you freshly mill the grain. Chew this to a liquid and you could possibly live on it.

Corn bread

Use 25 per cent fine maizemeal or freshly ground cornmeal. It should be fine if fresh-ground. Mix flours and proceed as for sourdough, using 3 teaspoons of shoyu instead of salt. Add this with the liquid.

Make into a shape 12 –15 cm round and 1–2 cm high. Top with sunflower seeds. Serve with pumpkin soup, page 53.

Can also be baked in a tin — not too high. It is a good idea to cook this in a pan on top of the stove over low heat for 10 minutes before baking. This makes the bread lighter.

Cornmeal becomes more accessible to baking when mixed with boiling water and allowed to cool. Then mix in other flours.

Flat bread — an ancient recipe

> 4 cups sifted wholewheat flour
> 1 teaspoon sea salt   )
> 1 tablespoon vegetable oil) can be omitted
> water

Add salt to flour, mix well and rub in oil thoroughly. Add water and mix with a wooden spoon until the dough leaves the sides of the mixing bowl. Add water slowly, as the flour you use may not absorb as much water as the flour I use. Knead the dough gently for 10 minutes until it holds together well and has a smooth, elastic quality. Break off pieces of dough and roll into a ball about the size of a large hen's egg. Flatten this with your hands until ½–1 cm thick, being careful not to split or separate the dough. Prick numerous holes in both sides of dough. Place on a pre-heated griddle. The temperature of the griddle should be sufficient to slowly cook the bread and at no time should it burn or scorch. When one side is golden and crust-like, turn over and cook the other side. Cooking time should be 10–15 minutes.

By crumbling toasted nori seaweed into the dough when mixing, a delicious savoury bread results. For variation, use a mixture of flour, but always 50 per cent wholewheat. Freshly ground flour is by far the best.

The Vegetarian Inn, an excellent restaurant in Melbourne, makes a variety of this bread which they call 'hot primitive' bread.

Basic yeasted bread (1)

There are many methods of making yeasted bread, all of which usually work. The method you choose will depend on the extent of your obsession. The best yeasted bread results from a long fermentation and a minimal amount of yeast. Not everybody has the time or the enthusiasm, however, so use a method which fits your schedules or you will give up baking bread.

Place 5 cups of wholemeal flour, preferably strong or high-gluten flour, in a heatproof bowl. Put it in a low oven for about 5 minutes. Meanwhile, dissolve 1 teaspoon of dried yeast or 2 teaspoons of fresh yeast in 1 cup of lukewarm water or soyamilk. Mix the flour with the yeast and enough lukewarm water or $^1/_2$ water/$^1/_2$ soyamilk, to form a very thick batter. Stir this vigorously with a wooden spoon for a few minutes until you see strands of gluten developing in the dough. Cover with a cloth and set aside to rise, preferably in a warm place.

If you put less yeast in this bread, it can be left overnight or all day while you work. When the batter is active and bubbling, stir vigorously to punch it down, add salt to taste (1 teaspoon would be average) and enough wholemeal or unbleached white flour to form a smooth dough. This dough should not stick to your hands nor should it be in any way tough or dry. Knead it gently but thoroughly for a few minutes. Form into a loaf and place in tin(s). Half fill the tin with dough and it should rise to the top. Cover with a cloth and leave to rise. This should take 1 hour.

Alternatively, if you don't have much time, mix the yeast and flour and enough warm liquid to form a dough which does not stick to your hands when you knead it. Be sure that it is not too dry, however. Shape this into a loaf, with the seam at the bottom, place it in a tin. Return 3 −4 hours later and the dough should have risen enough to bake. Follow baking instructions set out above.

Bake at 190°C (375°F) for one hour.

Basic yeasted bread (2)

This bread is at its best using 80 per cent freshly ground wholemeal wheat flour and 20 per cent unbleached white flour. This mixture is sometimes called 80 per cent wholemeal in the shops, but the 80 per cent flour available in Australia tends to be lower in gluten than the unbleached white flour you mix yourself. Either is suitable but the loaf made with 80 per cent flour will go stale more easily. Biodynamic's Falcon hard wheat or the red wheat from NSW and Queensland are the best to grind. Lowan Wholefoods market an unbleached white flour which is available in some retail outlets such as Soulfoods in Melbourne. A hundred per cent wholemeal is just as suitable as the mixture I have suggested; it depends upon your personal preference at the time of making. This also gives you the ability to bake different compounds without too much anxious premeditation. The recipe works well with 20 per cent barley, oat or rye flour: oat flour imparts a particularly delicious flavour. A really excellent combination given to me by a Yugoslavian miller is $^1/_3$ wholemeal wheat flour, $^1/_3$ wholemeal rye flour and $^1/_3$ unbleached white flour. This bread can be made without using salt if you prefer, or by using shoyu or miso. Make sure you use good quality unrefined sea salt, preferably from your own geographical vicinity.

Chapatti

This is Indian flat bread, at its best with freshly ground flour.

> 2 cups wholemeal wheat flour
> pinch salt
> water to make a smooth elastic dough (about $^3/_4$ cup)

Add salt to flour. Slowly add water and mix with your fingers until the dough holds together and is slightly moist. Knead for 10 minutes. The dough should be elastic and smooth. Roll into balls 5 cm in diameter. Heat a thick pan or skillet until quite hot. Roll out each ball into a circular, flat shape, thin or thick as you prefer. Use a floured board to prevent sticking. Place in the hot pan and pat the 'up' side with a paddle. It will bubble or puff up slightly. Lift and turn over. Cook until freckled with brown on both sides. Indian people smear the hot chapatti with ghee before serving. Seaweed such as crumbled nori or vegetable purée can be incorporated into the dough for variation. Vegetable oil may be rubbed into the flour for a richer chapatti. Use 2 tablespoons for 2 cups of flour and proceed as above. Try to keep your chapatti round and serve as soon as possible.

Puris

This is a delicate, puffed Indian flat bread which is deep-fried.

> 2 cups wholewheat flour
> 1 tablespoon vegetable oil
> good pinch salt
> ½–¾ cup water

Follow directions for chapatti, but take special care to knead well. Envisage a smooth elastic dough. Roll out into 8 cm rounds, carefully slip into hot oil at 170°C (350°F). The puri will go to the bottom, rise and usually puff up. Carefully turn over with a mesh spoon and remove.

They will not always puff up, but will still taste great.

Puris can be served with steamed and puréed or mashed sweet vegetables such as baked carrot, parsnip or pumpkin or sweet potato.

Indian people serve them with shrikand, which is a delicious sweet yoghurt dish. It can be made with thick tofu or bean curd if you prefer.

Shrikand

> 8 cups plain yoghurt or tofu
> 4 cardamom pods
> ½ cup cooked puréed dates
> ½ cup chopped pistachios, cashew nuts or almonds
> pinch nutmeg
> 1 teaspoon rosewater

Place yoghurt or Tofu in cheesecloth and hang up with a string for 6 hours. The water will drip out and the yoghurt/tofu will become quite firm. Pressing the tofu under a board will achieve the same effect. Crush cardamom seeds, chop nuts and add with the dates, nutmeg and rosewater. Mix until smooth. Chill for one hour before serving.

This tofu filling can also be put in samosa.

Pastry

Basic Pastry

> 4 cups wholewheat flour
> 2 – 3 tablespoons vegetable oil
> pinch salt
> 1–1½ cups water (depending on flour)

Add salt to flour. Rub in oil. Add water slowly while mixing with a wooden spoon. When dough starts to form lumps and comes away from the sides of the bowl, form into one piece with hands and start kneading in the bowl. Add more water if necessary — the texture should be elastic or slightly sticky.

Continue kneading until unified and pliable — about 2 minutes. If the pastry is too heavy, use more of a stretching, rolling knead. You may need more water, especially if the pastry will not roll out properly.

Flatten out the dough a little and roll with a rolling pin on a lightly floured board/table. Flouring the board and top of pastry prevents sticking and enables more rolling. Don't leave thick patches as you roll, keep all of the dough the same thickness as best you can. Roll, don't press.

When completed, roll the pastry on to rolling pin — place on edge of pie dish and unroll over dish — avoids lifting and breaking.

Bake at 190°C (375°F) for 15 minutes.

In hot water pastry

> 2 cups flour
> ¼ cup oil
> ⅔ cup boiling water
> pinch salt

Blend oil with water to form a creamy liquid, add slowly to flour. Mix with a wooden spoon. Knead for 5 minutes. Leave for 30 minutes.

Bake at 205°C (400°F) for 15 minutes.

Sourdough pastry

Follow directions for basic pastry. Allow to stand covered for 2 –3 days until sour and light. Knead for 10 minutes. Roll out and use as normal pastry. This is especially good for flan bases or for layering, with each layer brushed with oil and rolled very thin, as in phylo pastry. It has the tendency to flake or bubble, making it very attractive and satisfying to those who miss puff pastry.

Thin pastry

Use fine wholewheat flour.

    2 cups wholewheat flour
    2 tablespoons vegetable oil
    pinch salt
    1 cup water

Rub oil into flour and salt mixture. Add water, mixing with a wooden spoon. Make into dough and knead thoroughly. Add more water if necessary. Roll out the pastry quite thick, brush thinly with oil then fold it over in itself twice and roll out thick. Repeat this process six times.

Then roll out thin, fold up, brush with oil, and roll out thin again.

Repeat this process two or three times. Roll out very thin using a lightly floured board and rolling pin. If you repeat this process for 2–3 hours, your pastry will be thin enough for Lebanese goodies.

You may also use fine wholemeal flour and boiling water. High protein or hard wheat flour is good here as it develops more gluten and will stretch without breaking.

Nut pastry

When making any basic pastry mix, add 1–2 tablespoons of finely crushed, freshly toasted walnuts, hazelnuts or almonds to the flour mixture before adding liquids.

Yeasted pastry

    4 cups wholewheat flour
    1 teaspoon dried yeast
    2 tablespoons oil
    2 teaspoons sea salt
    1 cup water

Dissolve yeast in $1/2$ cup warm water with 1 teaspoon rice syrup, maltose or maple syrup and $1/2$ teaspoon flour. Set aside until it froths. Meanwhile add salt to flour and rub in oil. Add yeast and the cup of water.

Mix well with a wooden spoon and then knead for 10 minutes until a smooth, elastic dough. Add more water if necessary. Set aside for 1 hour. Knead for 5 minutes and roll out into desired shape. Bake at 170°C (350°F) for 30–40 minutes.

With this pastry you can make tea rings or braided loaves.

Tea rings

Roll yeasted pastry into a rectangle. Spread with filling (usually dried fruit cooked with ginger or spice or lemon rind). Roll this up to form a cylinder. Join the ends of the cylinder and make cuts around the ring. If you imagine the cylinder formed into a ring, make the cuts at two-hour intervals as on a clock face.

Turn small cylinders made by the incisions onto their base, still joined with each other and form a ring of small cylinders. Cover with a cloth and allow 45 minutes to rise.

Bake on an oiled tray for 30 – 40 minutes at 170°C (350°F).

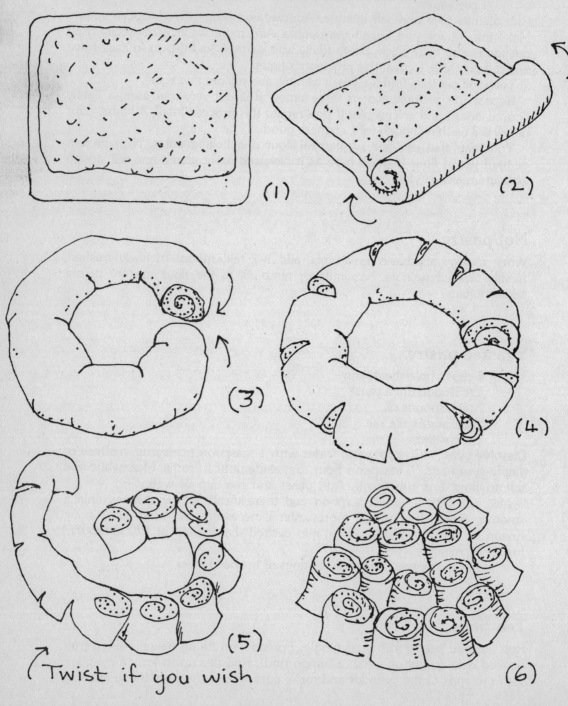

(1)

(2)

(3)

(4)

(5)

Twist if you wish

(6)

Spring roll skins (1)

   1 cup very finely ground wholewheat flour (sieve if necessary)
   1 cup water
   1 teaspoon salt
   1 tablespoon oil
   1 beaten egg

Mix well to form a batter. Heat a heavy frying pan and turn heat to low. Ladle in just enough batter to thinly cover pan. By turning the pan as you add batter it will be quite thin. Heat until batter is set, not brown or cooked, then turn over and heat the other side for 1 minute or less. Remove and repeat until you have enough skins.

Spring roll skins (2)

   2 cups of very fine-ground wholewheat flour
   or 1½ cups of flour and ½ cup of well ground kuzu arrowroot
   ½–¾ cups of boiling water

Add boiling water slowly until the dough starts to cling together. The texture should not be sticky. Knead carefully so as not to burn your hands. It is advisable to have a bowl of cool water handy to plunge your hands into! Knead for 5–10 minutes. Cover with a cloth and allow to cool. Flour the table when rolling out the pastry, and it can be rolled very thin. Brush off excess flour before deep-frying.

14

Baked sweets

Buns, scones and muffins

Byron buns

6 cups wholewheat flour
2 teaspoons dried yeast
1 teaspoon finely ground star anise (remove seeds and grind these, not the 'star')
$\frac{1}{2}$ teaspoon freshly grated nutmeg
1 teaspoon sea salt
4 tablespoons oil
1 cup currants
1 cup sultanas
2 teaspoons grated ginger
2 teaspoons finely grated orange rind added to 2 – 3 cups apple juice

Dissolve granulated yeast in $\frac{1}{2}$ cup warm water with 1 tablespoon flour and 1 teaspoon maple syrup or honey or grain syrup. Cover with cloth and set aside in a warm place to rise. Add salt to flour with star anise and nutmeg. When yeast has risen (about 10 minutes) add this to the flour and distribute evenly. Add fruit and ginger.

Blend or emulsify oil and water and slowly add to flour. Alternatively, rub the oil into the flour before adding water. The amount of water varies with flour — some wholewheat flour absorbs much more water than others. The texture should be wetter than pastry dough, but firm enough to handle — it should just stick to the table as you knead it — so sprinkle with a little flour, and flour your hands. If you have a suitable surface you can oil it lightly to prevent sticking.

Knead for 10 minutes until elastic but not dry — if the dough goes dry add more water. Do this by poking holes in the dough with your fingers and putting water in the holes. Cover carefully with more dough and knead.

Roll out onto a floured board with a rolling pin dusted with flour. The dough should be 2–3 cm thick. Cut out into shapes with an inverted glass, also dusted with flour, or a scone cutter, or shape into buns with your hands by rolling into a ball.

Place in an oiled tray and set aside in a warm place for 2–3 hours. Cover with a cloth. Make sure to eliminate draughts.

When buns have risen, brush with a glaze made from a beaten egg with 1 tablespoon water, mixed well. Bake at 190–205°C (375–400°F) for 15–20 minutes. Some ovens are more severe than others so it is hard to estimate exact temperature or time. The oven must be hot rather than slow. Bake them on a high rack.

Hot cross or cold happy buns

Make in the same way as Byron buns, but don't add any dried fruit. Use 1½ teaspoons ground cinnamon, ½ teaspoon ground nutmeg and ½ teaspoon ground cloves as the spice instead of star anise. Glaze with beaten egg.

For the cross, simply mix wholewheat flour and water to a paste and apply in a cross shape with a cake decorator or spoon. Do this before you set them to rise. Dust with cinnamon just before you bake.

Another Byron bun

Follow directions for Byron buns, but omit the spices, orange rind and dried fruit.

Cook 1 cup chopped Chinese dates or Iraq dates or 1 cup blackcurrants, raisins or sultanas or dried apricot with 3–4 cups water (depending on how dried the fruit is), 2 star anise, 3 cloves, 2 sticks cinnamon, 2 teaspoons finely grated ginger root, and a squeeze of lemon juice.

When soft and almost a purée (strain off excess water and use in the buns themselves), add 1 teaspoon orange rind. Remove spices (if whole) and spread mixture on the rolled out bun mix.

Have the dough in long rectangles 15 cm wide. Roll up and slice the roll every 6 cm. Stand them on end. Dust with ground cinnamon. Treat as Byron buns for rising and cooking. These are called Chelsea buns in bakeries.

Yeasted fruit bread

Follow directions for Byron buns or hot cross buns, but knead into one shape. Place in an oiled baking tin, cover and set aside 3 hours to rise. Bake at 205°C (400°F) for 45 minutes. Tap the top and bottom, this should make a hollow sound when ready.

Savoury yeast buns

Follow the directions for Byron buns, but omit the spices and dried fruit. Add 1½ tablespoons shoyu, 2 finely chopped onions and 4 sheets toasted nori, crumbled.

Sourdough scones

Follow the directions for Byron buns but use 2 cups sourdough starter instead of yeast (see page 125). Don't dissolve in water, simply add. They will need a little less water. Omit the spice and dried fruit for plain buns. Halve the ingredients if you are cooking for less than six.

For savoury scones, add finely chopped onion and cooked sea vegetables (hijiki) or crumbled toasted nori and 1½ tablespoons shoyu or 1 tablespoon miso (kome or mugi). A dozen soaked fermented black beans with soaking water, or fine chopped cooked shitake mushrooms for a delight. Allow 6–8 hours to rise or overnight. For this purpose, put the dough in a gem scone tray or special cake tray with 9 or 10 cake moulds on it.

These buns can also be steamed if made golf ball size.

Mugwart buns

Follow the directions for sourdough buns. Use mugwart tea instead of water. If you have any good quality mugwart (like the Japanese variety which comes in a hard green mass of leaves the size of a 50 cent piece) then soak 3 pieces in hot water and break it up very thoroughly. Use this, including mugwart strands, as liquid in bread.

Eating mugwart rapidly builds good blood. It is most effective for pregnant women and those nursing children.

Buckwheat muffins

Use 50 per cent buckwheat flour (or barley flour for barley scones) in the sourdough scone mixture. For sweet ones add 2 cups grated apple and a little extra flour.

For savoury, ½ cup grated matured cheese (rub well into flour), 1 finely chopped onion, 1 finely diced red capsicum, ½ teaspoon dried or 5 or 6 sprigs fresh basil or oregano.

Pumpkin scones

Following sourdough scone or buckwheat muffin procedure, use cooked pumpkin (baked is best) and add this instead of liquid — it may take 3–4 cups or more depending on how thin or thick the pumpkin purée or soup is.

Or add 2 cups very finely grated pumpkin to the mixture and add a few pinches freshly ground cummin. Use parsnip or carrot for variation.

Nut scones

Add 2 cups finely ground roasted almonds, peanuts, Brazil nuts, hazelnuts, macadamias, sesame or sunflower seeds to the sourdough scone mixture. Rub the nuts into the flour. Add ½ teaspoon extra salt.

You can also use roasted, coarse coconut strands or freshly grated coconut.

Sweet scones

Using the sourdough scone recipe, add 2 cups finely grated or cooked apple, pear, orange juice and rind — which requires more flour — puréed strawberries or blackberries, cooked raisins, dates, currants or apricots.

Cakes

When baking cakes, remember that you will not be making anything that resembles what are called cakes today. The cakes described here will be heavy and sometimes moist. The textures of modern cakes are only possible using fine white flour, sugar, dairy products and chemical risings. If you wish to make these, there are plenty of books which go into such methods. I see them as undesirable in terms of health and prefer to eat chewable, heavier cakes which are more satisfying all round. Baking powder and chemical risings cause swollen intestines, thirst, acidity and wind.

Any cake can be made very simply using sourdough. Follow the directions for sourdough scones. Basically, mix dry and wet ingredients, including sourdough. Cover, and leave overnight in a warm place to rise. Bake at 190°C (375°F) for 45 minutes–1½ hours depending on thickness of cake.

You will need only half of the ingredients necessary for sourdough scones, unless baking a monster. Add more liquid for cakes as cake dough or batter should be wetter than bread dough — spoonable rather than kneadable. Mix cake batter smoothly with a wooden spoon. If you wish to use a beaten egg or two for lightness, mix with liquid and add to dry ingredients.

Basic to all cakes — mix liquids together and add to dry ingredients. Extra oil and a little less liquid will give better results for cakes.

Cakes can also be made without oil or nuts. Substitute extra liquid, soya milk or skim milk for oil, and rolled oats for nuts.

Here are suggestions for combinations.

Basic liquids	Basic dry ingredients
Pear juice which is boiled with finely grated ginger, cooled. Sourdough Oil	Wholewheat flour, roasted coconut, roasted ground nuts or roasted chopped nuts and broken seeds (e.g. almonds, hazel, Brazil, sunflower and sesame is a good combination). Some sea salt in each case
Dates ⎫ Orange juice ⎪ Water ⎬ purée Natural tahina ⎪ Sourdough ⎭	Wholewheat flour Orange rind
Date purée Sourdough Oil	Wholewheat flour Carob powder Orange rind
Cooked apple and ginger purée Sourdough Oil	Wholewheat flour Roasted rolled barley Lotus root powder
Grated apple ⎫ Apple juice ⎬ purée Oil ⎪ Sourdough ⎭	Barley flour, roasted rolled oats, toasted sunflower seeds Cinnamon Blackcurrants
Goat's milk ⎫ purée Honey ⎬ Sourdough Vanilla essence	Wholewheat flour Lightly toasted ground sesame seeds Caraway seeds
2 eggs ⎫ Water ⎪ Oil ⎬ purée Vanilla essence ⎪ Sourdough ⎭	Wholewheat flour Lemon rind Roasted finely ground hazelnuts Toasted coconut
Cooked bananas ⎫ Oil ⎪ Vanilla essence ⎬ purée Water ⎪ Sourdough ⎭	Wholewheat flour Cinnamon Nutmeg

Basic liquids

Coconut oil
Water
Vanilla essence
Cooked dates
   or honey
Sourdough
} purée

Parsnip or
   pumpkin
Cooked apples
Vanilla essence
Oil
Water
Sourdough
} purée

Basic dry ingredients

Toasted coconut
Wholewheat flour

Wholewheat flour
Buckwheat flour
Lotus root powder

Examples:

Carob date cake

> 2½ cups flour
> 1 tablespoon oil
> 2 cups date purée
> ½ teaspoon salt
> 1 cup sourdough
> 1 cup apple juice
> ½ cup carob powder

Carob powder is very drying to cakes — it seems to absorb much liquid, so in order to get a good texture cook in 1 cup apple juice for 15 minutes. Leave overnight to rise. Bake at 170°C (350°F) for 1 hour.

I hope you can see from this how important basic technique is. Recipes are most valuable when you have to put your own thought into making them work — don't rely on quantities, all ingredients can vary.

My flour will need more oil or water than yours. I could add a drier date purée, or more carob powder. Therefore, in order to get the correct texture more or less liquid may be required.

The dates could have been cooked in 5 cups water and simply added to the liquid — or puréed with the carob and oil and used as the liquid. Or an egg could be added with the liquid, etc.

This is how we learned to cook, and each of us cooks differently. We still use the same ingredients — even in the same quantities, and the results are different. Rely on your own judgment and use the recipes as a guide. You will soon find how to develop your own technique with ingredients, times, textures.

Combinations in cakes are important. Too many fruit and nut combinations cause intestinal gas and fermentation — if this happens you have learnt what combinations to avoid. Try again.

Miso cake

2 cups sultanas, blackcurrants or raisins
5 cups water
1 vanilla pod split
1 umeboshi plum
1 teaspoon powdered lotus root (lotus root tea)
1 teaspoon finely grated ginger

Combine the above ingredients and bring to the boil. Simmer for 15 minutes. Allow to cool till lukewarm. Add 1 tablespoon barley or rice miso and 1 tablespoon corn oil. Place in a bowl and add 1 cup sourdough, 6 cups wholewheat flour (preferably freshly ground) and 1 cup uncooked, washed sultanas.

Mix methodically with a wooden spoon until an ideal cake texture is formed. This must not be too wet. Pour into a baking tin.

Cover and leave overnight to rise (on a warm spot for longer if the weather is cold). Bake at 170°C (350°F) for 45–60 minutes. Do not remove from tin until completely cooled. Ensure that the tin is high enough so the dough will not spill out when it rises.

Fresh fruit cake (adapted from *Tassajara Bread Book*)

An excellent cake. Make sure you let it stand for 3–4 hours before eating. It can be very light depending on ingredients chosen and method. It is adaptable to all kinds of fruits and/or nuts.

1 cup oil (corn germ oil is definitely best)
1 cup roasted chopped nuts
or 1 cup roasted coconut strands
1 cup raisins or currants or sultanas
2 cups lightly toasted or raw rolled oats
3 cups fruit purée, pulp and juice (here you can use orange, lemon, pineapple, apple, apricot, nectarine, banana, lychee, etc.)
(carrot or pumpkin juice work too, *or* goat's milk if you like)
1 teaspoon natural vanilla extract
2–2½ cups wholewheat flour (or ½ buckwheat or barley flour)

Lightly rub oil into oats, flour, coconut. Add nuts, dried fruit and liquid. It is a soft, crumbly dough. Press or spread into one large or two small, round pans. Bake at 170°C (350°F) for 30–40 minutes. This can be split and filled or simply spread with cooked and puréed fruit, dried fruits or sweet tofu cream.

Brown rice fruit cake

4 cups cooked brown rice (use extra water as this needs to be soft)
1 cup chopped or cooked dried fruit
1 cup kokkoh or wholewheat or buckwheat flour
1 cup toasted rolled oats
1 cup apple juice

Mix together with a wooden spoon, put in a baking tray and bake at 170°C (350°F) for 40 minutes.

In this recipe you can use roasted chopped nuts, kinako or seeds instead of dried fruit, or alternatively cooked pumpkin or parsnip.

Or use 2 tablespoons rice honey dissolved in 1½ cups apple juice instead of fruit and apple juice *or* fresh fruits pulped

Soft-cooked mung beans or azuki beans are very tasty. Use 1 cup beans and 3 cups rice. You could also use 1 cup of soft, cooked wheat or buckwheat or millet with 3 cups of rice.

Apple or apricot macaroon

1 cup rolled oats toasted
1 cup coarse coconut toasted
2 cups wholewheat flour
½ cup toasted ground hazelnuts
½ cup corn germ oil *or* walnut *or* coconut oil
1 cup apple juice
pinch salt
2 teaspoons natural vanilla essence

Rub oil into oats, coconut, flour, nuts and salt. Add juice and vanilla. Mix well. Spread 2 cm thick onto a flat baking tray. Bake at 160°C (325°F) for 20 minutes.

Spread with cooked apples or your choice of cooked dried fruit.

Topping:

1 cup roasted coconut
½ cup toasted flour
pinch salt
½ cup toasted, finely ground hazelnuts
2 teaspoons oil
2 teaspoons vanilla essence

Rub oil into other ingredients. Sprinkle thickly over fruit. Bake at 170°C (350°F) up high for 15 minutes or until top is golden.

Or: 6 egg whites
2 cups roasted coconut
½ cup apple juice
2 tablespoons wholewheat flour

Beat whites with apple juice. Fold in flour and coconut. Spread on top of fruit. Bake as above.

Tahina shortbread

$^1\!/_2$ cup natural tahina
1 teaspoon sea salt
3 cups wholewheat flour
2 teaspoons natural vanilla essence
1 tablespoon honey
1 cup sourdough
2 cups water or apple juice
2 teaspoons finely grated orange rind

Rub tahina into flour and salt. Mix vanilla, honey, sourdough, water. Add to dry ingredients and mix thoroughly with a wooden spoon until smooth.

Press into an oiled tray until 2 cm thick. Leave in a warm place for 4–5 hours. Bake at 190°C (375°F) for 30 minutes.

Apple walnut slice

2½ cups wholewheat flour
1 cup walnuts
½ tablespoon corn oil
pinch sea salt
6 apples, cored and chopped
½ cup sultanas
1 tablespoon rice honey or maltose
1 umeboshi plum
3 tablespoons kuzu arrowroot

Toast the walnuts in the oven until golden and fragrant. Cool and crush well with a rolling pin. Mix with the flour, oil and sea salt. Rub together until well mixed. Cook the apples with sultanas, plum and maltose and enough water to cover the apples, until soft. Mix approximately ¾ cup of the hot liquid from the apples with the flour mixture until a crumbly dough is formed. Press this into a rectangular pie tray about 2½ cm thick. Bake at 170°C (350°F) for 20 – 30 minutes until cooked. Strain remaining liquid, which should be about 3 cups, from the apples. Place in a saucepan.

Dissolve kuzu in a little cold water and add to the apple liquid. Bring this to the boil while stirring and simmer for 10 minutes until kuzu has cleared and thickened. Add apples and mix well. Pour this mixture over the walnut slice and refrigerate until the kuzu sets firm.

Rice crisp

6 cups cooked brown rice (or 4 cups cooked brown rice and 2 cups glutinous)
1 cup dates cooked in 3 cups water with star anise or cloves or cinnamon, till soft
½ cup blackcurrants
1 cup toasted rolled oats
½ cup kokkoh or lightly roasted wholewheat flour
½ cup toasted ground sunflower seeds
½ cup orange juice
½ cup roasted ground nuts or coconut

Mix all ingredients, including date water, and then knead with hands until quite sticky. If too loose, add more rice or kokkoh or flour. Press into a tray — the crisp should be about 3 cm thick.

Bake at 170°C (350°F) for 40 minutes — allow to cool and set.

This can be made with a variety of cooked whole grains, e.g. buckwheat, glutinous rice and cooked dried apricots. You can add 1 tablespoon carob powder for a carob crisp.

Baked fruit

This makes a really excellent dessert. I have included two varieties; there are as many more as cooks!

Apples

Core apples, leaving whole. Stuff with:
> 1 teaspoon finely grated lemon rind
> ½ teaspoon finely grated ginger
> ½ cup blackcurrants
> 1 cup cooked brown rice
> 1 tablespoon kokkoh

Rub the apples with a little oil, prick each several times with a skewer, sprinkle with sea salt, place in a pan with a little water on the bottom, cover and bake slowly at 150°C (300°F) for 40 minutes to 1 hour.

Apples in a blanket

Wrap the above in a thin pastry blanket and bake at 170°C (350°F) for 30 minutes. Or use apples without stuffing.

Pears

Wash pears and coat with a very thin film of ginger-oil. To make this, finely grate some ginger root and squeeze out 2 teaspoons of juice. Mix with 1 teaspoon dark sesame oil and 1 teaspoon vegetable (corn or sesame) oil.

Mix well, rub on pears and bake as for apples or bake in ¹/₂ cup saké for a treat.

Crumbles

Basic crumble

> 2 cups rolled oats
> ½ cup coconut or other crushed nuts
> ½ cup wholewheat flour
> pinch salt

Mix well. Add ½ cup fruit juice or water. Rub until small pebbles are formed — toss and separate with your fingers. Place on top of sliced soft fruit or cooked fruit and bake at 190°C (375°F) for 15 – 20 minutes. If you prefer a firmer top, add more water. You can layer the bottom of the baking tray for a double crumble. Bake bottom lightly first.

Special crumble

> 2 cups rolled oats
> ½ cup coconut
> ½ cup wholewheat flour
> ½ cup toasted ground almonds or hazelnuts or Brazil nuts
> 1 tablespoon coconut or corn oil

Rub together. Add ¾ cup juice or water. Layer on the bottom if you wish, bake lightly first.

Favourite Crumble Fillings:
> cooked apples, pears or blackcurrants
> sweet pumpkin or sweet parsnip cooked with apple juice and a vanilla pod
> mulberries or blackberries are a seasonal delight

Cold crumble

Follow directions for crumble but add 1 cup boiling water. Mix well and press into bottom of pan. Fill with jelly-fruit mixture, page 153. Cool to set and serve.

Another crumble

Topping:
> 2 cups cooked azuki beans slightly mashed
> 1 tablespoon tahina
> 1 cup roasted rolled oats
> ½ cup toasted coconut
> ½ teaspoon sea salt

Mix well.

Filling:
> sweet pumpkin cooked with vanilla or aniseed or apple juice
> *or* parsnip, squash, carrot cooked in the same manner

Pastries and pies

'Cream' puffs

> ⅓ cup good quality oil
> ½ cup water
> pinch sea salt
> ½ cup wholewheat flour (using ½ arrowroot or buckwheat flour with the wholewheat produces good results)
> 2 free-range eggs

Bring water to boil then add the oil and salt. Stir vigorously until well blended and add all the flour. Continue to stir briskly and remove from the heat. Break one of the eggs into the mixture and stir until it is well assimilated. Add the other egg, stirring until quite a thick batter is formed. Drop spoonfuls of this mixture on a lightly oiled tray. The size of the 'puff' depends on the size of the spoon — they can be tiny or quite large. Bake at 220°C (425°F) for 15 minutes, turn the oven down to 170°C (350°F) and bake another 15–30 minutes. Split the top to allow steam to escape. When cool, slice and fill with your choice of 'cream'.

Fillings:

Finely mashed tofu blended with sesame purée and corn or rice syrup replaces the common sugar and cow's cream filling more than adequately.

Any firm fruit purée or vegetables (pumpkin, miso or shitake mushroom is quite delicious). Well cooked and puréed rolled oats are also an excellent 'cream' filling.

Eclairs

Simply follow the previous recipe, but lay the batter in a strip instead of a blob. This can easily be accomplished with a cake decorator. To complete the fantasy, top these with carob icing when baked. Mix carob, grain syrup and a little hot water. Spread on eclair after filling.

Fruit and sweet pies

Use any of the pastries from pages 130–1.

Fillings:

Apple — allow 2–3 apples per person.

Core and chop or dice. Add water to ¾ the level of the apples. Add 1 umeboshi plum. Bring to a boil over medium heat. Remove from heat and let stand for 15 minutes. Drain off the liquid. Place in a pie shell, top on, slit the top to allow steam to escape. Flute the edges of the pie with a spoon handle or fingers and cut out a small decorative shape and place on the pie before baking, or glaze with a beaten egg. Bake at 170°C (350°F) for 15–20 minutes. Or cook the apples with 3 or 4 whole cloves and ½ cup sultanas for a classic. Add 2 star anise for an exotic variation.

Pear and ginger (1 teaspoon finely grated ginger).

Apple and strawberry — add the strawberries (washed in salted water to remove sprays) when allowing apples to stand — don't cook them.

Apple and blackberry, fresh lychee, mulberry (add at end of cooking), blackcurrant or date (cook with apples).

Buckwheat and banana.

Pumpkin cooked with 1 star anise and a split vanilla pod.

Parsnip cooked with apple juice and a vanilla pod.

Rice and dried fruit.

Sweet potato cooked with vanilla.

It is a good idea to cook fruit with an umeboshi plum. Use strained off liquid and thicken to make a sauce for the pie. Thicken with kuzu, arrowroot, kokkoh or flour.

Your imagination and sense of balance are the only limits!

Mince pies

    1 cup dates
    1 cup natural sultanas
    2 cloves
    1 star anise
    1 teaspoon grated ginger
    1 teaspoon grated orange or lemon peel
    3 cups water
    1 umeboshi plum

Bring to the boil over high heat and simmer for 30 minutes. Strain, remove cloves and aniseed and mash fruit. Make small pie bases using basic pastry. A cookie tray with 8 or 10 depressions is ideal. Bake at 160°C (325°F) for 10 minutes, being careful not to let them become too crisp. Spoon filling into pies, cool and serve.

Pillows to dream on

Filling:

    2 umeboshi plums
    2 cups chopped dates
    ½ teaspoon finely grated ginger
    2 star anise
    2 chopped apples
    1 teaspoon orange rind

Cook until all fruit is soft. Strain and mix well. Remove anise. Use strained liquid for cake. Using thin pastry, roll out and cut into squares 10 x 10 cm. Place the mixture in the centre, wet the edges and join, pinching together.

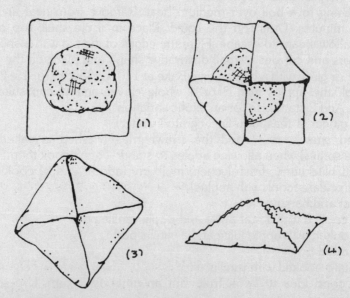

(1)   (2)   (3)   (4)

Glaze with egg and water — brush it on. Sprinkle with poppy seeds. Bake at 170°C (350°F) for 15 minutes or until golden and ready. Alternatively, spread this filling between layers of thin pastry to make a very succulent date slice.

Apple strudel — using yeasted pastry

Roll out pastry into a thin rectangle 20 cm x 15 cm. Spread this with a mixture of cooked apple, salt plum and sultanas, which has been very well strained. Roll this up, moistening the edges so as to seal. Make 2 or 3 slits across the top of the roll, sprinkle with ground cinnamon and bake for 30 minutes at 160°C (325°F).

Biscuits

Oat haggis

> 3 cups toasted rolled oats
> 1 cup wholewheat flour
> pinch sea salt
> ½ cup oil
> 2 cups date purée

Rub oil into oats, salt and flour. Add date purée. Mix well. Spoon onto oiled cookie sheet. Bake at 190°C (375°F) for 35 minutes.

Nut rocks

> 1 cup roasted ground peanuts
> 2 cups wholewheat flour
> 1 teaspoon sea salt
> 2 tablespoons oil
> 1 cup toasted Brazil nuts, ground
> 1 tablespoon honey
> 1½ cups water

Rub oil into flour and salt. Add nuts. Mix well. Combine water and honey and add to dry ingredients. Bake at 170°C (350°F) for 30 minutes.

High voltage biscuits

> 2 cups currants cooked in apple juice with 2 cups of their cooking liquid
> 1 cup toasted rolled oats
> 2 cups wholewheat flour
> ½ teaspoon sea salt
> 1 tablespoon oil

Rub oil into flour, salt and oats. Add blackcurrants and liquid. Mix well. Spoon onto oiled tray. Bake at 190°C (375°F) for 30 minutes.

Banana spraints

> 2 cups mashed bananas or cooked parsnip (cook parsnip in apple juice
>   with a vanilla pod and ½ teaspoon of finely grated orange rind)
> ½ teaspoon ground nutmeg
> ½ cup wholewheat flour
> ½ cup ground freshly roasted peanuts
> ½ teaspoon sea salt
> 1 cup kokkoh cereal
> 1 cup apple juice

Mix kokkoh, flour, nuts and nutmeg. Combine banana and apple juice. Add to dry ingredients. Mix well. Spoon onto oiled tray. Bake at 190°C (375°F) for 30 minutes. If you add 1 extra cup of flour, these can be deep fried.

Seed biscuits

> ½ cup sesame seeds, toasted and ground
> ½ cup sunflower seeds, toasted and ground
> 1 tablespoon toasted poppy seeds
> ½ cup ground roasted almonds
> 2 cups wholewheat flour
> 1 teaspoon sea salt
> 2 tablespoons rice syrup or 1 tablespoon honey or 2 tablespoons
>   maltose dissolved in warm water
> 2 cups apple juice
> 3 teaspoons natural vanilla essence
> 1 teaspoon finely grated lemon rind

Rub nuts, seeds and flour together. Add sweetener to water, mix in lemon rind and add to dry ingredients. Bake at 190°C (375°F) for 35 minutes.

Ginger snaps

> 1 cup rye flour
> 2 cups wholewheat flour
> 1 teaspoon sea salt
> 3 tablespoons finely grated ginger cooked with 2 cups apple juice
> 3 tablespoons of maltose or rice syrup
> ½ cup toasted ground Brazil nuts
> 1 teaspoon kinako
> 3 teaspoons oil
> 1 teaspoon dark sesame oil

Dissolve syrup in hot ginger and apple. Rub oil into flour. Add nuts and kinako. Mix. Combine dry and wet ingredients. Roll into balls with wet hands. Flatten, bake at 190°C (375°F) for 15 – 20 minutes.

Coconut Islands

    3 cups toasted coarse coconut (freshly grated is best)
    2 eggs, beaten
    ¾ cup sultanas
    2 cups wholewheat flour
    ½ teaspoon sea salt
    1 tablespoon coconut oil
    2 cups apple juice or 2 tablespoons palm sugar (gula malacca)
    3 teaspoons natural vanilla essence

Rub oil into flour and salt, then rub in coconut. Add sultanas, mix well. Beat eggs with vanilla and water. Combine dry and wet ingredients. Spoon onto oiled cookie sheet. Bake at 170°C (350°F) for 30 minutes.

Grain brains

    3 cups cooked rice, wholewheat, buckwheat, millet or whole oats
    1 cup kokkoh
    1 cup wholewheat flour
    2 teaspoons natural vanilla essence
    1 cup mixed fruit — currants, muscatels, raisins, sultanas
    2 cups carrot juice

Mix all ingredients well. Place on oiled sheet. Bake at 170°C (350°F) for 20 minutes.

Laver biscuits

    2 cups toasted rolled oats
    1 cup wholewheat flour
    pinch sea salt
    3 sheets nori (laver) seaweed, toasted and broken finely
    ½ cup toasted ground peanuts
    2 tablespoons shoyu
    ½ cup water

Mix dry ingredients. Combine shoyu and water. Add to dry ingredients — bake at 190°C (375°F) for 20 minutes.

Pumpkin biscuits

    2 cups mashed cooled sweet pumpkin
    1½ cups buckwheat flour
    ½ cup ground freshly roasted peanuts
    ½ cup cooked hijiki seaweed
    1½ cups water (or pumpkin cooking liquid)
    1 tablespoon oil
    1 tablespoon shoyu

Rub oil into flour. Add nuts, seaweed. Mix in pumpkin, shoyu and water if necessary. Bake at 170°C (350°F) for 30 minutes.

Sweet pumpkin or parsnip cookies

>2 cups mashed cooked sweet pumpkin
>   *or* parsnip (cooked as for banana spraints)
>1 cup hazelnuts, well toasted and ground
>1 cup buckwheat flour
>1 cup wholewheat flour
>1 teaspoon sea salt
>1 tablespoon oil
>1 cup toasted rolled oats
>1½ cups milk from 3-day wheat sprouts (blend with water and strain)
>½ cup sultanas

Mix pumpkin and wheat-sprout milk. Add oil to flours and salt and rub in. Combine with nuts, oats, sultanas. Mix well. Spoon onto oiled tray. Bake at 170°C (350°F) for 30 minutes.

Sesame crackers

>2 cups wholewheat flour
>2 tablespoons oil
>¾ cup lightly toasted sesame seeds
>1 teaspoon sea salt
>¾ cup water
>1 teaspoon shoyu

Mix flour and salt. Rub in oil. Add seeds. Combine water and shoyu. Mix all ingredients, knead, roll out thin, then cut into small pieces. Deep-fry. Drain well. Excellent with soup.

Nut slice

Toast well and finely grind:
>½ cup hazelnuts
>½ cup sunflower seeds
>½ cup almonds
>½ cup Brazil nuts

Mix with 2 tablespoons heated maltose or rice syrup, or 1 tablespoon honey (Leatherwood is best) and 2 tablespoons water. Mix well. Roll out dough from 'thin pastry' recipe on page 131, 30 x 30 cm — you will need four of these. Place pastry on an oiled tray. On a layer of pastry, thinly spread nuts and continue layering until all nuts and pastry are used. Make sure the innermost layers of pastry are very thin. Brush the top with oil. Slice the squares with a sharp knife, cleaning it after each cut. Don't separate the squares. Sprinkle with cinnamon. Bake at 170°C (350°F) for 30–40 minutes — longer if necessary.

Variations:

Use walnuts, pine nuts and pistachio nuts for a specialty.

Cook red beans or mung beans. Strain, mash and mix with sweetener. Use instead of nuts. This mixture must be very dry.

Mix carob powder with the nuts.

15

Desserts

I avoid the use of honey in sweets because it is a strong food and best left as a medicine. If honey is consumed regularly it cannot work as a medicine, in which capacity it is valuable. A small proportion in food occasionally is a delight. The consumption of sweet foods should be kept at a pleasant minimum in order to maintain a centred mentality and viable digestion. You will be surprised how sweet cooked (especially baked) vegetables, cooked and fresh fruit, grain honeys, sprouted grains and small proportions of dried fruit can be when you cease eating masses of sugared foods, honey and large quantities of fruit. It has been the experience of many that too much sweet food has been the cause of their disorientation and only after eliminating a sweet tooth is it obvious just how disorientated one can be from such foods.

Young children who eat much sweet food and fruit are mucusy and sleep a lot. William Dufty's book *Sugar Blues* is essential reading for anybody who is interested in what he/she eats.

Just a further note on honey. Many beekeepers feed their bees on pure refined sugar when food is in short supply. This produces a mutation of honey which should be avoided. Bees are victims of our agricultural industry in that their basic resource — flower pollen — is very often highly contaminated with herbicides, insecticides, hormone sprays and artificial fertilizers. In this way, they bring these chemicals, some of which are capable of altering genetic structure, into our food. Buy with thought.

Agar jelly

Agar is a blend of seaweeds or sea vegetables which grows on the tidal zone in many places of the world, including Australia. From agar you can make delicious jelly by flavouring with fruit or vegetables or beans. Australia's colonial ladies were renowned for the jellies they made from this seaweed, which abounds on our coast. It was used extensively in World War II when animal gelatine was in short supply. Scientists use agar to grow bacterial cultures — it is a pity they do not relate its obvious nutritive qualities to human diet.

Agar has a cooling effect, it contains valuable minerals, including much calcium, and has no calories. Within several weeks of eating agar three times weekly, you will notice tremendous fingernail growth. It makes a highly desirable form of dessert, especially in our hot climate. Because its preparation involves quite a bit of water or liquid, we can drink less and feel more comfortable if we consume it in the summer. I will outline a basic method of preparing it, with some examples, and you should develop your own jellies from there. Use more agar for a firmer texture.

Agar, called 'kanten' in Asia, is transparent and comes in bars from wholefood stores, or in bundles of clear fibres from Chinese or Asian stores. The powdered form is more readily available, but not as good quality. Agar sets at room temperature after 2–3 hours in winter, but usually needs refrigeration in summer. It will rarely melt if left unrefrigerated however.

All agar recipes quoted here will benefit immensely if used in conjunction with kuzu arrowroot. Simply dissolve 1 tablespoon of kuzu in a little water, juice or other cold liquid, and add it at the end of cooking. Stir over heat until it clears (usually about 5 minutes), or decrease the amount of agar used and increase the proportion of kuzu.

This is particularly effective for making glazed tarts. Kuzu improves the texture of the agar and aids the digestion of sweet foods.

Apple and strawberry jelly

>1 punnet strawberries
>3 apples, diced
>2 bars or ½ cup strands agar, chopped
>1 umeboshi plum

Wash strawberries well and soak in salted water for 10 minutes. (I poisoned myself picking and eating commercial strawberries, which are heavily sprayed.)

Cook apples and agar with 5 cups apple juice and the plum. Slowly bring to the boil and simmer over medium heat until the agar is dissolved. Then add strawberries and stir for 3 –4 minutes. Pour into a rinsed glass dish and allow to set in a cool place for 30 –40 minutes. Refrigerate for 15 minutes to set more quickly. Agar will remain as a jelly at room temperature and does not need to be kept refrigerated unless the weather is hot.

This jelly could be made of apple, pear, watermelon, strawberry, rock-melon, honeydew melon, apricots or nectarines, etc.

Purée honeydew, rockmelon or watermelon for a smooth, sweet texture, and add this purée with chunks of the diced melon at the end of cooking.

Apple and ginger jelly

>8 apples, chopped fine
>3 teaspoons finely grated ginger
>3 cups water or apple or grape juice
>2 bars or ½ cup strands agar, chopped

Bring all ingredients to boil slowly and simmer over medium heat until agar is dissolved. Pour into rinsed glass dish and allow to set. You may prefer to purée the apples after cooking for a smooth jelly.

Dried fruit jelly

This can be made with Chinese dates, Iraq dates, sultanas, blackcurrants (my favourite), raisins, bananas, figs, etc.

>1 cup chopped (or whole if small) dried fruit
>1 split vanilla bean
>1 star anise or 2–3 whole cloves (if required)
>2 bars or ½ cup strands agar, chopped
>1 teaspoon finely grated orange or lemon rind

Cook all the ingredients together with 5 cups water until agar is dissolved. Remove bean and spices. Pour into rinsed dish and set. Purée for smoothness.

Tofu jelly

>2 blocks tofu (about 1 cup of purée)
>1 cup raisin or dried fruit syrup
>*or* 2 tablespoons maltose or rice honey
>*or* 2 cups cooked fruit
>2 bars or ½ cup strands agar, chopped
>1 split vanilla bean
>1 teaspoon natural tahina

Boil tofu in water. Cook the rest of the ingredients together with 2½ cups water or apple or carrot juice until agar is dissolved. When cooked, add tahina and tofu, remove vanilla bean, and purée.

Pour into rinsed dish and allow to set.

Almond tofu

1½ cups blanched almonds, blended with 4 cups water until very milky
1 split vanilla pod
2 bars or ½ cup strands agar, chopped
2 – 3 tablespoons maltose or rice honey or 1 tablespoon bee honey

Bring puréed almonds and vanilla to the boil and cook over medium heat for 30 minutes. This will produce almond milk. Strain off the almond grounds and use for biscuits or cakes.

Put vanilla back into strained milk and return to heat. Add agar and sweetener and 1 cup water (or apple juice if not using honey) and cook until agar is dissolved. Remove vanilla, pour into a rinsed dish and allow to set.

Top with roasted chopped almonds. This could be made in a similar manner using roasted cashew nuts or ground, lightly roasted sesame seeds or sunflower kernels. To use coconut, cook 2–3 cups coarsely shredded fresh or dried coconut for 1–2 hours to extract the essence. With coconut the result is delicious. We call this Bali jelly. Top with roasted coconut.

Summer fruit jelly

1 cup chopped apricots
½ cup chopped nectarines
1 cup whole grapes (sultana grapes are best)
1 umeboshi plum
4 cups water or fruit juice
2 bars or ½ cup strands agar, chopped

Cook agar and plum in water until dissolved. Add fresh fruit and stir for 2–3 minutes. Pour into rinsed dish and set.

Yokan (red bean jelly)

1 cup cooked mashed azuki beans (there should be some whole beans remaining)
½ cup well-roasted fine ground nuts (hazel, walnut, almond, macadamia, peanuts)
2½ cups water or strained yannoh coffee or apple juice
2 bars or ½ cup strands agar, chopped
2 tablespoons maltose, honey, rice syrup or maple syrup
or 1 cup strong raisin or sultana or date syrup
(if using syrup use 1 cup less water)
1 split vanilla bean

Cook agar and vanilla with syrup and/or water until dissolved. Add beans and nuts, cook for 1–2 minutes. Place in rinsed tray. Cool, slice into bars and serve. When set this should be quite firm. This benefits from the use of kuzu arrowroot as well as agar — a delightful texture.

Liquorice jelly

> 2 cups strong liquorice tea
> ½ cup Chinese dates, chopped
> 3 star anise, broken up
> 2 cups apple juice
> 2 bars or ½ cup strands agar, chopped

Bring to the boil and simmer until agar is dissolved. Dissolve kuzu in ½ cup orange juice, stir into hot liquid until thickened. Place in dish to set.

Orange-sesame jelly

> 2 cups fresh orange juice
> 1 diced or slivered orange
> 2 bars or ½ cup strands agar, chopped
> 2 cups water
> 1 tablespoon natural tahina
> 2 tablespoons maltose or 1 cup raisin syrup

Cook agar in water until dissolved. Remove from heat. Purée tahina with orange juice and add to agar and water while hot. Add orange. Pour into rinsed dish. Cool to set. A decorative effect can be achieved by letting the jelly cool, and when it is slightly firm, place orange rounds on top with whole mint leaves. Press so these adhere to the jelly.

Troppo jelly

> 2 mashed bananas
> ½ cup finely ground roasted peanuts
> 1 cup shredded fresh or dried coconut
> ½ cup finely chopped sweet, ripe pineapple
> 1 bar or ½ cup strands agar, chopped
> 2 vanilla pods
> 2 umeboshi plums

Cook coconut in 4 cups water for 1 hour. Strain, and reserve the milk, which should make 2 cups.

Cook bananas, pineapple, coconut milk, plum, peanuts, agar and vanilla with 4 cups water. Slowly bring to boil, then simmer for 45 minutes. Pour into rinsed tray and allow to cool. This is wild made with custard apple or avocado.

For a specialty make this with banana as the only fruit, using 2 more bananas, and serve with ginger sauce — we call it Banana Float.
Sauce:

> 2 teaspoons finely-grated ginger
> 1½ cups water
> 2 tablespoons kuzu
> 3 tablespoons rice syrup or maltose

Cook ginger in water for 10 minutes. Add rice honey. Dissolve kuzu in a little apple juice. Add and stir over medium heat until clear.

Hazelnut mousse

1 cup roasted, finely ground hazelnuts
2 bars or ½ cup strands agar, chopped
1 vanilla bean, split
1 minced umeboshi plum
2 cups apple juice or puréed cooked apple
or   2 tablespoons maltose, rice syrup or maple syrup

Cook hazelnuts, plums, vanilla, agar, sweetener until agar is dissolved. Pour into small rinsed moulds for individual serves, or 1 large bowl. Add 1 table-spoon natural tahina for a very creamy mousse or ½ cup kokkoh. If using tahina add it at the end of cooking and mix well. Cook the kokkoh with the other ingredients.

Currant mousse

1 cup blackcurrants
3 cups grape juice
1 vanilla bean, split
1 tablespoon maltose, rice or maple syrup
2 bars agar
1 teaspoon finely grated ginger

Place blackcurrants, ginger, juice, vanilla, syrup and agar in a saucepan and bring to the boil. Simmer for 30 minutes until well cooked. Remove vanilla. Pour into a rinsed tray or mould and allow to cool and set.

Oat mousse

2 cups toasted rolled oats, well cooked with 4 cups water
½ cup roasted chopped almonds
1 cup dates
1 bar agar
1 umeboshi plum
1 split vanilla bean

Cook dates with agar, plum and vanilla and 2 cups water, until agar dissolves and dates are soft. Purée with oats. Add almonds. Pour into a rinsed mould, allow to cool and set. This is delicious made with thick buckwheat cream instead of oats, and dried apricots.

Kokkoh parfait

    1 cup cooked roasted rolled or whole oats, stirred to make creamy
    ½ cup kokkoh cereal dissolved in 2 cups water or apple juice
    1 cup currants cooked in apple juice
    1 cup cooked apple
    2 bars or ½ cup strands agar, chopped
    2 split vanilla pods
    1 tablespoon maltose or rice honey
    1 cup roasted chopped almonds

Cook agar in 4 cups water with vanilla pods and maltose or rice honey. When dissolved, add kokkoh cereal and cook for 5–10 minutes until kokkoh is done. Remove vanilla. Allow jelly to cool and almost set in saucepan. Remove and stir or whip when almost set with one tablespoon tahina.

    Now layer kokkoh, blackcurrants, oats, apple, etc. in tall glasses. Top with nuts and chill.

Flans

Almost all of the jellies described here are excellent poured into a baked flan shell or specially prepared base. Allow the jelly to set and you have a jelly tart of whatever thickness you desire. Here is a good flan base:

        ½ cup toasted rolled oats
        2 cups wholewheat flour
        ½ cup roasted ground hazelnuts
        ½ cup roasted coconut strands
        2 tablespoons corn or vegetable oil
        ½ teaspoon sea salt
        1 cup water

Rub oil into flour, oats, salt, coconut and nuts. Add water and mix well. Should be sticky and thick. Press into a baking dish and bake at 150°C (300°F) for 10 minutes — careful not to burn it, and don't leave holes or the jelly will run out. When cool, pour in jelly and set.

   Or use as a cake base:

        ½ cup sourdough
        2 cups fine wholewheat flour
        ½ cup arrowroot powder
      ¾–1 cup cold apple or carrot (or other fruit) juice
        1 tablespoon corn germ oil or vegetable oil
        pinch salt

Add salt to flour. Rub oil into flour and arrowroot, tossing and lifting to make light. Slowly add apple juice and sourdough, the texture should be a little loose or wet. Steam for 15 minutes and then bake at 170°C (350°F) for 30 minutes. Leave in pan and pour in jelly. Sometimes the jelly completely surrounds the cake. You can cut the cake up and mix with jelly when still liquid — which leads us to:

Just a trifle (Gerry's special)

        chunks of sourdough cake (old or stale cake is best, or use any cake
           or broken biscuits you have made)
        2 tablespoons carob powder
        2 bars or ½ cup strands agar, chopped
        1 split vanilla bean
        1 cup toasted, cooked rolled oats
        2 tablespoons rice honey or maltose *or* 1 cup
           raisin, date or sultana purée or syrup
           or 1 tablespoon honey
        1 cup toasted crushed but not ground walnuts
        1 teaspoon finely grated orange rind
      2½ cups water

Cook agar, water, vanilla, carob, rice honey, orange rind in a saucepan until agar dissolves. Stir to prevent carob from lumping. Cool to room temperature and purée with oats. Pour over walnuts and cake or cookies in a glass tray. Cool and allow to set for 3–4 hours. Refrigerate, covered, for faster setting or in summer.

Custard tart

Use flan base described.
Filling:

>   2 eggs, well beaten
>   3 teaspoons pure vanilla extract
> 2½ cups apple juice
>   1 tablespoon kuzu or arrowroot
>   1 teaspoon finely grated lemon rind

Dissolve kuzu or arrowroot in apple juice. Add lemon rind. Place in a saucepan and stir over medium heat until mixture starts to thicken. Add eggs and vanilla and stir until thick. Pour into flan base and cool. Top with ground cinnamon. Or use 1 cup yellow marrow purée and 1 tablespoon buckwheat flour instead of egg.

Tofu 'cheesecake'

> 1½ bars agar, chopped
>   2 cups tofu purée
>   1 vanilla pod, split
>   1 teaspoon orange rind, finely grated
>   2 tablespoons rice syrup, maltose or maple syrup
>   2 cups apple juice
>   chopped, roasted almonds

Soak agar in apple juice for 10 minutes. Add vanilla, orange, syrup and bring to a boil. Cook until agar is dissolved. Add tofu and mix well. Pour into a special base (*see* Pastry, page 130) or a pastry base and allow to cool. When almost set, sprinkle with chopped roasted almonds.

Dried fruit tart or flan

>   1 cup currants or sultanas or raisins
>   3 cups apple or grape juice
>   1 teaspoon finely grated lemon or orange rind
> $^1/_3$ cup arrowroot or kuzu dissolved in $^1/_2$ cup apple or grape juice

Cook dried fruit over medium heat in juice until just soft. Add arrowroot dissolved in juice and stir until thickened and clear. Add a few small grains of sea salt. Stir. Spread on pastry base and allow to cool.

Tarte aux pommes

Core and then slice one or two apples into rings. Drop into boiling water and let stand (off heat). Meanwhile, to 1 cup water or apple juice, add 1 teaspoon lemon rind, 1 tablespoon rice syrup or maltose, 1 vanilla pod, split, and 1 umeboshi plum. Bring to the boil and add 4 tablespoons kuzu dissolved in 1 cup apple juice. Ensure the texture is quite thick but just able to be poured. Arrange apples in the bottom of the flan, pour on mixture and cool. This sometimes requires refrigeration to set properly. The same effect can be achieved with any other fruit, especially strawberries.

Strawberry glacé flan

4 cups water
2 grated apples
2 tablespoons maltose or rice syrup
1 vanilla pod, split
1 bar agar (kanten) shredded
2½ tablespoons kuzu arrowroot
½ cup apple juice
1 punnet of strawberries, washed and halved

Bring water, apples, maltose, vanilla, agar to the boil and simmer until agar dissolves. Mix kuzu with ½ cup of apple juice and add to the simmering liquid. Stir until this begins to thicken. Add ½ the strawberries. Stir gently for 5 minutes. Layer the rest of the strawberries on a pre-baked flan base and pour the kuzu mix over them. Refrigerate until the glacé sets.

Using a pastry base, a large variety of quick, easy flans can be prepared. There is usually some pastry left over when making a pie for example — instead of storing it or throwing it out, simply roll out a flan base and bake at low temperature to ensure it does not become rock hard. While this is baking, make the flan filling.

Other flan fillings

Cooked, creamed rolled oats, or buckwheat, layered with toasted and crushed almonds.
Any thick and syrupy dried fruit mixture.
Sweet vegetables, tofu, sea vegetables, kneaded with grains.
Nut or sesame tofu make wonderful fillings.

Other desserts

Grain halva

Basic:

2 cups toasted and finely ground brown rice, barley or wheat
1 cup sultanas, raisins or chopped dates
2 cups apple juice or dried fruit purée
4 cups water
1 cup toasted chopped nuts
1 bar agar, chopped

Add water to cereal and agar with ½ teaspoon sea salt, and stir over medium heat until it starts to thicken. Add apple juice or purée, nuts and dried fruit. Cook just below boiling, stirring constantly, until this thickens — usually takes 10 minutes. Then turn heat down to low and simmer for 30 minutes, stirring occasionally to prevent sticking or burning. Stir well, and pour or spoon into a rinsed tray. Allow 2 hours to set. This can then be removed and sliced.

Clearly, there are endless variations of dried and fresh fruits which could be added to this. Personally I consider barley cream, barley-brown rice or millet-rice cream makes the best halva.

This can also be made savoury by using vegetables such as carrot or parsnip purée with miso or shoyu. Cooked with shitake mushrooms, this is similar to turnip slice, which demonstrates the adaptability of recipes.

Semolina or polenta can be used for this recipe, but should first be toasted slowly in a heavy skillet with 1 tablespoon oil. These produce delicious results, especially the polenta.

Sweet black rice

This is commonly sold in Indonesia and Thailand, where sugar is used as the sweetener. Originally, and sometimes still, it is made with palm sugar (gula malacca).

> 2 cups black rice, soaked overnight – discard soaking water
> 6 cups fresh coconut milk
> 6 small ripe bananas
> 3 whole star anise
> ½ cup Chinese dates, chopped or ½ cup palm sugar (this is best)*
>   or ½ cup maple syrup or honey
> 1 vanilla bean, split and cut into 4 pieces
> pinch sea salt

Mix all ingredients in a saucepan, bring to the boil. Simmer, covered, for 45 minutes.

Banana oat custard

> ½ cup chopped toasted walnuts
> 3 cups toasted rolled oats
> 2 split vanilla pods or add 3 teaspoons pure vanilla extract at end of cooking
> 5 cups water
> ½ tablespoon natural tahina
> 6 bananas, mashed not puréed
> 1 cup cooked raisins and 1 cup of the juice from cooking them

Cook all ingredients except walnuts over medium heat until oats are well cooked – this will take 30 minutes or longer if you use ground whole oats. Cooking rolled oats should take 10–15 minutes. If the porridge becomes too sticky, add more water. Stir in nuts and ½ tablespoon tahina.

Ladle into a rinsed dish and let set, or serve hot. Sprinkle with nutmeg or cinnamon.

*Palm sugar can be bought in some Asian food stores where it is called gula malacca. It is brown and in cylindrical form. Made from a variety of palm.

Soft rice custard

>   6 cups cooked rice
>   1½ cups dates or dried fruit
>   1½ cups diced apple
>   2 star anise
>   1 cup water
>   2 teaspoons finely grated lemon rind

Cook soft rice, following directions on page 26.

Cook other ingredients over medium heat for 15 minutes. Remove anise, stir thoroughly and add soft rice. Serve, or cool first.

To this you can add agar while cooking the other ingredients to produce a jelly on cooling. It is excellent made with pear, ginger and Chinese dates.

Pumpkin custard

>   ½ cup chopped agar
>   2 cups apple juice
>   4 cups sweet pumpkin purée
>   1 egg beaten (optional)
>   2 tablespoons kuzu or arrowroot
>   2 teaspoons finely grated lemon rind
>   ½ cup finely ground roasted hazelnuts or cashews

Soak agar for 10 minutes in apple juice. Then bring to boil. Remove from heat. Dissolve kuzu or arrowroot in 3 tablespoons water with lemon. Stir in juice and agar on medium heat for 1–2 minutes, until kuzu begins to thicken. Add purée and stir constantly until thick. Add beaten egg, nuts and vanilla, whip quickly over heat for 5 minutes. Remove from stove and pour into a rinsed dish. Serve hot or cold. This will set as it cools.

Goat's milk custard

>   4 cups unrefined goat's milk
>   2 split vanilla pods
>   3 tablespoons kuzu
>   1 tablespoon buckwheat flour or kokkoh
>   1 teaspoon orange or lemon rind
>   1 tablespoon roasted coconut
>   1 cup cooked raisin purée *or* 1 tablespoon bee honey
>   *or* 2 tablespoons maltose or rice honey

Place goat's milk, vanilla, rind and purée or honey in a saucepan and bring to boil very slowly.

Dissolve kuzu or arrowroot and flour in ½ cup apple juice or water. Remove milk from heat and stir in arrowroot/flour, being careful not to make lumps — stir quickly. Simmer while stirring, until thick. Remove pods, pour into rinsed dish, top with coconut. Serve hot.

Sago

The best quality sago has larger beads than that commonly available. Chinese food stores usually have a good variety.

Add sago to boiling water until clear balls are formed. This is then poured into a fine sieve and washed with cold water. It is then ready for use.

> 1 cup sago
> 5 cups water (or 3 water, 2 apple purée or juice)
> 2 tablespoons maltose or rice syrup
> 1 teaspoon finely grated lemon rind
> 1 vanilla bean, split
> 1 cup raisins or other dried fruit
> pinch sea salt
> ½ bar agar, chopped

Bring all ingredients to the boil. Cook over medium heat for 5 minutes, stirring. Place in a rinsed dish and leave 3–4 hours to set.

or

> 1 cup sago (precooked and washed)
> 5 cups coconut milk
> 1 vanilla bean, split
> 3 bananas, mashed
> pinch sea salt
> 3 or 4 cinnamon quills
> 2 bars agar

Boil sago with coconut milk, cinnamon, vanilla and salt. Add bananas, cook for 10 minutes. Remove quills. Place in a rinsed dish. Leave 3–4 hours to set. Sago can also be put on pre-baked pastry or crumble bases. It will set and make a novel flan or cold crumble.

Yannoh blancmange

> 3 cups water
> 1 tablespoon yannoh
> 1 vanilla pod, split
> 2 beaten eggs
> 1½ tablespoons maltose or rice syrup
> *or* 2 tablespoons natural muscatels (or other dried fruit)
> 1 tablespoon kuzu

Bring yannoh, water, vanilla pod and grain syrup (or dried fruit) to the boil over medium heat and simmer covered for 20 minutes. Dissolve kuzu in ¼ cup cold water. Stir into the simmering liquid and continue to stir for 5 minutes. Add eggs and stir rapidly for a further 5 minutes. Chop one banana and lay in a glass dish. Pour mixture over banana and set aside to cool. This can be refrigerated for faster cooling. If not using a refrigerator, leave overnight.

Extension:
Cook 2 cups toasted rolled oats with 3 cups water and a pinch of sea salt. Bring to the boil slowly, stirring often. This should be quite thick. Pour into a tray. Cool for 10 minutes. Pour the blancmange mixture on this. Cool very well before serving.

Sesame and/or nut 'tofu'

> 6 tablespoons lightly toasted sesame seeds
> 2½ cups water
> 5½ tablespoons kuzu *or* 7 tablespoons arrowroot
> ½ teaspoon sea salt
> 1 tablespoon honey *or* 1 cup Iraq date purée *or*
> 3 tablespoons grain syrup

Carefully toast sesame seeds over low heat until light gold. Don't burn any as they will spoil the tofu. Purée or blend seeds and water several times until well ground — you can grind the seeds by hand with a little water.

Strain to remove seed hulls and press hulls for any extra milk. Add kuzu or arrowroot, salt and sweetener to the milk and blend or mix very thoroughly.

Place in a saucepan over medium heat and stir until kuzu thickens. Reduce heat, keep stirring for 10–15 minutes. Pour into a rinsed dish or moulds. Best kept 2–3 cm thick. Cool, chill in refrigerator until firm.

Use ¾ cup roasted peanuts, finely ground, for peanut tofu. By adding 1 tablespoon shoyu and leaving out sweetener while heating, this is a delicious savoury dish.

By using 10½ tablespoons kinako (roasted soya flour) and 3 tablespoons oil you can create a really unusual sweet or savoury tofu.

It follows that any kind of nut or seed can be treated in this very simple manner — a book could be written on the variations alone.

Summer Ambrosia

> ¼ diced rockmelon
> 6 sliced fresh apricots
> 6 sliced fresh nectarines
> 6 sliced fresh peaches
> ½ tablespoon natural tahina
> 1 tablespoon rice syrup
> ½ tablespoon hot water
> 1 umeboshi plum

Mix plum, water, rice syrup and tahina. Pour over fruit and stir for 2 minutes so as to mix fruit juices with the syrup.

Cool and serve. Fresh figs are very good — omit the rice syrup and water, using only tahina and plum.

Ice glaze

Slices of firm peach or favourite fruit — apple works best. Put on skewer and dip into hot maltose. Immediately dunk in ice water. The maltose will solidify, making a very unusual dessert.

Maltose stickjaws — for fulfilling cravings

Use 4 cups maltose. This can't be measured out because of its stickiness, but use 2 of the earthernware containers you buy in Chinese stores.

Gently heat the maltose until it is quite runny. Add 1 cup ground roasted peanuts and 1 cup blackcurrants or sultanas. Stir for 3–4 minutes and ladle into paper patty pans.

Cool for 2 hours.

Banana flambe — a rich French-style dessert for a very special meal

    1 punnet strawberries
    juice of 2 oranges and 1 lemon
    6 ripe bananas sliced in 5 cm sections
    ½ tablespoon honey or 1 tablespoon maltose (the best!)
    1 teaspoon butter
    1 tablespoon brandy
    2 teaspoons vegetable oil

Heat oil in a frypan till quite warm. Add bananas, butter and honey, stir and cover for 2 minutes. Add juice, freshly squeezed from the fruit onto the bananas and honey, stir. Increase heat and cover for 5 minutes. Check and stir if necessary. Add strawberries when bananas are just cooked. Stir. Sprinkle brandy over mixture.

Heat ½ tablespoon brandy over a flame, set alight and pour onto bananas and syrup. Serve with scalded cow's cream.

Pancakes

If you have a blender you can make pancakes in 5 minutes. Otherwise beat or mix vigorously to form a smooth batter. Let stand for 30–40 minutes. Rub pan lightly with oil and heat. Pour on some pancake mix. Tilt pan to spread it. When bubbles appear on upper side, flip, but be careful not to break. Add a pinch of salt to all mixes.

Buckwheat

    1 cup buckwheat flour
    2 teaspoons oil
  1½ cups water
    pinch sea salt

Blend for 2–3 minutes or stir thoroughly and let stand 40 minutes. Stir and cook as above. Top with apple/tahina purée or hazelnut cream.

Wholewheat

Same as buckwheat. Top with blackcurrant purée.

Kokkoh-wholewheat (half and half)

Same as buckwheat. Top with a thick tofu and pumpkin purée. Sprinkle with cinnamon or nutmeg.

Orange or lemon

      1 cup wholewheat flour
      2 teaspoons oil
      pinch sea salt
      1½ cups orange (or lemon) juice
      1 teaspoon orange rind

Blend or mix and let stand for 40 minutes. Cook as above. Mighty with carob-tahina cream.

Carob

      1 cup wholewheat flour
      3 teaspoons oil
      1 tablespoon carob powder
    1¾ cups water
      pinch sea salt
      1 teaspoon orange rind

Blend or mix and let stand. Cook as above and serve with cashew cream.

Corn

      1 cup polenta or cornmeal
      1 cup wholewheat flour
      1 tablespoon oil
      pinch sea salt
      1 beaten egg (optional)
      2 cups water

Soak cornmeal in water for 30 minutes. Blend or mix. Cook as above and serve with pumpkin purée or with pumpkin and shoyu. Maple syrup is traditional on this one.

Apple

      1 cup wholewheat flour
      2 teaspoons oil
    ½ cup sourdough
      1 cup apple juice

Blend or mix. Cook as above and serve with hot toasted walnuts and apple sauce.

Fruit fritter aways

Banana

2 teaspoons finely grated ginger
2 tablespoons maltose
½ cup water
2 teaspoons kuzu or arrowroot
crushed seeds from 1 cardomon pod

Cook water, maltose, ginger and cardomon over medium-high heat for 5 minutes or until ginger acquires a sweet rather than sharp odour. Add kuzu, dissolved in 2 tablespoons water. Stir over heat until kuzu clears and thickens. Meanwhile, cut 1 banana in half. Rub with umeboshi plum. Dust with flour, dip in rice flour/wholewheat flour batter, and deep-fry until golden. Serve with the ginger sauce.

Apple

As for banana. Use buckwheat flour/wholewheat flour batter. Serve with thin tahina cream.

Steamed buns

4 cups fine wholemeal wheat
or   3 cups wheat flour and 1 cup very fine-ground brown rice flour
1½ teaspoons dried granulated yeast dissolved in 1 cup warm water with 2 tablespoons of flour
or   1½ cups sourdough liquid
1¼ cups warm water
¼ teaspoon salt

Allow yeast to rise and bubble in the water. When the yeast has doubled in volume, mix with the flour and salt. Rub in gently to distribute yeast. Add warm water, mix with a wooden spoon to form one mass of dough. Knead until smooth. Place in a bowl, cover with a tea towel and set aside in a warm place to rise, 2–3 hours. When the dough has doubled in size, knead gently till smooth. Flour the board or table if necessary. Roll out into a long cylinder 5 cm in diameter. Break off 5 cm sections and roll into balls.

While holding the ball in the palm of one hand, poke your thumb into the ball almost to the bottom. Thin the dough around the hole, so you have an 'empty eggshell' shape. Insert filling of your choice, but make sure it is dry. A sloppy filling will burst out during steaming.

Seal the top with a pinch and place on a small piece of grease-proof paper in a bamboo steamer — or arrange on a cake rack for steaming. Allow 20 minutes for it to rise. Steam with medium intensity for 30–40 minutes — make sure your steaming device does not leak drops of water into the buns or they will be soggy. When ready, spray with a fine mist of cold water. This glazes the buns.

To make smooth buns when using a dry filling, after sealing the vent gently roll the bun between your hands so as to make a smooth ball — you can't see the seal. The Chinese make these buns, so to get an idea of them, find a Chinese shop or restaurant which has them. They are usually made from white flour — yours will be slightly heavier and brown.

If you don't have an oven, these buns can be steamed without a filling and used for bread; this is the bread of northern China.

Savoury steamed buns

> fine ground wholemeal wheat flour or 80 percent wholewheat
> or unbleached white flour
> boiling hot water

Carefully mix boiling water into the wholewheat flour and stir until the dough begins to cling together. Then knead carefully to avoid burning fingers. Knead for 10 minutes until a smooth, elastic (not sticky) dough is formed. Form the dough into golf ball sizes. Press your thumb into these to make a deep bird's nest, thin the pastry by revolving the dough on your thumb and pressing. Imagine a tennis ball with the top quarter removed ... this is what you should be left with after all this thumb work.

Alternatively, roll this pastry quite thin into small circular shapes. Place mixture in the centre and draw the edges together above the filling. Give a twist to the seal and steam.

Fill your three-quarter ball with finely chopped cooked vegetables and miso, and seal by stretching the pastry together. Steam for 20 minutes. Chinese bamboo steamers are the best for this.

There are endless variable fillings. These fillings should be chosen carefully, and cooked to ensure they are strong tasting as this blends well with the blandness of the dough.

Favourite filling

> 2 tablespoons finely grated ginger
> 2 brown onions finely chopped
> 2 cups finely chopped vegetables (pumpkin, carrot, parsnip, cabbage are very good)
> 1½ tablespoons of mugi (barley) miso
> ½ tablespoon of shoyu (tamari)

Sauté the ginger and onion in 1 tablespoon of peanut oil over medium heat for 5 minutes. Add ½ tablespoon of rice syrup or maltose, the vegetables, and shoyu. Cook over medium heat until the vegetables are quite soft. Strain to remove excess liquid, which you can make into a gravy by thickening with flour, and mix in the miso to the vegetables. This should taste quite salty.

Fill buns and steam.

If you want to have a gravy filling, simply make up a savoury miso gravy with onions, miso water and flour. Chop onions, fry in oil, add flour, stir for 5 minutes.

Meanwhile, add shreds of agar to the water and bring to a boil. Simmer until agar is dissolved, add miso or shoyu, add to flour and onion mix, stir till thick.

Place in a tray to set. Cut into small pieces when cool and place in the middle of the buns. These will just be hot gravy when the bun is ready. Make sure you put the sealed part of the bun upwards or leakage may occur.

Sweet ginger filling

> 1 teaspoon finely grated ginger
> ½ teaspoon finely grated orange peel
> 1 tablespoon maltose
> 1 tablespoon coarse coconut, preferably freshly grated
> 1 tablespoon vegetable oil

Heat oil, add ginger, orange, maltose, coconut. Stir-fry till thick — ginger must be cooked. Add a tiny amount of water if necessary, but cook until quite dry. Mix with 1 cup mashed red beans.

Other fillings

Prawns, fish, mashed salted vegetables, sweet potato, red bean or mung bean mashed with chopped dates, chopped dried fruit, lotus seed jam, ground nuts.

The Chinese stores in Dixon and Hay Streets, Sydney, and in most other large cities have an interesting array of steamed, baked, boiled and fried buns, cakes and savouries. It is worth trying all of them so that you can create your own variations at home — without using dyed pork, sugar and monosodium glutamate! It is a pity that so much of the delicious natural food which was once prepared by the Chinese has been allowed to degenerate into a 'chemical feast'. The use of flavour-improving chemicals indicates that we can no longer taste natural food and that the manufacturers have become less generous with the natural ingredients, because chemical flavour boosters disguise the shortage. Thus the manufacturers make more money and so do the hospitals — treating you!

Lotus cakes

These are made from lotus seeds and rice pastry. Lotus seeds are available in Chinese food stores.

To prepare lotus seeds, split them if not already done. Remove the centre green pip. Soak with water and 1 teaspoon salt for 15 minutes. Boil for 15 minutes in clean water. Drain and rub off the red skins (if still on). Steam or simmer for one hour till soft. Cool seeds and mash.

For each cup of mashed seeds mix in half a cup finely chopped or crushed Chinese dates. Mix well.

Pastry:

> 4 cups cooked glutinous or sticky rice
> 1 cup cooked brown rice
> 1 cup kokkoh cereal or very fine wheat flour
> *or* 2 tablespoons finely ground kuzu arrowroot
> *or* 3 tablespoons good quality arrowroot

Knead this mixture well. With wet hands roll into balls the size of a golf ball. Hollow out with your finger, fill with lotus-date mixture. Seal up. Roll gently to smooth the surface where sealed. Deep-fry until golden, or bake at 170°C (350°F) for 25 minutes.

Alternatively, fill with mashed, cooked red or green beans (azuki or mung) and finely ground or chopped dates. The bean mash must be dry.

Sweet potato lotus cakes

    4 cups glutinous rice flour
    1 cup buckwheat flour
    2 cups boiling water
    4 tablespoons vegetable oil
    4 cups cooked, drained, mashed sweet potato or Japanese pumpkin

Add boiling water to the flour mixture. Mix to a dough. When cool, add oil and knead well. Add sweet potato and knead. Follow rolling procedure for previous cakes, using lotus-date or date and orange peel filling. Bake at 170°C (350°F) for 25 minutes, or deep-fry.

Ice creams

If you are prepared to forget the chemical taste and texture of commercial ice creams, you can enter a new realm with these concoctions.

The methods are basic and the variations are endless.

Use agar or simply make gelati-style ice creams with kokkoh or flour or flavoured water.

Carob-hazelnut

    1 cup ground roasted hazelnuts
    1 tablespoon carob powder
    2 tablespoons rice syrup *or* ½ cup Iraq date purée
    ½ cup kokkoh or toasted soya flour
    3 cups apple juice

Purée all ingredients until very fine. Pour into a tray and freeze. Serve, or purée again and freeze. This can be repeated several times with worthwhile results. The more you purée, the creamier the mixture.

Use 1 cup yoghurt for variation and only 2 cups apple juice. Add 1 egg for a familiar texture.

Red bean gaytime

Soak 1½ cups rolled oats in 3 cups apple juice for 3 hours. Stir frequently. Strain off the liquid and reserve the oats. Add to the liquid:

½ cup water
3 bars or 1 cup strands agar, chopped
2 vanilla pods, split
3 tablespoons maltose *or* rice syrup
or   1 tablespoon honey
½ cup of the soaked oats

Cook until 'milk' thickens and agar dissolves. Add 3 cups cooked red beans (azuki) mashed and pressed through a sieve. Purée. Freeze. Purée again and insert an ice cream stick into each block. Freeze. When frozen again, soak oat strainings with 1 tablespoon natural vanilla essence and 1 tablespoon carob powder. Toast until dry and fragrant. Moisten ice blocks. Roll in oats. Chill. Serve.

Pear and ginger ice cream

2 vanilla pods, split
6 chopped pears
1 cup water
2 teaspoons finely grated ginger
3 cups apple juice
3 bars or 1 cup strands agar, chopped

Cook these ingredients over medium heat until agar is dissolved. Remove 2 cups liquid and purée it with 1 tablespoon tahina and ½ cup kokkoh or soya flour. Mix together, purée, place in trays and freeze. Remove, chop, purée and freeze again. Delicious

Other ice cream combinations using this method are:
Strawberry and apple, apricot, nectarine, watermelon, rock or honeydew melon, sweet pumpkin, cashew.

Creamy ice cream

3 cups puréed tofu
3 vanilla pods, split
2 cups Iraq date purée
(*or*   if you want it white, omit date purée and add 2 cups apple *or* fruit juice and 1 tablespoon honey)
1 cup apple juice
2 bars or ½ cup strands agar, chopped

Scrape insides from vanilla pods and add to tofu, water, juice and honey (or purée), and agar. Stir and cook until agar dissolves. Cool. Purée. Freeze.

Dice and purée, add chopped strawberries. Place in prepared square moulds. Insert an ice cream stick and freeze.

If you insist, dust with carob powder before serving.

Ice cream fritters

Use cubes of ice cream you have made, 5 x 5 cm. They must be totally frozen, rock hard. Dip in thick batter and drop into hot oil 170°C (350°F). Remove quickly. If you are expert enough the result will be amazing.

Creams for desserts

Kuzu creme — best of all!

>   3 cups water or juice from cooked fruit or soy milk
>   2 tablespoons kuzu arrowroot
>   1 teaspoon sesame purée (thick natural tahina)
>   pinch sea salt

Dissolve kuzu in water or juice (use 1 tablespoon of rice honey or maltose if not using juice) and bring to the boil slowly while stirring. Turn heat down and simmer while kuzu clears and thickens.

When kuzu is clear and thick, remove from heat. Thoroughly mix the tahina with 1 tablespoon of kuzu and mix in with the rest of the kuzu. Stir thoroughly until creamy, but do not heat or the tahina will flocculate.

Add the sea salt, stir and serve. If allowed to cool this becomes thicker.
or

Toast and cook rolled oats into porridge. Cook thoroughly. Blend with fruit juice or dried fruit purée to make a creamy consistency.

Tofu

>   2 blocks tofu parboiled in water
>   1 tablespoon maple syrup
>   1 teaspoon natural tahina
>   *or*   homemade peanut butter

Purée till creamy.

Sesame yoghurt

>   1 cup yoghurt
>   ½ tablespoon honey or 2 tablespoons rice or corn syrup
>   ½ tablespoon natural tahina

Blend well.
or

>   2 tablespoons natural tahina
>   4 tablespoons water or fruit juice purée

For example, if you wanted this rich cream on apple pie, you could use the juice strained from the apples to blend with the tahina.

A sweet for young children

I think it is a good idea to give very little sweet food to young children, as this, combined with fruit, makes them slow and sleepy. Sugar is absolutely out, unless you want to damage your child's developing organs, and honey is too strong. A little cooked fruit and grain honey such as maltose are ideal sweeteners, as are baked or steamed sweet vegetables. To make your own grain sweetener, wash some organic wheat and soak overnight. Place in a tray, cover with a cloth and put in a dark cupboard. Flush the seeds daily. After two or three days, you should have root and stem sprouts. Crush these very finely or blend, and cook with a little water over medium heat for 5 minutes. Strain and sieve. Serve as is or mix with cereals, or thicken with kuzu.

This is a good basic source of easily assimilable sugars. Barley can be treated in this way. It is important for children to develop basic strength. This can be ruined if they are fed poorly in their first years of solid food. More importantly, their health is determined by what their mothers nourished them on in pregnancy.

Wheat sprout milk

A good sweet drink, especially for children.

Soak, then sprout organic wheat for 2 days. Blend with clean water. Strain. Heat if you like.

16

Drinks

Drinking

Perhaps the greatest undoing of all of us is that we drink to excess. A hot climate such as Australia's makes us drink a lot, but more satisfaction and cooling is obtained from drinking little rather than becoming awash with teas, juices, alcohol, milk, etc.

The huge gut is characteristic of most Australian men over 30, and some younger — this is swollen intestines often from over consumption of beer. I believe that the stomach region is our centre of balance, and this balance is washed away with gallons of fluid.

But this is obvious excess. Most people reading this will not be in this category, but how much have you thought about drinking and its relation to digestion and health? Drinking is necessary to maintain body fluid levels and clean kidneys. The amount most of us drink today is damaging to both of these factors.

If you are eating grain and vegetable foods, basically your grains are cooked with water, as are vegetables, porridge, fruit, breads, etc. So in fact you are receiving plenty of fluid from the foods you eat. The same is not true of a meat-eater, who craves liquid to balance the effect of refined salt and meat.

Some criticise grain and vegetable diets because they often recommend a reduction in consumption of liquid. This criticism, and the idea that we should drink volumes (especially water) to clean ourselves, is both non-traditional and simple-minded. It is important that we learn about physiology from those who have experienced it from prehistory, as well as from science. Man's experience has led to conservative ingestion of liquids among traditional peoples. It is a leisure-filled society which has brought on the drinking drug to fill in time which should not really need filling in. The demands of the beverage manufacturers and their subversive propaganda: 'It's the real thing', have duped a whole generation of sugar addicts. If you find what I am saying hard to swallow, cut out all sugared drinks, sugar, sweet beverages and cut down on your drinking for one week. Why not, for just one week out of your allotted 2–3000 weeks? Or is there something to be afraid of? Maybe it's yourself!

Asian peoples take their teas and liquids in small cups and in small portions. I have found this most practical, and am sure you will too. Many glasses of liquid make you sweat to excess in hot weather and flush everything, including nutrients, from your system. Drinking volumes also produces indigestion if your food is basically grain and vegetables.

While fasting, drinking only one or two small cups of liquid for one day can increase elimination severalfold — but be careful of cutting out drinking altogether as you will eliminate very rapidly (although I have done this and not suffered). If liquid and food are chosen sensibly and used in small quantities, particularly in summer, they will refresh, and you will be more active with less hot-weather lethargy.

How often have you felt you could drink a whole flagon of apple juice or cordial or beer during hot weather — then done it, and felt just as thirsty five minutes later? The Aborigines have survived our climate without such excess and it is only lack of judgment on our part which leads to over-indulgence in liquids.

Teas

Herbal teas are commonplace and usually can be prepared by adding 1 teaspoon of herbs per cup of boiling water.

Place the required amount of herbs in a teapot. Pour on boiling water. Cover and let stand or 'draw' for 5 minutes.

Serve without milk or any kind of sweetening. Some sweetened teas are simply hot honey liquid, and the herb is not actually being employed. Such sweetenings interfere with the function of many herbs.

Herbs must be brewed in an earthenware or glass pot — don't ever use metal for teas.

Root herbs used to relieve physical discomfort need to be brought to the boil and simmered for up to 30 minutes. This concentrates the herb and makes it effective.

Chinese black or green tea

Follow above directions but let stand 2–3 minutes. China tea loses its taste after 5 minutes and is quite bitter after 10 minutes.

Chinese stores have wonderful teas — ones we enjoy are pu-erh, koo loo (favourite), green tea, oolong, jasmine, lichee's, 'China black' and lok-on.

Enjoy tea, black, in small Chinese teacups. The flavours are quite different from our common 'tea', which is often dyed with chemicals and quite rank in taste. This *has* to be mixed with milk and sugar or honey to hide its flavour.

The Chinese claim that their fermented black teas are good for the digestion, particularly after eating oily or fried food. I believe this is true, having been saved by such tea during a Yum Cha or Chinese Sunday breakfast.

Mu tea

Mu tea can be bought in sachets from health food stores. It appears expensive but the sachets make a large pot and can be rebrewed 3 or 4 times. It is very effective drunk first thing in the morning and 1 hour before meals in the winter. It will warm you up and provide protection from flu and colds if you also eat well.

Mu tea is a blend of traditional Asian herbs and you should not eat within an hour of consuming it. This tea is very delicious chilled in summer.

Mu tea contains ginseng and is an excellent way of consuming this herb.

Bancha or kukicha tea

Bancha is made from the older twigs from the tea plant, whereas Chinese, Sri Lankan and Indian teas come from the leaves.

We may grow this in Australia soon, or at least procure it here. Bancha is my favourite tea and has a quality which can be appreciated only from experiencing it.

Use 1 teaspoon bancha twigs per person. Toast them first if you wish. Slowly bring to a boil then simmer for 5 minutes. Also very good mixed with herbs, especially peppermint, and is excellent hot or cold.

Kashmiri chai

Aids indigestion and is cooling in summer.

>   1 teaspoon green tea
>   ¼ teaspoon chopped fresh ginger
>   3 cups boiling water

Stand for 5 minutes. Brew it over low heat for a few minutes if you want. Strain off ginger.

Spice tea

>   1 teaspoon good black tea
>   1 whole cardomon pod
>   2 whole cloves
>   1 small stick cinnamon

Prepare as for chai. Strain off spices. Use sparingly.

Root decoctions

Yannoh coffee

Made from ground beans and grains. Coffee is merely a substitute for it.

>   1 teaspoon yannoh per person
>   1 cup liquid per person

Bring to a boil then simmer for 5 minutes. Strain and serve.

Dandelion coffee

Superlative medicinal drink and a pleasing beverage. It is a little bitter, but effective for liver and kidney trouble. Make as for yannoh.

Burdock

Used to cleanse the lymph and eject poisons. Prepare as for dandelion.

Liquorice

Take this in combination with a leafy herb such as peppermint or sage. Used for liver complaints. Do not use if you contain too much fluid as it causes the cells to retain liquid. Infuse with hot water for a mild tonic or prepare as for dandelion and use in small quantity as a medicine.

Barley 'coffee'

Slowly roast whole barley until it is quite black. Grind and prepare as for yannoh. Very cooling when drunk cold in summer.

Ginseng

This is a very strong herb and you should not use it indiscriminately. If it doesn't appear to affect you, do not drink it.

Ginseng works very well if you eat balanced vegetal food. It simply increases blood pressure if you consume much meat. Those who take it to increase sexual vigour are fooling themselves if they do not eat well at the same time.

Don't eat great lumps of ginseng daily as this merely increases your tolerance to it. If used occasionally and in proper measure, it will work for you.

When making this tea use another herb — preferably a leafy one — to make it available to you in a balanced fashion. Do not take ginseng if you are sick — wait till you are recovering.

For Sexual Endurance:
>   1 ounce ground ginseng
>   1½ cups dried orange rind (organic and unwaxed)
>   3 cups clean water

Gently bring to a boil and simmer slowly for 30 minutes. Very strong. Use sparingly.

Ginseng-liquorice

Used to remove thought impairments
>   1 teaspoon liquorice root
>   ½ teaspoon ground ginseng *or* 1 cm of root, broken
>   3 cups water

Bring to boil. Simmer for 20 minutes.

Beverages to relieve physical discomfort

Fatigue remedy

>   1 cup hot bancha tea
>   ½ teaspoon shoyu

Mix and drink hot.

Helpful in a crisis

>   1 cup bancha tea
>   5 drops ginger juice (grate ginger root and squeeze out 5 drops)
>   1 teaspoon shoyu
>   ½ umeboshi plum
>   1 teaspoon kuzu, dissolved in 1 tablespoon water

Bring bancha to high heat, add other ingredients and stir gently over medium heat for 5 minutes.

Very good if you are not well and you don't know why!

'Reducing the yang' beverage

Good for the end of winter.

> 1 cup hot bancha tea
> 1 teaspoon very finely grated radish

Drink it for three mornings (chew the radish!). Wait for 30 minutes before eating.

Radish drink

> 1 cup radish juice
> 1 cup water

Bring to high heat and remove just before boiling. Drink warm. Good for inducing urination, the kidneys, swelling and skin problems. Take once a day for 3 days and then wait for 3 days before using again. Don't eat within one hour of drinking. This is an old European remedy believed to dissolve kidney and bladder stones.

Cornsilk tea

> 2 cups water
> handful dried organic cornsilk

Boil till one cup remains. This is a kidney and bladder tonic which is very effective if you have dark rings under your eyes.

Wheat grass

A cleansing tonic.

Grow some wheat in a box of soil — this is very easy. Fertilise with liquid seaweed fertilizer. When wheat is 15 cm high, cut it down. Chop and blend this with water or carrot juice or put through a special juicer. Drink a small quantity, 1 tablespoon per glass of juice or water initially, and slowly increase the amount. This is most effective for those who have been consuming much meat and for people with strong, heavy constititutions

Indulgences

Vegetal flash

> *Juice:* 3 carrots, 2 spring onions, small portion pumpkin, small radish,
> ½ bunch parsley

Add one teaspoon shoyu.

Watermelon mouth water

Extract juice from one watermelon and one orange. Blend with 2 teaspoons tahina.

Sesame milk

>   1 tablespoon tahina
>   1 pint water

Blend very well.

Spicy lassi

>   3 cups yoghurt
>   1 cup water
>   pinch salt
>   pinch ground cummin

Blend well. Good with hot foods (Indian style).

Sweet lassi

>   3 cups yoghurt
>   1 cup water
>   1 teaspoon rose water
>   seeds from 2 cardomon pods

Crush seeds, mix and blend well. Serve with ice cubes. Incredible with curry.

Sherbet

Very rich and all-consuming — the complete indulgence.

>   1 cup yoghurt
>   2 teaspoons natural tahina
>   juice of 1 orange
>   ½ cup apple juice
>   1 teaspoon honey (optional) or 1 tablespoon rice syrup
>   1 cup water
>   1 banana

Blend well.

Substitute milk shake

>   1 cup cooked, toasted, rolled oats
>   1 tablespoon rice syrup, maltose or maple syrup
>   1 teaspoon natural tahina
>   2 teaspoons natural vanilla essence (or cook the oats with 1 split vanilla
>   pod)
>   1 cup apple juice
>   1 cup clean water

Blend very well.

17

Food for pregnancy and travel

Pregnancy

Pregnant and lactating mothers have a responsibility to eat sensibly. From the moment fertilisation takes place, until the fully formed infant is born, the whole process of human evolution, which took x million years, is duplicated. By eating extreme foods at any stage of the development, the mother is subjecting this evolving human to extremes of environment which effect radically its constitutional development. If the mother eats chemically produced industrial food for a few days, then the child is nurtured for the equivalent of several thousand years on such foods. Many have noticed how different the children of their vegetarian friends are compared to the children of people who eat processed foods.

But some mothers, aware of their diets, do not understand what it means to eat well during pregnancy. They go onto extreme dietary regimes which in my opinion cause a development which is not harmonious with the mother's usual pattern of living. It is more advisable for a woman to change her diet before becoming pregnant, so as to give herself and her child a better start. Altering diet during pregnancy can be a load on the system when hormonal and other functions are already undergoing massive changes.

If you wish to eat well during pregnancy firstly exclude all refined sugar from your diet. Then continue to eat your normal diet and, over a period of 4 to 6 weeks, reduce your intake of all animal quality foods to an absolute minimum. At the same time, substitute for your past diet, cooked whole grains in all forms, ferments such as miso and sourdough, cooked and sprouted beans, sea vegetables, fresh and cooked fruit, cooked and raw vegetables, nuts and seeds. If you need flesh, eat fish.

The proportions should be 40–50 per cent whole grains and 30 per cent vegetables, with sea vegetables, beans, fruit and nuts filling in the remaining amount. Ensure that you eat adequately and do not fast or practise self-denial. Fulfil cravings with natural foods, but do not eat any particular foods in great excess. Abstain from smoking and drugs.

Those living with a pregnant lady must be aware of her needs and be considerate but not overly indulgent. Pregnancy does not exclude activity so don't use it as an excuse for laziness. Practise simple Yoga and breathe well. Attempt to maintain serenity, for your child while developing, is you.

Some women develop discharge and other such problems during pregnancy. These can be controlled with hip baths containing (a) green leafy vegetables, (b) cooked sea vegetables, (c) bancha tea and sea salt, and exposure of the region to sunlight. Shitake mushrooms, tekka and mugwart rice are helpful foods.

Breast-feeding

When breast-feeding, some modern mothers are victims of the 3 month milk shut-off syndrome, which means that after 3 months of breast-feeding, breast milk seems to diminish. This is usually associated with a physiological and psychological period of readjustment for both mother and child.

Milk does not cut off at all. You must relax more during this readjustment, and if the child does not seem to be getting enough milk, feed more often for longer periods and remain in a calm frame of mind. What you eat is exactly what your child eats, so be considerate of its development. Baby faeces should be golden colour and in young days soft, becoming firm as the baby grows. Green faeces means unbalanced or extreme food which is too Yin, e.g. too much sugar, dairy food, rich sauces, ice cream, raw fruit or salad — not enough well chewed grain. Baby faeces which are brown and firm suggest the mother is eating too much food such as meat, cheese, bad salt, hamburgers, processed gumbo, not enough vegetables and grain or lighter quality food.

If your child cries too strongly, this tea is effective:

> 20 g organic wheat
> 6 g dates (Chinese red, not the sweet black variety) including pits
> 5 g liquorice root

Mix with 3 cups water, bring to the boil and simmer for one hour. This will be soupy. Be sure to do this in a non-metal pot. Give 1 or 2 teaspoons 3 times a day for 1 or 2 days.

Travelling

Vitality is lost when travelling by eating poor quality food. Often the tendency is to submerge the actual experience of travelling in a host of stimulants from food to fags. It is easier to travel longer and further by not continually munching because of boredom. You will see more, and be less tired as a result of overeating. Overcome 'travel sickness' with umeboshi plums, which regulate acidity and settle the digestive system. It takes a while to become accustomed to plums, so place one or part of one, under the tongue, and don't suck.

Unless travelling in a cold climate, make brown rice your principal food. This will smooth the effect of any poor food and centre you. Buckwheat is recommended for cold-weather travelling. Both are easily prepared in transit. Add the grain to boiling water in a thermos flask. Seal for 6–8 hours. A plum will act as a preservative, keeping the rice fresh for days. Other grains, and especially noodles, can be prepared in this manner. Add land and sea vegetables if available. Carry miso always, as it need only be stirred into hot water for an invigorating soup. If dining out, eat some fish or plain vegetables and steamed rice in a Chinese restaurant. Ask them to leave out the monosodium glutamate. Munching on dried fruit and nuts, which many a traveller does for convenience, causes fermentation in the intestines, and undue discomfort.

Friends who travel in Asia report that they have no digestive complaints, dysentery or hepatitis, because they can eat grain (rice) and cooked vegetables almost anywhere. Any discomfort can be allayed with miso, mu tea or an umeboshi. These products are easily carried and prepared. Such traditional foods are being rejected by some Asians in favour of Western industrial food. It is important that knowledge concerning the debilitating effect of industrialised food be spread through Asia ... it is really a duty for those of us who have contact with Asian peoples.

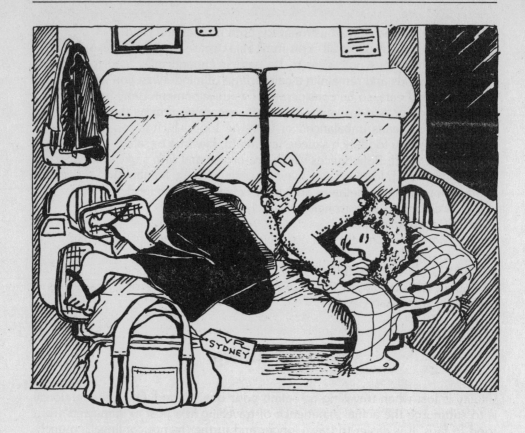

Food in transit

Whole grains prepared in a thermos
Rolled oats or millet meal cooked same way
Vegetables, noodles, seaweed in a thermos
Pre-made biscuits of a hard, non-sweet nature will keep for many days,
   as will toasted grains and seeds (granola minus the dried fruit)
Miso-water soup
Fresh vegetables and fruit

If travelling in a car, take picnic lunches, as these are more fun than the offal available at roadhouses.

18

Shopping

Victoria
Melbourne

Albert Park Health Foods, 103 Bridport St., Albert Park. 690 4038.
Biodynamic Organic Fruit, Vegetables, Grains, 14–16 McAdam Sq. (off Plymouth Road),
  Croydon.
Caulfield Health Foods, 103 Hawthorn Rd., Caulfield. 523 9050.
*Ceres Wholefoods, 116 Chapel St., Prahran. 529 2206.
Cippola (for pasta), 99–102 Station St., Malvern. 500 0262.
d'Agostino, A. (organic produce), 601 Station St., Box Hill.
Demeter Meats (free-range), 18 McAdam Sq., Croydon North. 725 6975.
Down to Earth Whole Foods, Camberwell Shopping Centre, 614 Burke Rd., Camberwell.
  82 1831.
Elsternwick Health Foods, 338 Glenhuntly Rd., Elsternwick. 528 5528.
Eltham Health Food Store, 929 Main Rd., Eltham. 439 8693.
Europa Cheese Factory (fresh natural cheese), 12 Lynch St., Hawthorn. 818 5734.
Greens and Grains (vegetables), 123 Greville St., Prahran.
'Health Food Stall', Victoria Market, Melbourne.
Japan Mart, The, 568 Malvern Rd., Prahran. 51 9344.
Lesley's, 225 Lygon St., Carlton. 347 3585.
Lotus Foods, 324 Brunswick St., Fitzroy. 419 5526.
Lygon Foodstore (cheese), 263 Lygon St., Carlton. 347 6279.
Melbourne University Food Co-op., 1st Floor, Union Building,
  Melbourne University, Parkville.
Mitcham Village Store, 28 Britannia St., Mitcham. 874 3303.
Mount Eliza Health Foods, 60 Mount Eliza Way, Mount Eliza.
Natural Tucker Bakery, 809 Nicholson St., North Carlton. 380 4293.
Nature's Store-House, Shop 8, Floriston Ave., Boronia. 762 4333.
Natural Tucker. 527 7121.
Pantry, The, Union Building, Monash University, Clayton.
Piatek Health Foods, 77 Glen Eira Rd., Ripponlea. 523 6416.
Prahran Health Foods, 201 Commercial Rd., South Yarra. 241 5983.
Prahran Market Health Foods
Rainbow, 808 Glenferrie Rd., Hawthorn.
Shakti Health Foods, corner Terry Ave. & Main St., Belgrave. 754 4732.
Small Planet Food Store, 326 Lygon St., Carlton. 347 8482.
*Soul Food, 279 Smith St., Fitzroy. 419 5347.
    "   "   , 322 Toorak Rd., South Yarra. 241 4519.
*Spiral Foods (distributor), Richmond (Vic). 429 8655.
Sustenance Health Food Shop, 282 Queens Pde., Fitzroy North. 489 2978.
Various Chinese grocery stores in Little Bourke St., Melbourne.
Williamstown Health Foods, 20 Douglas Pde., Williamstown. 397 7363.

Victorian country

Aviva Health Foods, 39 Chute St., Diamond Creek. 438 2978.
Bendigo Trading Co., Myers St., Bendigo.
Good Foods, 238 Barker St., Castlemaine.
Henderson's Health Foods, Ryrie St., Geelong.
Honeymead, Main St., Bacchus Marsh.
Jillong Wholefoods, Donnys Lane, Geelong.
*Lowan Wholefoods, 58 Nelson St., Nhill. (053) 91 9781.
Rivergum Health Foods, 2 Mt. Joy Pde., Lorne.
Wodonga Health Food Centre, Shop 7, Wodonga Mall, 1 Stanley St., Wodonga.

* Recommended

New South Wales
Sydney

Gerardis Health Foods, 31a Kingsgate, Kings Cross. 358 6129.
Graham's Health Foods, Shop 33, Village Shopping Centre, Neutral Bay. 90 2244.
Graham's Health Foods, Shop 10, Crows Nest Plaza, Willoughby Rd., Crows Nest. 438 3285.
*Harmony Wholefoods, 230 Oxford St., Woollahra. 387 1785.
Health and Healing Foods, 22 Perouse St., Randwick. 399 3538.
Herb 'n' Health Centre, 148 Norton St., Leichhardt. 569 5828.
Nutra Health Foods, 15a Burns Bay Rd., Lane Cove. 427 4420.
Rainbow Groceries, 509 Willoughby Rd., Willoughby. 95 0257.
Russells Health Mart, 55 Glebe Point Rd., Glebe. 692 0824.
Russels Bulk Buy, 184 Liverpool Rd., Enfield. 74 8561.
Sirius Earth Foods, Shop 5, Hilltop Rd., Avalon. 918 0800.
True Health Aids, 443 George St., Sydney. 29 8676.

Country

Bambu Wholefoods, 86 Summerland Way, Kyogle. (066) 321 1881.
Byron Bay Health Foods, Marvell St., Byron Bay. (066) 85 6429.
Fundamental Foods, 140 Keen St., Lismore. (066) 21 6760.
Laughing Buddha, The, Shop 10, Albury Shopping Centre, Olive St., Albury.
Munchies Health Foods, Jonson St., Byron Bay.
Nimbin Emporium, Cullen St., Nimbin. (066) 89 1205.
Nuthouse, The, 228 High St., Coffs Harbour. (066) 52 4455.
Olive Bulk Health Foods, The, 512 Olive St., Albury.
Peterson, T. & D., 94 North St., Casino.
Santos Trading, 91 Stuart St., Mullimbimby. (066) 84 2410.

(N.B. The Good Food Shop at Bellingen burnt down recently and is closed for an indefinite period.)

A.C.T.

ANU Nutrition Society, c/- Australian National University, Canberra.
Healthy Life, Belconnen Mall, Belconnen.
Mawson Health Foods, 'Southland', Mawson.
Mountain Creek Wholefoods, 14 Barker St., Barker Centre. (062) 95 1474.
Peter Gardiner's Health Foods, Monaro Mall, Monaro.
Sesame, 122 Allinga St., Canberra.

South Australia
Adelaide and Country

Athens Gourmet Foods, Central Market, Adelaide.
Cleanlight Foods, 201 Rundle St., Adelaide.
Farmhouse, The, 414 King William St., Adelaide.
From the Earth, 195 Magill Rd., Marylands.
Good Health, North East Rd., Windsor Gdns.
Harvest Wholefoods, P.O. Box 764, Nairne.
Healthy House, O'Connell St., North Adelaide.
Healthy Life, Norwood Pde., Norwood.
Organic Vegetable Stall, Central Market, Adelaide.
Ti Tree Health Foods, 25 Albert Place, Victor Harbour.

* Recommended

Queensland

Caterpillar Shop, Atherton, North Qld.
Earth's Corner Health Foods, 61A Scarborough St., Southport, South Qld.
Simply Bazaar, Shop 8, 78–80 Bulcock St., Caloundra.
Whole Earth Store, The, Hospital Rd., Nambour.
Wholefoods, Milton Rd., Auchenflower, Brisbane.

Tasmania

Health Food Shop, The, 18 Criterion St., Hobart.
Healthy Life, Shop 206, Centrepoint, 70 Murray St., Hobart.
Prasad Wholefoods, 249 Elizabeth St., Hobart.
—— 249 Sandy Bay Rd., Hobart.
Wynyard Health Foods, 52 Goldie St., Wynyard.

Western Australia

Ceres Wholefoods, 7 South Terrace, Fremantle.
Hawthorn Wholefoods, Shop 12, Hawthorn Plaza, Mt. Hawthorn.
Joby's Natural Foods, 967 Beaufort St., Inglewood. (09) 272 1670.
Scarborough Wholefoods, 66 Scarborough Beach Road, Scarborough.
Sundance Wholefoods, The Old Church, Margaret River.

New Zealand

Alexandra Health Foods, Alexandra Street, Te Awamutu.
Ambrosials, Karamu Road, Hastings.
Bryce and Chapman, Main Road, New Plymouth.
Ceres Health Foods, Haupapa Street, Rototua.
Susan Clare Health Foods, Sturdee Street, Wellington.
Corn Rigs Health Foods, Main Street, Palmerston North.
Cornucopia Health Ltd, Centre Court Complex, Devon Street East, New Plymouth.
Country Health Foods, New Brighton Bazaar, Seaview Road, New Brighton, Christchurch.
Culpeper House, Mainstone Mall, Geange Street, Upper Hutt.
Edgeware Health Food Centre, Colombo Street, Christchurch.
Fine Foods, Devon Mall, Tauranga.
Fundamental Foods, Parnell Road, Parnell, Auckland.
Glenfield Vitamins & Health Foods, Glenfield Mall, Glenfield, Auckland.
The Good Life Health Shop, 246 Buildings, Queen Street, Auckland.
Good Stuff Health Shop, Guiness Street, Greymouth.
Greerton Health Foods, Chadwick Road, Greerton, Tauranga.
Hadlums Nutrition Store, Oxford Street, Levin.
E.W. Hall & Son Ltd, Armagh Street, Christchurch.
Hamilton Health Food Shop, Victoria Street, Centre Point, Hamilton.
Hans Health Food Shop, Devon Street East, New Plymouth.
Harvest Health Foods, Main Road, Mt Maunganui.
Harvest Homestead Natural Foods, Bank Street, Whangarei.
The Health Food Shop, Bridge Street, Nelson.
Health Food Specialists, Broadlands Centre, Napier.
The Health Shop, Elizabeth Street, Warkworth.
The Health Shoppe, Clyde Road, Browns Bay, Auckland.
Healthy Life Ltd, Queens Road, Panmure, Auckland.
Healthy Living, The Strand, Whakatane.
Heretaunga Health Foods, Heretaunga Street East, Hastings.
Ideal Foods, Gordon Street, Mosgiel.
Invercargill Health Foods, Pall Mall Arcade, Dee Street, Invercargill.
Karori Mall Health Foods, Karori Mall, Main Road, Karori, Wellington.
Kosmea Health Shop, Stafford Arcade, Palmerston North.

New Zealand continued

Levin Healthrite Foods, The Mall, Levin.
Lynmall Health Foods, Lynmall Centre, New Lynn, Auckland.
McLeods Health Food Centre, Karangahape Road, Auckland.
Merivale Health Food Shop, Clyde Road, Merivale Mall, Christchurch.
Modern Health Foods, Tutanekai Street, Rotorua.
Natural Foods, Columbo Street, Christchurch.
Naturally Health Foods, Broadway, Newmarket, Auckland.
Northland Health Food Centre, Water Street, Whangarei.
Peerswick Health Foods, Peerswick Lane, Church Corner, Upper Riccarton, Christchurch.
Ready Health Foods, Broadlands Centre, Napier.
Real Foods, Anderson Bay Road, Dunedin.
Rebirth Health Shop, Cuba Street, Wellington.
Remuera Health Foods, Remuera Road, Remuera, Auckland.
Sanitarium Health Food Co, Pah Road, Royal Oak, Auckland.
Sanitarium Health Food Co, Harewood Road, Papanui, Christchurch.
Sanitarium Health Food Co, George Street, Dunedin.
Sanitarium Health Food Co, Dee Street, Invercargill.
Sanitarium Health Food Co, Lambton Quay, Wellington.
The Sesame Seed, Mt Eden Road, Mt Eden, Auckland.
Somerset Health Foods, Plaza Centre, 11th Avenue, Tauranga.
Source and Essence, Colombo Street, Sydenham, Christchurch.
Specialty Foods, Gt South Road, Papatoetoe, Auckland.
The Sunflower Health Foods, Victoria Street, Devonport, Auckland.
Suzanne's Health Foods, Pembroke Mall, Ardmore Street, Wanaka, Central Otago.
Taradale Health Foods, Gloucester Court, Taradale.
True Foods Ltd, Gardens Shopping Mall, North Road, Dunedin.
Tudor Health Foods, Victoria Avenue, Wanganui.
Vita Health Foods, Ponsonby Road, Three Lamps, Auckland.
Vita Health Foods, Downtown Shopping Centre, Queen Street, Auckland.
Vita Health Foods, Clyde Road, Browns Bay, Auckland.
Vita Health Foods, BNZ Mall, Moore Street, Howick, Auckland.
Vita Health Foods, Pakuranga Shopping Centre, Pakuranga, Auckland.
Vita Health Foods, Manukau Shopping Centre, Manukau City, Wiri, Auckland.
Vita Health Foods, Kitchener Road, Milford, Auckland.
Vita Health Foods, Great South Road, Papakura, Auckland.
Vita Health Foods, West Coast Road, Glen Eden, Auckland.
Vita Health Foods, Plaza Shopping Centre, Queen Street, Auckland.
Vita Health Foods, Southmall Shopping Centre, Manurewa, Auckland.
Vita Health Foods, Cnr Anzac & Como Streets, Takapuna, Auckland.
Vita Health Foods, Highland Park, Pakuranga, Auckland.
Vita Health Foods, Great South Road, Otahuhu, Auckland.
Vita Health Foods, Cnr Maheke & Polygon Roads, St Heliers, Auckland.
Vita Health Foods, National Mutual Arcade, Hereford Street, Christchurch.
Vita Health Foods, Main North Road, Papanui, Christchurch.
Vita Health Foods, Collingwood Shopping Centre, Collingwood Street, Hamilton.
Vita Health Foods, Moana Court Shopping Centre, Orewa.
Vita Health Foods, King Street, Pukekohe.
Vita Health Foods, Horomatangi Street, Taupo.
Vita Health Foods, Devonport Road, Tauranga.
Vita Health Foods, Lambton Square Shopping Mall, Wellington.
Vital Foods, Maxwell Road, Blenheim.
Vitality Foods Ltd, Gladstone Road, Gosborne.
The Wheatsheaf, Gladston Road, Gisborne.
Whole Earth Foods Ltd, Dickens Street, Napier.
Wholefoods Ltd, Gloucester Street, Christchurch.
Wholefoods Naturally, Richmond Mall, Richmond, Nelson.
Wild Rice Health Foods, Dominion Road, Mt Eden, Auckland.

England

Ceres Bakery, Portobello Rd., London.
Dandelion Bakery and Store, 123 Newington Green Rd., London.
Healen Centre, The, 39 Park Rd., Crouch End, Hornsey N8 8TE.
Infinity Bakery, 23 North Rd., Brighton, Sussex.
Lotus Foods, 29–31 St Lukes Mews, London.
Neils Yard (off Neil St.), Covent Garden, London.
Sesame Food Shop, 128 Regent Park Rd., London.
Springhill Bakery, Dinton (near Aylesbury).
Sunwheel Natural Food Store, 196 Old St., London EC1V 9BP.
Sunwheel Restaurant, 3 Chalk Farm Rd., London NW1 3AA.

International

American Health Food Centre, 301, 3rd Floor, Orchard Towers, Orchard Rd., Singapore 0923.
—— M-79 Lucky Plaza, Singapore.
Muso Co. Ltd., Otedori 2-5-1, Higashiku, Osaka, Japan.
Ohsawa Japan Inc., 11–5 Ohyama-cho, Shibuya-ku, Tokyo, Japan.
Whole Earth Cafe, 93/3 Soi Langsuan, Bangkok.

There are great problems involved with recommending eating houses. The ownership changes often and restaurants close and open with delightful regularity. Personally, I dislike most of the health food or vegetarian restaurants in Australia because the experience of the cooks is generally very limited and the combinations of foods tends to be indiscriminate. However, you may find something to your liking or some food which will be all right if you have to eat out — for example, a salad or a soup. I prefer to eat in ethnic restaurants where the food is usually fresh, the cooks are well grounded in techniques and the dishes themselves are representative of traditional cooking.

A good restaurant will bend over backwards to please you — most of the health food or vegetarian restaurants are disappointing in this respect. It is a good idea to ring up or go to the restaurant in advance if you want some special cooking done. A good restaurant will be only too pleased to help, especially if you are good natured with your requests. Apart from that, ethnic restaurants (Chinese, Greek, Indian, Italian, Japanese, South-east Asian and Spanish) nearly always have some foods or dishes which are well worthwhile. You can ask Chinese and Japanese restaurants not to include sugar, MSG (monosodium glutamate) or Aji no-moto in your food — to provide rice with steamed or boiled vegetables or fish. Southern European or Middle Eastern restaurants can do wonderful fish or vegetable cookery or salads if you ask in a reasonable fashion, for example, fry with less oil, or oil and not butter, or grill (broil).

Above all remember that you are the customer who is paying. Don't be afraid to send food back if it is not what you ordered — good restaurants will serve you and do not become unpleasant.

Glossary

Substances should be used medicinally only after a proper and adequate diagnosis of the condition.

Agar (or kanten): Sea vegetable gelatin. Actually a blend of five different seaweeds. High in calcium and other minerals. Used as food for making jellies and thickening; or medicinally to cool, and reduce blood pressure.

Animal quality salt: Salt which is absorbed into the system combined with animal fats. This can be stored for many years, even while on a vegetarian diet. It causes hard conditions in personality, and arteries, bones and joints.

Arrowroot: The root is ground and the starch is washed out. This starch is the flour used to thicken sauces. It is not as good a quality nor as nutritious as kuzu arrowroot.

Azuki beans: Small, hard, red beans. Very nutritious and excellent kidney food. Can be used for sweet as well as savoury dishes. Obtainable in oriental food stores. High quality azuki beans are available in natural food stores, but are very expensive. Use this type medicinally.

Barley: A cooling grain which is easy to digest. Grown widely for making beer. Can be cooked whole or ground into meal for porridge. Used in making miso (mugi).

Basmati rice: *see* page 28.

Batter: Mixture of flour and water using wholewheat flour as the base, and adding other flours for variation. Used to cover food for deep-frying.

Bechamel: A basic sauce made from oil, flour and water. Sauté 2 tablespoons wholewheat flour in 1 tablespoon oil with ½ teaspoon sea salt until it begins to brown and emit a nutty fragrance. Cool. Add 2 cups water or soup stock (e.g. miso stock) and stir over medium heat until this thickens. Excellent with noodles, baked or stuffed vegetables.

Besan: Fine, yellow chick pea flour. Produces an attractive red-coloured batter when used in deep-frying.

Biodynamic: A system of agriculture which establishes a harmonious relationship between cultivated crops and the environment. This is done with the careful selection of companion plants and the use of herbal compounds for sprays and composting. Our ancestors practised biodynamic farming. Modern farming techniques exclude nature with the use of chemicals and gross mechanisation.

Black beans (1): Do-shee. Fermented and salted. A traditional Chinese product. Black soya beans are cooked, fermented, salted and dried. A very strong savoury taste, especially good with seafood.

Black beans (2): A black soya bean available in oriental groceries. Extremely tasty and nutritious. Require overnight soaking and 3–5 hours' cooking. Fermented black beans are made from these.

Blanch: Pour boiling water over salad vegetables, then strain. Or soak almonds in boiling water so as to make the skins easily removable.

Buckwheat: A small pyramid-shaped seed, not truly a grain. A good winter food as it produces heat quickly. It is said to be responsible for the volatile nature of Russian people, as it is their principal grain (called kasha). Contains vitamin E and is beneficial to blood building and good circulation.

Bulghur wheat: *see* cous-cous.

Burgers: Another name for rissoles — a rice burger, for example, is a cylindrical mass of rice and vegetables 4 cm in diameter and 4 cm high.

Carob powder: Flour made from the Carob bean which grows in Mediterranean Europe, Africa, the USA and Australia. Sweet and nutritious, used as chocolate powder. Available from Greek and Natural Food stores.

Chapatti: Round Indian flatbread, originally made from wholewheat flour. There are many varieties of chapatti.

Chick peas: Hard, fawn coloured peas. Soak before cooking. Available in continental food shops and 'health' shops. Beware of stones — clean chick peas well.

Chilli oil: Oil, usually peanut, which has chilli steeped in it for several months. This gives the oil a reddish colour and a very, very hot taste. Use sparingly. Available in oriental groceries. Easy to make your own.

Coconut milk: Please don't use the canned variety. Boil shredded coconut (freshly grated is best) in water for 1 hour and strain.

Congee: Breakfast dish of Chinese origin. Basically it is soft rice with vegetables or eggs or seafood or pork added and cooked together. A savoury rice porridge.

Corn: The summer grain, sweet and cooling in hot weather. Often sprayed excessively, so get it as clean as possible. Cornmeal or polenta makes good bread and pudding. Has a favourable effect on the heart.

Cous-cous: Steamed, dried and cracked or ground wheat. Coarse semolina or cracked millet can be substituted. Used in Middle Eastern and African cooking.

Curry powder: So easy to make your own by grinding a selection of spices. Pre-packaged curry powder varies endlessly. Each region of Asia has produced its own special variety. I enjoy roasted curry powder from Sri Lanka. This is a dark brown powder which contains pieces of lemongrass and curry leaves. Ingredients for curry can be selected from: cummin, cloves, turmeric, coriander, mustard, dill, ginger, asafoetida (hing), laos, lemongrass, curry leaves, aniseed, chilli, cayenne, cardamon, etc. Slowly toast your home made variety in a heavy skillet before use.

Daikon: Oriental white radish, sometimes 60 cm long. Good as food and excellent medicinally. An aid to digestion and contains far more vitamin C than any citrus fruit. Available in oriental food stores, where it is sometimes called turnip. Several dried, pickled varieties are available. The commonest is called 'takuan', and is available from natural food stores.

Dandelion: Dried, chopped or ground root of the dandelion plant. Made into a dark, almost bitter beverage with water. Traditionally, and I can vouch for it, a tremendous tonic and blood builder. An excellent replacement for coffee. Buy the authentic product, i.e. the actual chopped roots, not the instant beverage form. Dandelion leaves are very good salad greens if picked before the plant flowers. These contain more nutrients and healthful properties than almost any other vegetable.

Deep-fry (or tempura):   This involves placing the object to be cooked in a batter, usually made from flour and water. This is then immersed in heated oil at 170°C (350°F) until cooked. The best oil to use is cold pressed. Place an umeboshi plum in deep-fry oil and store in a jar with a tight lid. This keeps fresh for a month or more.

Dulse: Red seaweed widely used in traditional cooking. Available in USA and Europe but only rarely seen in Australian Natural Food stores, *see* page 44.

Fish sauce (Nam Pla): A condiment made in South-east Asia by fermenting fish and water. It is salty and essential to Thai dishes.

Fu: *see* Kofu.

Genmai miso: *see* Miso and page 11.

Ginger juice: Juice squeezed from finely grated fresh ginger root.

Ginger root: Many-branched tuber or root spice widely used throughout Asia. A very healthful vegetable, particularly good with seafood. Australia has wild varieties which have excellent flavour but a very stringy texture.

Glutinous rice: *see* 'sticky rice'.

Gô: This is the first stage in the tofu-making process. Soaked soya beans are ground with water. This is boiled to produce a creamy liquid. If you require gô for cooking, simply add less water than when making tofu. This will produce a paste or batter.

Gomasio: Condiment made from roasted and ground sesame seeds and sea salt. Proportions vary from 5–15 of seed to 1 of salt. We use 10:1. The oil from the sesame seeds coats the sea salt and enables a proper intake of salt without consequent thirst. Excellent made with black sesame seeds. Try to use unhulled sesame seed which is grey, not bleached white.

Green beans: Mung beans, small and green. Cooling in hot weather. Widely eaten in the orient.

Green leafy vegetables: Chinese spinach, wild greens, savoy cabbage, spinach, beet greens, radish tops, turnip tops, Chinese cabbage, mustard cabbage, kale, etc. These help develop good blood. The harder ones such as Chinese spinach, wild greens such as dandelion leaves, spinach and radish tops, help to remove excess mucus deposits from the body. They are best eaten blanched, sautéed or raw. Green vegetables should be served when they turn brilliant green in cooking — not grey!

Green prawns: Uncooked or raw prawns. Preferable to red or cooked ones which are often cooked in sea water on the trawler. Green prawns go off faster than cooked ones, so are usually freshest. Be sure to remove the spinal column before eating.

Groats: The whole kernel of grain as opposed to meal or broken grains. Oat groats means the whole oat grain which is crushed to produce oats. The best way to consume grains.

Hijiki: Black wiry seaweed harvested in Japan. Delicious and unique flavour. Available in Natural Food, Japanese and Chinese stores, *see* page 44.

Hatcho miso: *see* Miso and page 11.

Hulled millet: *see* millet.

Jelly: A jelly made with agar seaweed.

Kanten: *see* Agar.

Kibblewheat: Soaked or steamed dry wheat.

Kinako: Roasted, fine-ground, unsoaked soya beans. Delicious savoury flavour. Make your own. Add to soups and sauces.

Knead: Rhythmic mixing of bread or pastry dough by hand. Requires calm, purposeful actions and the idea of creating unity — the dough becomes one and does not separate. Beginning with a round piece of dough 7 cm thick and 20 cm in diameter, bring the furthest edge from you over to the edge closest to you. Push the edges together gently and roll away from you. Spin the dough a half circle and bring outside edge to inside edge and roll. This becomes a continuous rhythmic motion. Good kneading eliminates acidity in bread and pastry and allows a better rise. This is because water is thoroughly mixed with the grain and gluten forms into long elastic strands which allow expansion or stretching. *See* pages 124 – 9.

Kofu or Fu: Wheat gluten — *see* recipe, pages 122 – 3.

Kokkoh: Basically a combination of brown rice, sweet brown rice and sesame. Sometimes it contains millet and sometimes it is merely brown rice and sweet brown rice. Excellent children's food, tempura batter without equal, for baking and in desserts. Available in natural food stores, and some 'health' shops.

Kombu: Flat, broad green sea vegetable. Used in soups or when cooking grains. Delicious deep-fried alone or used to roll vegetables in. High in minerals. Roast, grind and incorporate in sesame salt. *See* page 44.

Kome miso: *see* Miso and page 11.

Kuzu: An arrowroot which is grown in mountainous regions in Asia. It is used for thickening foods and as a wonderful medicine for stomach complaints and runny noses in children. Dissolve in cold water before adding to hot liquid for thickening purposes.

Laver: *see* Nori.

Lotus root: Edible tuber of the aquatic Lotus plant noted for its scented and beautiful flowers. An oriental specific for lung disorders.

Macrobiotics: A much misunderstood term. Michio Kushi, a leading figure on the natural foods frontier, says:

'Macrobiotics is not brown rice. Macrobiotics is to dream or envision yourself as whatever you want to be, and then to realise that dream. If you wish to see yourself as a sick person, you can eat accordingly to make yourself sick. If you would like to become healthy, if you wish to realise that dream you can do it. When you wish to see this universe as infinite, then you can eat accordingly and begin to see it as so . . . Macrobiotics is being able to freely make ourselves whatever we want in order to fulfil our dream . . . In order to have a happy dream you have to eat according to a certain way.'

From this you could summarise that macrobiotics is the practice of eating correctly to make yourself completely functional. Eating correctly means to use grains and vegetables as your principal foods, supplemented with beans, sea vegetables, nuts, seeds, fruit and small proportions of lean animal food. Diet must vary according to a person's constitution, age, activity, outlook — different people require different quantities of certain foods. Macrobiotics is finding your own requirements, eating accordingly and becoming totally efficient.

Unfortunately macrobiotics is widely misunderstood by lay people and professionals. Many folk think macrobiotics means 12-day rice fasts and a diet of 90 per cent brown rice.

The recommended basic diet, from which we all develop our own, more than adequately fulfills all nutritional requirements set out by the UN World Health Organisation and every other body which has attempted to define a man's nutritional requirements. Unfortunately the same cannot be said of the food eaten by most people in industrial society — particularly young people today.

All traditional diets were macrobiotic — natural, balanced and seasonal.

Maltose: A grain sweetener extracted from sprouted wheat. Needs to be heated to make it usable, as it sets firm. To heat it, place the container in hot water and simmer over medium heat. A more than adequate replacement for honey or sugar, especially on porridge. Available mainly in oriental food stores in small earthenware, and sometimes plastic containers.

Mame miso: *see* Miso and page 11.

Millet: Small, yellow grain which is alkaline. Millet has to be hulled as the outside shell is indigestible. High in protein and good for the spleen, therefore for those who sing, e.g. canaries. Must be lightly toasted before use or it is bitter.

Minerals: Elements and compounds of elements which can affect the balance of body functions, even in minute quantities. Seaweed and green vegetables are an excellent source of minerals.

Mirin: Sweet saké or rice wine used for cooking.

Miso (pronounced meeso): Purée made from fermented soya beans and grain. Miso is an excellent source of vegetable protein, B vitamins and essential amino acids. It has numerous healthful properties which include the ability to implant necessary bacteria in the digestive tract to ensure complete digestion of food. It combines with poisons in the body which result from bad food or chemicals, and neutralises them for easy elimination. Miso dissolves cholesterol and keeps arteries pliable. It contains valuable minerals, especially when eaten with sea vegetables and natural ferment sugars which provide energy. There are numerous varieties of miso available in the orient. The variety depends on what is mixed with the miso during fermentation, and for how long fermentation goes on. Rice (kome) miso can be very light in colour and only fermented for 2–3 months. Soya (hatcho) miso is very black and fermented for 3 years. Vegetables and other beans can be mixed with miso during fermentation for variation. Sea salt is added to inhibit further biological action and to age the miso. The common varieties available in Australia in natural food stores and some 'health' stores are kome (soya-rice) miso, which is red or light brown; mugi (soya-barley) miso which is brown, and hatcho (soya) miso, which is black.

Kome and mugi miso are most suitable for Australians to consume. This is because our weather is warm and most of us contain too much animal-quality salt. Mugi and kome miso have much less salt than hatcho miso. Kome is high in glucose. Both of these are combined with grains and it appears that legume (beans) protein and grain protein complement each other to make more complete food. Excessive consumption of hatcho miso can cause short temper and impatience. The Japanese produce about 100 different varieties of miso.

Mugi miso: *see* Miso and page 11.

Mugwart: Herb used to eliminate worms. One of its many varieties is cooked with rice. *See* page 28.

Mu tea (pronounced moo): A blend of traditional Asian herbs including ginseng. Used medicinally for respiratory problems or as a tonic for weak people. Fragrant and tasty, it is an efficient way to consume ginseng. Available in natural food stores. Some mu tea may be polluted; contact Spiral Foods or the East West Foundation for validation of this.

Natto miso: *see* Miso and page 11.

Nigari: This is sold in grey 'scales'. It is the leftovers from refining natural sea salt. Magnesium chloride, calcium chloride, calcium sulphate and magnesium sulphate are the major mineral salts. Nigari is used as a solidifier in making tofu.

Noodles: Thin, cylindrical strands usually, but flat or in bundles in the orient. Made from grain flour, commonly wheat and buckwheat. Sweet potato and other vegetable starches are sometimes used. Wheat noodles are called 'udon' in Japan and buckwheat noodles are 'soba'. There are a few excellent varieties of Italian whole rye noodles available. These are usually called bucatini (hollow), tagliatelli (flat), or vermicelli (cylindrical). Real Foods, Spiral, Ceres Wholefoods and Harmony Foods have these. Eggs are often added to flour to produce egg noodles. Noodles are most nutritious made from freshly ground flour at home. This process is very easy to master.

Nori: A seaweed which is available in sheets 30 cm by 15 cm. These range in colour from the purple Chinese to dark black-green Japanese nori. Japanese nori is best. Widely consumed in past times by Europeans, still eaten in coastal Scotland and Ireland.

Oats: Staple of many European peoples. High in fat and good for those suffering dairy products withdrawal. Best consumed as the whole grain, toasted then cooked. Can be soaked overnight. Toasted rolled oats make good porridge or additions to soup or in baking.

Okara: Strainings from the tofu-making process. These have to be strained from the soya milk to give smooth curds (tofu). Okara is delicious incorporated in bread or baked goods, and deep-fried.

Organic: Widely misused term. In this book it simply means grown without chemicals, sprays or industrial pollutants. Only those who grow and eat 'organic' foods regularly are aware of the superior quality of such food. Scientific analysis can reveal little about actual quality, only chemical constituents, so 'scientific' thinkers usually refute 'organic' ideas.

Pilau: Grains and/or beans and vegetables cooked together in one pot.

Polenta: Coarse yellow cornmeal, *see* page 35.

Porridge: Coarse ground grain meal which is cooked with water to produce a thick, creamy texture. Rolled oats are perhaps the most common cereal porridge. It is good to toast cereals for porridge.

Purée: Liquidised or blended ingredients made into a fine paste or liquid.

Phylo or Philo pastry: Extremely thin wheat flour pastry used widely in Middle Eastern cooking.

Red Beans: *see* azuki beans.

Red peppercorns: Chinese peppers which have an unusual and spicy flavour. Often used in dishes originating in Szechuan province. Available in oriental groceries — very good in egg dishes.

Rice: The most complete grain food and basic food of Asian people. There are many varieties. Short-grain brown rice is the best everyday rice. The long-grain brown rice is good in summer. Rice has a very noticeable effect after eating it as your basic grain for some time. It contains B vitamins and in this case B stands for BEING! Avoid using white rice, but when eating out Chinese style, use it to balance out rich sauces and flavours.

Rice Flour: Finely ground rice. To be useful in baking, this must be fine to allow easy water absorption. If you are grinding it at home, as you should, grind three or four times for baking quality. Chinese grocery stores sell white rice flour and glutinous rice flour, which are the right texture but the wrong colour! They are useful for steamed breads and buns, however.

Rice syrup: Sold commercially as 'yinnies' with Chico San label. Also available mixed with malt syrup, and much harder. This is specially fermented rice from which a sweet liquid is extracted. Being a complex sugar, it enters the blood slowly. A desirable form of sweetening.

Rye: Traditional grain of many Europeans. It makes beautiful dark sourdough bread. Can be treated in a similar manner to wheat. Both these grains provide energy, endurance and muscle power.

Salad: Commonly a raw vegetable mixture. Traditionally the vegetables were blanched with boiling water and sea salt.

Sauté: To fry food in oil over medium heat while stirring gently. This is often done prior to adding liquid for further cooking and softening. Sautéeing coats the vegetables with a thin layer of oil which preserves their nutritive value in cooking. Sautéeing flavours the oil and therefore spreads this flavour through the rest of the food. Onions, garlic, ginger and spices are the first vegetables to sauté. Then add others, from hardest to softest, e.g. carrot before zucchini, and greens last of all.

Sea salt: Natural sea salt which is not refined or bleached. This contains many minerals. The best way to get it is to go to a clean beach, collect sea water and boil it away on a driftwood fire while you play.

Sea vegetables: Commonly, seaweed. Wakame, nori (laver), kombu, hijiki, agar (kanten), are the most widely consumed species. Most seaweeds are edible. A common one found on Australian coasts, known as sea-lettuce, is edible. Very fine-filament seaweeds are best avoided. All are high in mineral content.

Seitan: Savoury kofu (fu or wheat gluten) flavoured with shoyu and ginger. Cut into small pieces, it resembles dark meat.

Semolina: A uniform, coarse-ground, hard wheat. Used widely for cooking, especially in the Middle East and India.

Shitake Mushrooms: Dried Chinese and Japanese mushrooms. Incredible flavour and good for kidneys taxed by too much animal food or salt.

Shoyu: Black or red-brown liquid made by fermenting soya beans and wheat. Sea salt and water are added and this is aged for 6 months to 2½ years. A valuable vegetable source of protein, B vitamins, enzymes, and good quality salt. Used in food and cooking, and medicinally, to replace animal quality salt. Commonly known as soy sauce, but most soy sauce is heavily laced with additives and not naturally fermented. *See* tamari.

Simmer: A slow-cooking process, in which the food being cooked is kept moving slowly by heat.

Skillet: A heavy, usually cast-iron, frying pan.

Soba: *see* noodles.

Soba miso: *see* Miso and page 11.

Soft rice: Rice cooked with 6 times its volume of water for 3–5 hours. Good infant and invalid food. *See* congee.

Solidifier: *see* nigari.

Sommaque or semak: Ground flower used in Middle Eastern food. Dark purple colour with a pleasant lemon sharpness. Good with tabboule, page 70.

Sourdough: A rising agent made by allowing a mixture of flour and water to ferment naturally. Used in place of yeast, carbonate soda or baking powder.

Soya milk: A by-product of the tofu-making process. More than a substitute for cow's milk, which is meant for calves.

Star Anise: Star-shaped spice. Aromatic with true 'aniseed' flavour. Use whole or remove seeds and grind.

Sticky rice: Pearl-white variety of rice. Also called glutinous rice. Unpolished variety not yet available in Australia. Widely consumed in sub-tropical and hot climates in Asia. Truly delicious.

Stir-fry: Method of cooking, usually done in a wok. Ingredients (usually onion first, greens last) are stirred in a little hot oil and then water is added to create steam. Requires fairly high heat, constant watching and a lid for the wok.

Stored salt: This is usually animal quality salt which is deposited in the body in fatty tissue. Pads on the hips and back are common repositories, as are the kidneys. This can be eliminated through correct eating and its elimination brings about great capacity for health.

Sugar: Sugar exists in natural form in whole grains, fruit, vegetables, some beans, maple syrup and other foods. This sugar is in disaccharide or polysaccharide form, which means, respectively, 'two' and 'many' sugars — referring to the amount of molecules bonded together. Such sugar, when ingested, is released slowly into the blood stream after going through normal digestion. Refined white and brown sugar is a monosaccharide, which means 'one' sugar. This sugar requires no digestion but is instantaneously injected into the blood stream. Thus it is a 'high energy' food.

Natural sugars, through slow release, provide consistent energy as they are digested. Refined sugar provides an energy 'hit' then a relapse. Because natural sugars go through the digestive process, they do not tax the system. Refined sugar actually stops the digestive process and draws acid to the stomach and blood in an attempt to neutralise its effect. Consequently minerals, mostly calcium, are drawn from the bones and teeth in an attempt to neutralise the acid. When the sugar moves into the duodenum, it creates bacteria which destroy the intestinal flora responsible for the production of B vitamins. The overall effect of this process is to create an inflamed stomach prone to ulcers, weak bones, vitamin B deficiency, acidic blood, over-stimulation of the liver and pancreas, deposits of fatty acids in the heart, kidneys and ovaries, formation of stones in organs, advanced diseases such as leukaemia, Hodgkin's disease, diabetes, hyper- and hypo-glycaemia and cancer.

Is that too much for you? Go off all sugar and sugar foods for two weeks and see if I am wrong. By going off all foods which contain refined sugar you may find you have an empty kitchen. At least this may indicate something — we are a nation of sugar addicts. Almost all of our food contains refined sugar in some form — examine labels — and if it does not contain sugar, we usually add it. But if you are on a 'health kick' and use only raw sugar, who is being fooled? 'Raw' sugar is white sugar which is recoloured. There is no raw sugar produced in Australia, you are still a junkie.

Sugar consumption has soared through the western world since its introduction in early medieval times. It is at an all-time high today, along with its allies, meat and dairy food consumption. These two go hand-in-hand usually, as each tends to mask the effect of its counterpart, until they finally unite to cause the typical diseases of industrial society at increasingly early ages. How many of you have healthy parents? Why shouldn't they be healthy? Old age used to mean venerable and wise folk; we also have our 9-year-olds with diabetes, heart disease, leukaemia, tuberculosis, arthritis and uncontrollable or hyperactive mentalities.

Such mayhem is my definition of sugar. I recommend strongly that you read *Sugar Blues* by William Dufty for further illumination.

Sunflower salt: A condiment made from ground and roasted sunflower seeds and sea salt. Ratio 10 units of seed to one unit of salt. Use as a variation from sesame salt (gomasio). Add roasted seaweed in the same proportion as salt for a difference.

Suribachi: An oriental grinder, the equivalent of our mortar and pestle. This has a grooved grinding surface to break seeds and grains efficiently.

Szechuan pepper: Small black peppercorns with a black seed which have a unique flavour. Available in some Asian grocery shops.

Tahina: A purée of sesame seeds and oil. Often the oil used is of very poor quality and contains an emulsifier. If the tahina has oil floating on top and the oil is golden in colour, it is probably of good quality. It is better to buy sesame purée, such as that marketed by Spiral foods, which is made solely from unhulled sesame seeds. This can be diluted with water or cold pressed oil to make tahina.

Tamari: This label is given to what is actually shoyu. Tamari is the liquid which can be scooped from the miso keg. It is very tasty, especially in soup.

Taro or albi: A type of potato tuber which is grown in more sub-tropical and tropical areas; can be found in oriental groceries and grows in NSW and Queensland, Australia.

Tekka: Condiment made from lotus root, burdock, carrot, dark sesame oil, ginger and miso. This is sautéed for hours until a dry, almost black substance remains. Very delicious sprinkled on grains, in baking and it is also a valuable medicine for heart and blood.

Tempe: Fermented soya bean cakes used only in Indonesian cooking. A delicious flavour. High in B vitamins and protein. *See* page 92.

Tempura: *see* deep-fry.

Toast: As in 'toasting sesame seeds', means to heat seeds over low to medium heat in a skillet or saucepan, while stirring, until seeds are golden and fragrant.

Tofu: A white gelatin-like substance made from soya beans. The process involves making soya bean milk by heating ground, soaked soya beans in water to make a milky liquid. Strain this to produce soya milk, and curdle the milk with a solidifier — usually sea water or nigari. The curds are laid on cloth in a special container and pressed to produce a solid 'cake'.

Tofu is good quality protein and sensually satisfying. Oriental people believe it can reduce sexual appetite. Chinese and Japanese Buddhist vegetarian cuisine employs it to a large extent — sometimes by pressing it in specially shaped containers to resemble chicken or pork or fish. I know of one dish in which the tofu is placed in a fish mould. It is then split and layered with bamboo 'bones'. The two pieces are joined, wrapped in nori seaweed and deep-fried. There are many varieties of tofu available. It is called 'tahu' in Indonesia and 'dow-foo' in China. It can be pressed and firm, jelly-like, smoked, fermented or flavoured. Most dried and instant tofu is chemical. Best of all, make up your own.

Udon: *see* noodles.

Umeboshi plums: This is the product of a Japanese method of pickling what used to be the wild plum or apricot, used now for fruit of domesticated trees. Umeboshi plums are available in Asian food stores in many forms. The South-east Asian variety is usually dried. The Chinese variety is similar to the Japanese, but not pickled with the beefsteak leaves (chiso) which give the Japanese product its distinctive colour and flavour. Some Chinese plums are sold in a very citric brine which makes them unsuitable for direct consumption as a corrective for stomach trouble like the Japanese plum. Chinese plums are suitable for sweet and sour but generally the Japanese plums, particularly those from natural food outlets, are the best for all-round use. Most commercial Japanese plums contain chemicals and should be avoided. Umeboshi can act as a preservative, e.g. in keeping oil used for deep frying, and are useful in cooking fruit. Cooked with inorganic food, umeboshi are supposed to neutralise harmful chemicals. Generally you break the plum up with your fingers in the cooking liquid and remove the stone after cooking. To make umeboshi paste, remove the flesh from the stone and chop finely. Keep the stone as a remedy for indigestion. The stones are a good replacement for chewing gum. Umeboshi should be given to children in very small quantities and only as a medicine as they are very salty. It is best to mix them with a liquid for children as they seem to irritate the teeth. To reduce their salinity, soak them in water for an hour or two.

Vegetal quality salt: Sea salt combined with vegetal oils and fats. This is high in minerals, easily and safely digestible, because the salt is combined with vegetable oil.

Wakame: Green-brown Japanese seaweed available in dried form from Natural Food, Japanese or Korean stores. *See* page 44.

Wheat: The basic grain for most European and Middle Eastern peoples. High in protein and the acknowledged food for thinking. Usually ground to flour for various breads. Many varieties from hard to soft have varying protein content. Hard wheat is usually best for bread flour. Soft wheat is better for pastry.

Wholefood: As opposed to incomplete or non-whole food. The word 'wholesome' sums it up. White rice is not whole as it has had the valuable bran and germ removed, as has white flour. These are therefore not wholesome food.

Wok: An Asian cooking implement made from cast iron or rolled steel. The latter are best. It is adaptable to all types of cooking, except baking. It utilises heat very efficiently. The wok is like a smooth metal bowl with handles. Use a wok ring over electric stove.

Yannoh: *see* page 177. Available in Natural Food stores under the Lima brand.

Yinnies syrup: Rice 'honey' malted cereal syrup made from rice. *See* maltose.

Yin-Yang: Volumes could, and have been written in an attempt to explain these terms. In the orient, 'Yin' is the name given to the forces which produce expansion. 'Yang' is the force which makes things contract. These forces are each other's opposites; harmony is produced when Yin and Yang are balanced. In winter when the weather is cold (Yin) we tend to be less physically active, stay inside and withdraw from the cold. This is because the Yin force of cold produces an harmonious opposite within us, we contract from the cold and try to make ourselves more Yang by using fire and heat. In summer, weather is hot (Yang). We tend to become active, outgoing and seek cool refreshment (Yin).

Cooking is our most fundamental way of balancing Yin and Yang. Look at the example of foods. Tomatoes, ripening in summer, juicy and refreshing to some in hot weather, are Yin food. Carrots, growing underground, maturing in cold weather, are, by comparison, Yang food. There are within this category, Yin fruit and Yang fruit, Yin grains and Yang grains. Apples, being harder, less sweet and juicy than oranges, are more Yang than oranges. Corn kernels, juicy and large, are Yin compared to millet, tiny and dry. Yin is that force which tends to make us dizzy — drugs, alcohol, sugar. Yang is a more binding or together force — salt, time (as in longer cooking) and heat.

Some confusion can arise when comparing the macrobiotic idea of applying Yin-Yang to the ideas expressed in the *I Ching* for example. This can be avoided if you can see Yin-Yang as opposite, complementary forces. Actually Yin could be called Yang and vice-versa and the idea would not have changed at all.

Most European people today are more Yang because they consume excess meat, animal-quality and refined salt, processed food and dairy products. Such a diet requires extreme Yin to make it balanced — i.e. sugar. Then we have today's typical diet, basically meat and dairy products and sugar. This is indeed balanced, otherwise death would result. But such a balance is walking a tightrope and is hard to maintain, as is evidenced by those who consume such a diet. They are dying in hordes from cancer, artery degeneration, blood diseases, acute organ failures, strokes, etc., which are merely indications of imbalance. Eating grain and vegetables as principal foods puts you more towards the centre as far as Yin-Yang is concerned. Balance is easier to maintain and health is permanent. People consuming vegetal quality (Yin) food use heat (Yang) for cooking food to produce balance. Many vegetarians become Yin from eating large amounts of raw food and fruit. Often such people have stored animal-quality salt (Yang) which makes such a diet appealing initially.

I recommend that you take time to develop your conception of Yin-Yang and do not try to apply its idea as a rule. Read *The Looking Glass God*, a study in Yin-Yang, by M. Nahum Stiskin.

Zaatar: A Lebanese spice made by grinding sesame seeds and coriander. Used on top of kebbe, *see* page 63.

Bibliography

Valuable guide books

Aihara, Cornelia — Macrobiotic Childcare, George Ohsawa Macrobiotic Foundation (GOMF) San Francisco, California, USA, 1971.

Aihara, Herman — Milk — A Myth of Civilization, GOMF, San Francisco, California, USA, 1977.

———————— — Acid + Alkaline. Is acid Yin? Is alkaline Yang?, *ibid*, 1971.

———————— — Seven Macrobiotic Principles, *ibid*, 197?.

Aihara, Ohsawa, and Pulver — Marijuana and Drugs, GOMF, San Francisco, California, USA, 1977.

———————— — Seven Macrobiotic Principles, Smoking, Marijuana and Drugs, GOMF, San Francisco, California, USA, 1977.

East West Foundation — A Dietary Approach to Cancer, Boston, Mass., USA, 1976.

Feinberg, Alice — Macrobiotic Pregnancy, GOMF, California, USA, 1973.

Kervan, Louis C. — Biological Transmutation, Swan, New York, USA, 1972.

Kervan, Louis C., and Ohsawa, George — Biological Transmutation, GOMF, San Francisco, California, USA, 1975.

Kushi, Michio — The Book of Macrobiotics — The Universal Way of Health and Happiness, Tokyo, Japan, 1977.

———————— — Food for Spiritual Development, Order of the Universe, USA, 1968.

———————— — The Teaching of Michio Kushi, vol. I, II, III, East West Foundation, Boston, Mass., USA, 1977.

———————— — Seminar Reports, Kushi International seminars — distributed by East West Foundation.

———————— — Macrobiotic Seminars of Michio Kushi: Acapuncture; ancient and future worlds, East West Foundation, Boston, Mass., USA, Winter 1973.

———————— — Macrobiotic Seminars of Michio Kushi: Disease — origin, causes and cures. Principles of the Ancient World Calendar. The theory and practice of natural agriculture, East West Foundation, Boston, Mass., USA, Fall, 1972.

Langre, Jacques de, The first book of Do-In — Guide Practique, Happiness Press, Canada, 1971.

———————— — Second book of Do-In, *ibid*, 1974.

Moon, J. Yogamundi — A Macrobiotic explanation of Pathological Calcification — the great industrial epidemic, GOMF, San Francisco, California, USA, 1974.

Muramoto, Naboru — Healing Ourselves, Swan House, Avon Publications, New York, USA, 1973.

Nyoiti, Sakurazawa — Macrobiotics — you are all Sanpaku, Tandem, London, UK, 1965.

Ohsawa, George — Acupuncture and the Philosophy of the Far East, Tao Publications, USA, 1973.

_____ — Macrobiotic — an invitation to health and happiness, GOMF, Canada, 1971.

_____ — The Philosophy of Oriental Medicine, GOMF, San Francisco, California, USA, 1965. (Volumes 1. Zen Macrobiotics, 2. The Book of Judgment, 3. Guide Book for Living.)

Stiskin, M. Nahum — The Looking Glass God: A Study in Yin-Yang, Autumn Press, Kyoto, Japan, 1971.

Magazines

The order of the Universe (Boston, Mass., USA); East West Foundation, East West Journal (East West Foundation, Boston, Mass., USA); Spiral (Red Moon Publications, London, UK). All dates.

Useful Books on Natural Healing and Medicine

Chen, Li Shih — Chinese Medicinal Herbs, Georgetown Press, California, USA, 1973.

Lui, Da — Taoist Health Exercise Book, Links Books Music Sales Co., London, UK, 1974.

Oki, Masahiro — Healing yourself through Okido Yoga, Japan Publications, Tokyo, Japan, 1977.

_____ — Practical Yoga, _ibid_, 1970.

Richards, L., Baumann, A., and others — Rice and the 10 day rice diet, George Ohsawa Macrobiotic Foundation, San Francisco, California, USA, 1975.

Togushi, Masaru — Oriental Herbal Wisdom, Pyramid Books, New York, USA, 1973.

Yellow Emperor's Classic of Internal Medicine, University of California Press, California, USA, 1949. Translated by Ilva Veith.

see also 'Valuable Guide Books' section.

For interest

Altman, Nathaniel — Eating for Life — a book about vegetarianism, Theosophical Publications, USA, 1973.

Beau, Georges — Chinese Medicine, Avon Publications, USA, 1973.

Brandt, Johanna — the Grape Cure — for cancer and other diseases. Religious Liberty Publications Association, New South Wales, Australia, 1968.

Burang, Theodore — The Tibetan Art of Healing, Watkins, London, 1974.

Chan, Pedro — Finger Acupressure, Ballantine, New York, USA, 1975.

Daigram Group — Man's Body — An owner's manual, Paddington Press, New York, USA, 1976.

Ekret, Arnold — The Mucusless Diet Healing System, Ehret Lit. Publishing Co., California, USA, 1953.

Wei-Kang, Fu — The story of Chinese Acupuncture and Moxibustion, Foreign Language Press, Peking, China, 1975.

Hall, Dorothy — The Natural Health Book, Nelson, Melbourne, Australia, 1976.

Hashimoto, M. — Japanese Acupuncture, Liveright, New York, USA, 1968.

Houston, F. M. — The Healing Benefits of Acupressure, Keats Publications, USA, 1958.

Jain, K. K. — Health Care in New China, Rodale Press, USA, 1973.

Kadans, Joseph — Encyclopaedia of Natural Herbs, Arco, New York, USA, 1970.

Kourrennoff, Paul — Secrets of Oriental Physicians, Health Research, California, USA, 1950.

Kulvinskas, Viktoras — Love your Body, Hippocrates Health Institute, USA, 1972.

_____ — Nutritional Value of Sprouts and Grasses, Omangod Press, New York, USA, 1976.

_____ — Survival into the 21st Century.

Law, Donald — A Guide to Alternative Medicine, Turnstone Books, London, UK, 1974.

Lucas, Richard — Ginseng — the Chinese 'Wonder Root', R & M Books, USA, 1972.

Lust, John — The Herb Book, Benedict Lust Publications, New York, USA, 1974.

Macon, Nathanial, and Chang, I-Lok — Acupuncture and Moxibustion. A handbook for the barefoot doctors of China, Shocken Books, New York, USA, 1975.

Manaka, Y. and Urquahart, I. A. — Quick and Easy Chinese Massage, Shufunotomo Co. Ltd., Tokyo, Japan, 1973.

Nanking Army Ear Acupuncture Team — Ear Acupuncture — the Complete Text, Rodale Press, USA, 1974.

Palos, Stephen — The Chinese Art of Healing, Herder and Herder, New York, USA, 1971.

Price, Joseph M. — Boronaries, Cholesterol, Chlorine, Pyramid, USA, 1976.

Rodale, J. J. — Guide to better food and nutrition, Rodale Press, USA, 1966.

Shelton, Herbert M. — Food combining made easy, Dr. Shelton's Health School, USA, 1951.

Shook, Edward — Advanced Treatise on Herbology, Health Research, California, USA, no date.

Szekely, E. D. — The Essene Gospel of Peace, Academy Books, California, USA, 1974.

Venings, Louise — The Ginseng Book, Ruka Publications, California, USA, 1976.

Wallnofer, Heinrich and von Rottauscher, Anna — Chinese Folk Medicine, Signet Crown Publications, USA, 1965.

Wade, Carlson — Hypertension (High Blood Pressure) and your diet, Keats Publications, USA, 1975.

Books Worth Reading

Alexander,   — Farmers of Forty Centuries, publishing details not available.

Aykroyd, W. — The Story of Sugar, Quadrangle Books, Chicago, USA, 1967.

Bernard, R. W. — The Dead Sea Scrolls, Continental Health Research, California, USA, 1956.

Cribb, A. B. and J. W. — Wild Food in Australia, Collins, Sydney, Australia, 1975.

Diesendorf, Mark, and Furnass, Brian — The impact of environment and lifestyle on human health, Society for Social Responsibility in Science, Canberra, Australia, 1977.

Dufty, W. — Sugar Blues, Chilton, New York, USA, 1975.

Licata, Vincent — Comfrey and Chlorophyll, Continental Health Research, California, USA, 1971.

Maiden, J. H. — The Useful Native Plants of Australia, Compendium Pty. Ltd., 1975. (Originally published 1851.)

Ricegrowers Co-op Mills Ltd. — Rice — the Riverina Miracle, Sydney (no date).

Rodale, J. I. — Natural health, sugar and the criminal mind, Pyramid, New York, USA, 1968.

Thomas, Pete — The big crush — what everybody should know about CSR sugar monopoly, Queensland Guardian, Australia 1965.

Wilhelm, Richard — The secret of the Golden Flower — a Chinese book of life, Harvest/Harcourt & Brace, New York, USA, 1962.

Wood, Beverley M. — Tucker in Australia, Hill of Content, Melbourne, Australia, 1977.

Cookbooks

Abhesera, Michael — Cooking for Life, Avon Publications, New York, USA, 1967.

Aihara, Cornelia — Chico-San Cookbook, Chico-San Incorporated, California, USA., 1972.

_____ — The Do of Cooking, George Ohsawa Macrobiotic Foundation, San Francisco, California, USA, 1972. 4 volumes.

Aihara, Cornelia and Herman — Soybean Diet, ibid, 1974.

Brown, Edward Espe — The Tassajara Bread Book, Shambala Publications, California, USA, 1970.

_____ — Tassajara Cooking, ibid, 1975.

Couffignal, Huguette — The People's Cookbook, Pan, London, UK, 1980.

Deadman, Peter and Betteridge, Karen — Nature's Foods, Rider & Co., Hutchinson, Victoria, Australia, 1973.

Farmilant, Eunice — The Natural Foods Sweet-tooth Cook Book, Pyramid, New York, USA, 1971.

Holt, Calvin and Caradine, Patch — Zen Hash, Pyramid, New York, USA, 1971.

Miller, Gloria Bley — The Thousand Recipe Chinese Cookbook, Hamlyn, London, UK, 1966.

Mori, Kisakv — Mushrooms as Health Foods, Japan Publications, Tokyo, Japan (no date).

Sakurazawa, Nyoti (George Ohsawa) — Macrobiotics — you are all Sanpaku, Tandem Books, London, UK, 1965.

Ohsawa, Lima — The art of just cooking, Autumn Press, Japan, 1974.

Sacharoff, Shanta Nimbark — Flavours of India, 101 Publications, California, USA, 1972.

Shurtleff, W. and Aoyagi, A. — The Book of Tofu, Autumn Press, Japan, 1975. (volume 1).

_____ — The Book of Miso, ibid. 1976.

_____ — The Book of Kudzu, ibid. 1977.

Cookbooks for Ideas and for Interest

Ayrton, Elisabeth — The Cookery of England, Penguin, Harmondsworth, UK.

Chu, Grace Zia — The Pleasures of Chinese Cooking, Pocket Books, New York, USA, 1969.

David, Elizabeth — English Bread and Yeast Cookery, Penguin, Harmondsworth, UK, 1978.

_____ — French Provincial Cooking, Penguin, Harmondsworth, UK, 1975.

_____ — Italian Food, Penguin, Harmondsworth, UK, 1972.

_____ — Mediterranean Food, Penguin, Harmondsworth, UK, 1974.

Davidson, Alan — Fish and Fish Dishes of Laos, Charles Tuttle & Co., Tokyo, Japan, 1975.

_____ — Mediterranean Seafood, Penguin, Harondsworth, UK, 1980.

Hunter, Beatrice Trum — Fermented Foods and Beverages, Keats Publishing Incorporated, Connecticut, USA, 1973.

Japanese Cooking Companions (comps) — Tempura and Sukiyaki, Japan Publications, Tokyo, Japan, 1965.

_____ — Teriyaki and Sushi, ibid, 1961.

Lee, Gary — The Chinese Vegetarian Cookbook, Nitty Gritty Publications, California, USA, 1972.

Lo, Kenneth — Chinese Food, Penguin, England, 1972.

Oles, Shayne — The New Zen Cookery, Shoyfer Corporation, California, USA (no date).

Owen, Sri — The Homebook of Indonesian Cookery, Faber, London, UK, 1976.

Pritikin, Nathan — The Pritikin Programme for Diet and Exercise, Bantam, New York, USA, 1980.

Ray, Elizabeth — The Best of Eliza Acton, Penguin, Harmondsworth, UK, 1978.

Rudzinski, Russ — Japanese Country Cookbook, Nitty Gritty Publications, California, USA, 1969.

San, W. Sou — Chinese Culinary in Plain English, Brisbane, Australia, 1965.

Whie, Merry — Pasta and Noodles, Penguin, Harmondsworth, UK, 1979.

Wu, Sylvia — Madame Wu's Art of Chinese Cooking, Bantam, New York, USA,

Index

Y

Z